Guilt and Shame

Basic Problems in Philosophy Series

A. I. Melden and Stanley Munsat
University of California, Irvine
General Editors

The Analytic-Synthetic Distinction
Stanley Munsat

Civil Disobedience and Violence
Jeffrie G. Murphy, The University of Arizona

Guilt and Shame
Herbert Morris, University of California, Los Angeles

Human Rights
A. I. Melden

Morality and the Law
Richard A. Wasserstrom, University of California, Los Angeles

War and Morality
Richard A. Wasserstrom

Guilt and Shame

Edited by

Herbert Morris

University of California, Los Angeles

Wadsworth Publishing Company, Inc.   Belmont, California

1971

. . . *it corresponds faithfully to my intention to represent the sense of guilt as the most important problem in the development of civilization . . . S. Freud,* Civilization and Its Discontents.

Shame is an emotion insufficiently studied because in our civilization it is so early and easily absorbed by guilt. E. Erikson, Childhood and Society.

© 1971 by Wadsworth Publishing Company, Inc., Belmont, California 94002. All rights reserved. No part of this book may be reproduced, stored in a retrieval system or transcribed, in any form or by any means, electronic, mechanical, photocopying, recording or otherwise, without the prior written permission of the publisher.

ISBN–0–534–00052–5
L. C. Cat. Card No. 75–164995
Printed in the United States of America

1 2 3 4 5 6 7 8 9 10 — 76 75 74 73 72 71

Series Foreword

The Basic Problems in Philosophy Series is designed to meet the need of students and teachers of philosophy, mainly but not exclusively at the undergraduate level, for collections of essays devoted to some fairly specific philosophical problems.

In recent years there have been numerous paperback collections on a variety of philosophical topics. Those teachers who wish to refer their students to a set of essays on a specific philosophical problem have usually been frustrated, however, since most of these collections range over a wide set of issues and problems. The present series attempts to remedy this situation by presenting together, within each volume, key writings on a single philosophical issue.

Given the magnitude of the literature, there can be no thought of completeness. Rather, the materials included are those that, in the judgment of the editor, must be mastered first by the student who wishes to acquaint himself with relevant issues and their ramifications. To this end, historical as well as contemporary writings will be included.

Each volume in the series will contain an introduction by the editor to set the stage for the arguments contained in the essays and a bibliography to help the student who wishes to pursue the topic at a more advanced level.

A. I. Melden
S. Munsat

Herbert Morris is a Professor of Law and Philosophy at the University of California, Los Angeles. He received an A.B. degree from the University of California, Los Angeles, a D.Phil. from Oxford, and an LL.B. from Yale University. He has published *Freedom and Responsibility* (1961), *The Masked Citadel* (1968), and several articles, including "Punishment for Thoughts" (*Monist,* Vol. 49, 1965), "Persons for Punishment" (*Monist,* Vol. 52, 1968), and "Guilt and Punishment" (*Personalist,* Vol. 52, 1971). He received a Fulbright Scholarship in 1954–1956, a Ford Foundation Law Faculty Fellowship in 1963–1964, and a Senior Fellowship from the National Endowment for the Humanities in 1970–1971.

Contents

Guilt and Shame

Introduction

Most of us are painfully familiar with the experience of guilt **1** from an early age. We have all on occasion had thoughts or acted in ways which have led to our *thinking* of ourselves as guilty, and we have then *felt* guilty. What is it, though, to feel guilty? Of course, we feel bad. We might say, not just bad, but rotten, depleted of energy, unable to stand upright and partake of life. But what is the source of these feelings? Is it hostility toward ourselves, hostility because we have damaged what we value? Is it that feeling guilty we see ourselves as separated from others and somehow from ourselves? Is it that we are weighted down with a sense of having to make amends, having to restore what has been damaged so that there is again union? Is it some combination of all these elements and perhaps more?

We know that there is a powerful need to be rid of guilt. We know that feeling this need we seek, on some occasions, to excuse ourselves, to make out that we are not, in fact, guilty. On other occasions we confess and seek and, perhaps, gain forgiveness. On still other occasions, we seek what some see as the essential consequence of guilt—punishment. These are only some of the familiar responses, but they make clear that any moral view of life which contains guilt must be one in which there are also responsible persons who sometimes act wrongly, who suffer because of it, who see themselves as owing something to others because of their wrong, and who are disposed to act to restore a relationship damaged by their conduct.

We may take all this for granted. Our thoughts, our feelings, run smoothly in accord with the logic of guilt. Still, there are those who raise powerful voices against this logic. They find barbaric a man's guilty suffering over what is done and finished. But what is more common to guilt than this? For these critics, it is to the future that the rational man must look. The harsh, unrelenting domination of the past must be overcome. Guilt and the whole morality of which it is a part may be seen as a self-imposed curse, an illness which must be cured if mankind is to live. But is it, as Nietzsche observed, an "illness" like pregnancy, a condition that can give birth to a man truly worthy of wonder and admiration, a man that can replace the withered creature produced by sub-servience to guilt?

Sometimes when we act in a way unacceptable to ourselves or others, a feeling of shame rather than guilt is evoked. We are familiar with this feeling as we are with guilt, though both Erikson and Lynd suggest in their essays why we may not wish to ac-knowledge the feeling and prefer instead to feel guilt. What, we may wonder, are the features of shame, and how do they relate to guilt? What does our capacity for feeling shame reveal about us, about our conceptions of ourselves, the values we hold, the way we see and respond to others? That shame differs from guilt seems apparent. There are a number of clues. With guilt we are disposed to confess; with shame to hide. We seem to rid our-selves of guilt, when we are fortunate enough to do so, by restor-ation; we seem to rid ourselves of shame by changing ourselves. Auditory images arise naturally in connection with guilt; visual ones with shame. These are only a few hints. The essays in this volume reveal much more about the differences and similarities between guilt and shame.

Analytic philosophers have devoted only offhand attention to the concept of guilt, and the almost total lack of philosophic interest in shame is, in a word, shameful. The moral world of beliefs, attitudes, and feelings of which these concepts are a part has not concerned analytic philosophers in England and the United States, who have proceeded, on the whole, as if moral emotions were unworthy of their attention, a matter best left, perhaps, for theologians, psychologists, and those muddle-headed philosophers with an interest in existentialism and phenomenology. A major focus of analytic philosophers for hundreds of years has been the probelm of free will and deter-minism, an issue connected with, to be sure, but hardly exhaust-ing the subjects raised in this collection. J. L. Austin in the early 1950s made a plea for excuses, a plea that philosophical ener-gies be directed away, at least for a while, from the large, tra-ditional metaphysical issues, to the more down-to-earth ques-tions about responsibility and the variety of concepts linked to it in law and everyday life. Many philosophers heeded his words. They turned to questions such as: What are the principles govern-ing ascription of responsibility? Are these principles justifiable? What is the nature of an act, omission, intention, punishment? What is it to do something inadvertently, absent-mindedly, acci-dentally, etc.? But this not unrewarding shift in philosophical activity left guilt and shame untouched. It would be well worth investigating why this was so. It may just be that philosophers are human too, and the subjects raised in this collection are resonant with personal significance for all people, and thus understandably difficult to approach. What is now unquestionably needed is a forceful plea for the examination of these subjects. In fact, we can claim a certain urgency for this plea. Pressed upon us by respected individuals are proposals for drastic reform of our criminal law. Central to much of the dissatisfaction with our present system is its foundation in what some see as an anachronistic, unacceptable morality — the morality of guilt and punishment because of it. We must ask ourselves what we should gain and what we should lose were we to attempt to cut the criminal law loose from its mooring in this morality. Perhaps even more fundamentally, we must ask what we should gain and what we should lose in raising children and living ourselves outside of a guilt morality (or a shame morality). We must carefully reflect upon these questions, for here more than perhaps anywhere else, philosophical positions cut a wide swathe through the real world of men relating to men.

The materials in this collection, drawn from literature, law, anthropology, history, philosophy, psychoanalysis, and sociology, demonstrate that guilt and shame are large and exciting topics, certain to repay investigation and certain, too, to set loose tremors of thought and feeling within us that will demonstrate indubitably the vital importance within us of these concepts. The range of different approaches and disciplines included here was, of course, a matter of design. If the subject is to be opened up for study, it should be done so in a way that permits the understanding and imagination of the reader to be stimulated and challenged by the widest assortment of materials.

There are a number of different theoretical inquiries undertaken by the authors included in this collection, and there are, too, materials that are less *about* guilt and shame than they are presentations *of* them. First, there is conceptual analysis. For example, what is guilt? What are guilt feelings? How is guilt related to feelings of guilt? Over what matters is it appropriate to feel guilt? What are the connections, if any, between legal, moral, political, and metaphysical guilt? What is unconscious guilt? Neurotic guilt? What is the relationship between guilt and crime, guilt and responsibility, guilt and fault, guilt and punishment? What are the connections between guilt and confession, repentance, atonement, regret, forgiveness, remorse, renunciation? What criteria guide us in determining degrees of guilt? What is it to have a conscience? To feel resentment? To blame? In brief, we may ask about the nature of each of the fundamental concepts comprising either a guilt or shame morality, and we may ask how these concepts are related to each other. Apart from the first three selections, all the essays in this collection concentrate to some degree or other on these conceptual questions.

Second, what are the presuppositions of guilt and shame morality? What is implied about persons who feel guilt or feel shame? What conceptions must they have of identity, of value, of time, of human relationships, if they employ these concepts? If they employ the one concept and not the other? Would, for example, a person's not feeling guilt, where it is normally believed appropriate to feel it, reveal something about that person's capacity for love and concern for his fellow man? In what situations might we anticipate that a guilt morality would arise and in what situations a shame morality? I find John Rawls' *The Sense of Justice* and Helen Lynd's *The Nature of Shame,* a work abundantly and sensitively illustrated with literary material, particularly suggestive on these questions.

Third, there are large and challenging claims about guilt and shame that deserve examination. Some claim, for example, that we should move beyond guilt, that to continue as we have for thousands of years is irrational. Some claim that we are all guilty, some that none of us is. Some claim that psychotherapy aims at ridding one of guilt or that it is concerned with "inauthentic guilt." On this last topic, the relationship of psychotherapy to guilt, Buber's *Guilt and Guilt Feelings* and Herbert Fingarette's direct response to Buber, are especially relevant. On the question of moving beyond guilt, there is Nietzsche's brilliant essay, full of insight and passionate concern for man. On shared and collective guilt I have included Karl Jaspers' moral appraisal of the guilt arising from the horrors of the Nazi period.

Fourth, a number of the selections raise questions of an essentially historical kind. They consider the origin and development of guilt and shame in either the life of an individual or the development of culture. A number of these selections directly raise questions about the process of socialization. While we engage in inquiry on this subject it is essential, I think, to remain sensitive to the variety of relationships into which we enter, voluntarily or otherwise—for example, those holding between parent and child, two adults with a mutual relationship of love and trust, two adult strangers, two or more persons related through participation in some joint activity in which there is an equal distribution of benefits and burdens. Rawls' essay sets out types of guilt, depending on types of relationships. Here he is following the suggestive work of Piaget in *The Moral Judgment of a Child.* The brief selection from Freud, taken from *Civilization and Its Discontents,* introduces us to the most influential theory yet propounded for the origin of the sense of guilt, which must be compared with

Section 16 of Nietzsche's essay. The selection by Erikson, *Autonomy v. Shame and Doubt,* is his characterization of the stage in the development of the child when shame makes its appearance. I include too few of his words, but they are rich in suggestion. Nietzsche's essay is concerned with the origin and development of moral concepts at different stages of cultural development. Different concepts have in different cultures and times dominated man's view of himself, his fellows, and his world.

We begin, however, not with generalizations of one kind or another but rather with the work of an artist (Dostoyevsky), and the work of a morally reflective person (Jaspers), individuals who are wrestling either with concrete issues of guilt and innocence or are concerned with vividly recreating and portraying, as with Stavrogin, the gripping play of feelings that makes us nod or even shiver with recognition, and think, "Yes, that is how it is; that is life; I, too, have felt and suffered and acted in such ways." We turn back to ourselves from such first-hand accounts and grasp in a deeper, fuller way, in a way we did not before, the role in our own lives of guilt and shame. And, then, perhaps, we are tempted to think, and not without some justification, that a careful look at ourselves would reveal more to us about these topics than many a tome.

But sometimes this process of self-discovery is helped by another, and sometimes what helps is what another has put down on paper. And so, these few essays may help illumine for us not merely these grand topics, but our very selves.

Fyodor Dostoyevsky

Stavrogin's Confession

6   That night Nikolay Vsyevolodovitch did not sleep, and he spent the whole of it sitting on the sofa, often staring hard at one point in the corner by the chest of drawers. A lamp was burning in his room all night. About seven in the morning he fell asleep sitting up, and when, according to the established custom, Alexey Yegorytch entered the room with the morning cup of coffee exactly at half past nine, and woke his master up by his appearance, the latter opened his eyes, seeming disagreeably surprised to find that he could have slept so long and that the hour was so late. He drank his coffee hastily, dressed quickly, and hurriedly left the house. To Alexey Yegorytch's cautious query as to whether there were any orders, he made no reply. Once in the street, he walked looking at the ground deep in thought, only at moments lifting his head and betraying a vague yet intense uneasiness. At one street corner, while he was still near home, a crowd of peasants, some fifty men or more, crossed his path; they marched with dignity, almost silently, in ordered formation. At a small shop where he was forced to wait a while, some one said that these were the "Shpigulin workmen." He hardly noticed them.

Finally, at about half-past ten, he reached the gates of the local Spas-Yefimyev Bogorodsky Monastery, on the outskirts of the town, by the river. It was only then that he seemed to recall something alarming and troublesome. He stopped short, felt for something in his side-pocket, and grinned. Having entered the enclosure, he asked the first servant who came along to direct him to the bishop, Tihon, who was living in retirement at the monastery. The servant bowed repeatedly, and immediately led

From *The Possessed,* by Fyodor Dostoyevsky, trans. by Avraham Yarmolinsky. Copyright 1936 and renewed 1963 by Random House, Inc. Reprinted by permission of the publisher.

the way. Near a little flight of steps, at the end of the long two-story monastery building, a stout, grizzled monk encountered them, and with bold dispatch snatched Stavrogin from the servant. The monk led him through a long, narrow corridor, bowing perpetually (although, because of his stoutness, he could not make a low obeisance, but simply kept jerking his head up and down) and continually inviting him to follow, in spite of the fact that Nikolay Vsyevolodovitch followed him anyhow. The monk kept on asking questions and talking about Father Archimandrite, but getting no response, he became more and more deferential. Stavrogin noticed that he was known here, although as far as he could recall he had only visited the place as a child.

When they reached the door at the very end of the passage, the monk opened it with an authoritative hand, as it were, inquired with a show of familiarity of the novice who sprang up at their appearance, whether they could come in, and without waiting for his answer threw the door wide open and bowing, let in the "dear" visitor. Upon receiving Stavrogin's thanks, he vanished precipitately as though fleeing. Nikolay Vsyevolodovitch entered a smallish room, and there appeared almost simultaneously in the doorway of the adjoining room a tall, lean man, about fifty-five years old, in a plain indoor garment which is usually worn under the cassock. He looked somewhat sickly, and had a vague smile and a strange, rather shy expression. This was Tihon, of whom Nikolay Vsyevolodovitch had first heard from Shatov, and about whom he himself had in the meantime collected some information by the way.

The information was varied and contradictory, but one fact stood out, namely, that both the people who loved him and those who did not (and such there were) spoke of him with a certain reserve: those who disliked him, perhaps out of contempt, and his admirers, even ardent ones — because of discretion, as though they wished to conceal something, perhaps a weakness of his, possibly something like saintly folly. Nikolay Vsyevolodovitch had learned that Tihon had been living in the monastery for some six years and that he was visited by people of both the lowest and the highest ranks, that even in distant Petersburg he had most ardent admirers, chiefly women. On the other hand, from one of our personable old men, a clubman who was yet devout, he heard that "this Tihon is half crazy, and undoubtedly drinks." Anticipating upon the course of events, let me add for my own part that this assertion was sheer nonsense, and that if Tihon suffered from anything it was from a rheumatic pain in his legs which was of long standing, and at times from obscure nervous spasms. Nikolay Vsyevolodovitch also learned that, whether because of weakness of character or "an unpardonable absent-mindedness inappropriate to his rank," the retired bishop failed to command any unusual degree of respect in the monastery itself. It was said that Father Archimandrite, an austere man, rigid in the performance of his duties as prior, and furthermore, known for his learning, cherished something like an animosity, as it were, against Tihon, and condemned him, not to his face but indirectly, for his careless way of living and for being all but a heretic. Furthermore, the brethren treated the invalid prelate not exactly disrespectfully, but rather with easy familiarity. The two rooms which formed Tihon's cell were oddly furnished. Alongside of clumsy, old-fashioned furniture upholstered in shabby leather, stood three or four elegant pieces; a luxurious easy-chair, a large writing-table of excellent finish, an exquisitely carved book-case, little tables, what-nots—all, of course, gifts. There was a costly Bokhara rug, and side by side with it, ordinary mats. There were engravings representing both secular and mythological subjects, and in the corner, a large shrine as well, holding ikons gleaming with gold and silver, one of them an ancient piece containing saintly relics. The library too, it was said, was of an all too varied and conflicting character: besides the works of the great saints and worthies of the Church, there were theatrical compositions and novels and "maybe something much worse."

After the first greetings, spoken for some reason with obvious mutual embarrassment in hasty and indistinct syllables, Tihon led the visitor to his study, and with the same apparent haste made him sit on a sofa before a table, while he himself took a seat nearby in a wicker armchair. Here, surprisingly enough, Nikolay Vsyevolodovitch completely lost his composure. It seemed as if he were making violent efforts to bring himself to do something extraordinary, something incontrovertible and yet almost impossible for him to execute. For a few moments he let his eyes wander over the room, obviously without seeing what he was looking at; then he grew thoughtful, but perhaps did not know what he was thinking about. The quiet roused him, and suddenly it seemed to him that Tihon looked down bashfully, as it were, and with an odd and altogether irrelevant smile. For an instant this moved him to disgust and rebellion; he wanted to rise and go; he fancied that Tihon was actually drunk. But the latter suddenly lifted his eyes and looked at him with a glance so firm and full of thought and, at the same time, so unexpected and puzzling that Stavrogin almost started. And now suddenly another notion occurred to him, namely, that Tihon already knew why he had come, that he had already been forewarned (although no one in the world could have known the reason) and that if he had not spoken first, it was in order to spare him, it was for fear of humiliating him.

"Do you know me?" he asked abruptly. "Did I introduce myself when I came in? Excuse me, I am so absent-minded."

"You did not introduce yourself, but I had the pleasure of seeing you once, some four years ago, here in the monastery . . . by chance." Tihon spoke in an unhurried, soft, even voice, articulating the words clearly and distinctly.

"I wasn't at the monastery four years ago," retorted Nikolay Vsyevolodovitch with unnecessary rudeness. "I was here only as a child, before you had come at all."

"Perhaps you have forgotten," observed Tihon cautiously and without insistence.

"No, I haven't forgotten. And it would be ridiculous if I had," insisted Stavrogin on his part, with excessive emphasis. "Perhaps you have only heard about me and formed an idea of me, and then you imagined that you had seen me yourself."

Tihon did not answer. It was only then that Stavrogin noticed that Tihon's features twitched from time to time, a symptom of a nervous disorder of long standing.

"I see only that you are not well to-day," he said, "and perhaps I had better leave." He even made a motion as if to rise from his seat.

"Yes, to-day and yesterday I have had severe pains in my legs, and I had little sleep last night."

Tihon stopped. His guest suddenly fell into a vague reverie. The silence lasted a long time, some two minutes.

"Have you been watching me?" he asked suddenly, alarmed and suspicious.

"I was looking at you, and I recalled your mother's features. Although there is no external likeness, there is much internal, spiritual resemblance."

"No resemblance, particularly spiritual. Not the slightest," said Nikolay Vsyevolodovitch, needlessly alarmed and with an over-emphasis for which he could not account to himself. "You say this just like that . . . out of pity for my situation," he suddenly blurted out. "Bah! Does my mother come to you?"

"She does."

"Didn't know it. Never heard about it from her. Often?"

"Almost every month, and oftener."

"Never, never heard of it. Haven't heard of it." (This seemed to upset him terribly.) "And of course she has told you that I am mad," he blurted out again.

"No, not exactly mad. Still, I have heard others say so."

"You must have a good memory to recall such trifles. And did you hear about the slap?"

"I heard something."

"You mean all about it. You must have plenty of time to listen to such things. And about the duel?"

"About the duel, too."

"You don't need newspapers here. Has Shatov warned you about me?"

"No; I am acquainted with Mr. Shatov, though, but I haven't seen him for a long time."

"H'm! What's that map there? Bah! a map of the last war. What good is that to you?"

"I used the map in connection with this text. A most interesting account."

"Let me see; yes, fairly good style. But this is rather odd reading for you."

He drew the volume toward him and glanced at it. It was a comprehensive and able account of the circumstances of the late war, presented rather from the purely literary than from the military angle. He turned the book about and suddenly with an impatient movement tossed it aside.

"I certainly don't know why I have come here," he said with disgust, looking straight into Tihon's eyes as though expecting an answer from him.

"You, too, seem to be somewhat indisposed."

"Yes, perhaps."

And suddenly, in words so brief and disconnected as to be somewhat obscure, he began to speak of how he suffered, especially at night, from certain strange hallucinations; how he sometimes saw or felt close beside him an evil being, derisive and "rational": "it shows different faces and assumes different characters, and yet is always the same and always infuriates me . . ."

These disclosures were wild and incoherent, and really seemed to come from a madman. And yet Nikolay Vsyevolodovitch spoke with such strange, unaccustomed frankness, with a candor so entirely foreign to him that it seemed as though his former self had suddenly and unexpectedly disappeared. He was not at all ashamed to show the terror with which the apparition inspired him. But all this lasted only a moment, and vanished as quickly as it had come.

"It's all nonsense," he caught himself up swiftly and with awkward chagrin. "I will go to see a doctor."

"No doubt you should," Tihon agreed.

"You speak so confidently. . . . Have you met people who had hallucinations like mine?"

"Yes, but very rarely. I remember only one case, an army officer; it happened after he had lost his spouse, his irreplaceable life companion. Of another case I know only by hearsay. Both men went abroad for treatment. . . . And how long have you been subject to this?"

"About a year, but it's all nonsense. I'll go to see a doctor. It's all nonsense, frightful nonsense. It's myself in various forms, nothing else. Since I have just added this last . . . phrase, you must surely think that I still have some doubt as to whether it's I or whether it's not really the devil."

Tihon looked at him inquiringly.

"And . . . and do you really see him?" he asked, thereby putting aside all doubt of its plainly being no more than a false and morbid hallucination, "do you really see a definite image?"

"It is strange that you should persist in asking me when I have already told you that I do." Again Stavrogin became more and more irritated with each word. "Of course I see him. I see him just as plainly as I see you . . . and sometimes I see him but I am not certain that I see him, although I do see him. . . . And sometimes I do not know who is real, he or I. . . . It's all nonsense. And you, can't you imagine that it really is the devil?" he added, laughing, and passing too abruptly into a derisive tone. "It would be more in keeping with your calling."

"It's more likely a disease, although . . ."

"Although what?"

"Devils undoubtedly exist, but our conceptions of them differ widely."

"Just now you dropped your eyes again," said Stavrogin with an irritable laugh. "Because you were ashamed for me, since, while I believe in the devil, by pretending I don't, I am slyly putting a question to you: does he really exist, or not?"

Tihon smiled vaguely.

"Well then, let me tell you plainly that I am not at all ashamed, and to make up for my rudeness I will say boldly and in all seriousness: I do believe in the devil, I believe canonically, in a personal devil, not in an allegory, and I don't need confirmation from anybody. That's the whole story."

He gave a nervous, unnatural laugh. Tihon looked at him interestedly, but with a timid and withal gentle glance.

"You believe in God?" Nikolay Vsyevolodovitch blurted out.

"I do believe."

"It is written, isn't it, that if you have faith and bid a mountain remove itself hence, it will do so. . . . However, pardon this nonsense. Still, I am curious to know: can you remove a mountain or can't you?"

"If God commands, I will remove it," said Tihon in a low, restrained voice, dropping his eyes again.

"Well, but that would be the same as if God Himself removed it. No, you — you — will you be able to do it, as a reward for your faith in God?"

"Perhaps I shall not."

" 'Perhaps'! That's not bad. Ha! ha! You are still a doubter then?"

"I doubt, because my faith is imperfect."

"What! Even *your* faith is imperfect? Well, I wouldn't have supposed it, to look at you." He suddenly stared at Tihon with wholly naïve amazement, which did not at all harmonise with the derisive tone of the previous questions.

"Yes. . . . Perhaps my faith is imperfect," answered Tihon.

"At any rate, you believe that, though if only with God's help, you could remove it, and that's no small matter. At least you wish to believe. And you take the mountain literally. That is a great deal. A good principle. I have noticed that the more advanced of our Levites are strongly inclined toward Lutheranism, and are quite ready to explain miracles by natural causes. Anyhow that is more than the *'très peu'* of one archbishop, who said it, true enough, at the sword's point. And of course you are a Christian, too."

Stavrogin spoke rapidly, his fluent words now serious, now derisive; perhaps he did not himself know why he was talking as he did, asking questions, getting excited, growing curious.

"Let me not be ashamed of Thy cross, O Lord," Tihon muttered in a strange, passionate whisper, bowing his head still lower.

"Is it possible to believe in the devil without believing in God?" asked Stavrogin with a laugh.

"That's quite possible. It's done right and left." Tihon lifted his eyes and smiled.

"And I am sure that you consider such a faith more estimable than utter lack of faith . . ." Stavrogin burst out laughing.

"On the contrary, outright atheism is more to be respected than worldly indifference," answered Tihon, with ostensible gaiety and candor; at the same time he scrutinised his guest carefully and uneasily.

"Aha! so that's where you stand! Decidedly you astonish me."

"Say what you may, but the complete atheist stands on the penultimate step to most perfect faith (he may or he may not take a further step), but the indifferent person has no faith whatever except a bad fear, and that but rarely, and only if he is sensitive."

"H'm. . . . Have you read the Apocalypse?"

"I have."

"Do you remember: 'And unto the Angel of the Church of the Laodiceans write . . .'"

"I remember."

"Where is the book?" Stavrogin grew strangely impatient and alarmed, his eyes wandering over the table in search of the Bible — "I'd like to read to you. . . . Have you a Russian translation?"

"I know the passage. I remember it," said Tihon.

"Do you know it by heart? Say it. . . ."

He quickly dropped his eyes, leaned his wrists on his knees, and impatiently prepared to listen. Tihon began reciting, recalling word after word:

"'And unto the Angel of the Church of the Laodiceans write: These things saith the Amen, the faithful and true witness, the beginning of the creation of God; I know thy works, that thou art neither cold nor hot; I would thou wert cold or hot. So then because thou art lukewarm, and neither cold nor hot, I will spue thee out of my mouth. Because thou sayest, I am rich and increased with goods and have need of nothing: and thou knowest not that thou art wretched, and miserable, and poor, and blind, and naked . . .'"

"Enough!" Stavrogin cut him short. "Do you know, I love you very much."

"And I love you," replied Tihon in a low voice.

Stavrogin grew silent, and suddenly again fell into a reverie. This occurred fitfully, as it were, now for the third time. He was practically in this state when he said to Tihon, "I love you," at least his words came as a surprise to himself. More than a minute passed.

"Do not be angry," whispered Tihon, touching Stavrogin's elbow lightly with his finger and appearing to grow timid himself.

The latter started and frowned fiercely. "How did you know that I was going to get angry?" he said quickly. Tihon was about to speak, but Stavrogin, suddenly overcome with inexplicable agitation, interrupted him:

"Why did you fancy that I must necessarily become angry? Yes, I did get angry. You were right. And angry precisely because I told you I loved you. You're right. But you are a coarse cynic, you have a low opinion of human nature. There might have been no anger if it had been anyone but me. However, we're not dealing with anyone else, but with me. And still you are an odd fellow and a saintly fool. . . ."

He grew more and more irritable and, strangely enough, he did not choose his words:

"Listen, I don't like spies and psychologists, at least such as pry into my soul. I don't invite anybody into my soul, I do not need anybody, I can shift for myself. Perhaps you think I am afraid of you." He raised his voice and threw his head back defiantly. "Perhaps you are fully convinced now that I have come to disclose a 'terrible' secret to you, and you are waiting for it with all the monkish curiosity of which you are capable. Well, then, let me tell you that I will disclose nothing, no secret whatever, because I can very well get along without you . . . because there is no mystery whatever . . . it exists only in your imagination."

Tihon looked at him steadily. "You were struck by the fact that the Lamb loves those who are cold better than He does the luke-warm," he said; "you do not wish to be merely lukewarm. I have a foreboding that you are struggling with an extraordinary, perhaps a fearful intention. I implore you, do not torment yourself, and tell everything."

"And you were certain that I had come with a story."

"I . . . guessed it," whispered Tihon, looking down.

Nikolay Vsyevolodovitch was somewhat pale. His hands trembled slightly. For several seconds he stared, motionless and silent, as if coming to a final decision. At length he drew several printed sheets of paper from the side pocket of his jacket and laid them on the table.

"Here are the sheets intended for the public," he said in a breaking voice. "If only one man reads them, then you may be sure that I will not conceal them, and everyone will read them. That's my decision. And I do not . . . need you at all, because I have made up my mind. But read. . . . Say nothing while you're reading. Tell me everything when you are through."

"Shall I really read them?" asked Tihon, hesitatingly.

"Do; I am calm."

"No, I can't make it out without my spectacles, the print is small, foreign."

"Here are your glasses." Stavrogin took them up from the table, handed them to Tihon and leaned against the back of the sofa. Tihon did not look at him and plunged into the reading.

II

It was indeed foreign print—three sheets of ordinary small-size note-paper, sewn together. It must have been printed secretly at some Russian printing-press abroad, and at first blush the pamphlet looked very much like a revolutionary leaflet. It bore the heading: "From Stavrogin."

I insert this document verbatim into my chronicle. I have allowed myself only to correct the mistakes in spelling, which are rather numerous and which somewhat surprised me, for the author was, after all, an educated and even well-read man (of course, relatively speaking). As for the style, I made no changes in it, in spite of the errors. At any rate, it is obvious that the author is by no means a man of letters.

I shall allow myself one more remark, in anticipation of what is to follow.

In my opinion, the document is a morbid thing, the work of the devil who had taken possession of this gentleman. Thus a man suffering from acute pain tosses in his bed, eager to find a position which would bring him relief, at least momentarily—indeed, not to find relief, but merely to exchange one kind of suffering for another, if only for a minute. And, of course, in a case like that, one doesn't care how graceful or sensible the position is. The fundamental idea of the document is a terrible undisguised need of punishment, the need of the cross, of public chastisement. Meanwhile, this need of the cross in a man who doesn't believe in the cross—why "that in itself is an idea," as Stepan Trofimovitch once expressed himself, on an occasion of a different sort, however.

On the other hand, the entire document is at the same time something wild and reckless, although ostensibly written with a different purpose. The author declares that he "couldn't help" writing it, that he was "forced" to do it, and this is fairly plausible: he would have been glad to have had this cup pass from him if he could, but he seems really to have been unable to avoid it, and he took advantage of this opportunity to engage in a fresh outburst of violence. Yes, the sick man tosses in his bed, and wants to exchange one kind of suffering for another—fighting society seems to him the least uncomfortable position and so he flings down a challenge to it.

Indeed, in the very existence of such a document one senses a new, unexpected and irreverent challenge to society. Just for the sake of finding an enemy . . .

And, who knows, perhaps all that, to wit, those sheets intended for publication, are nothing else but another way of nipping the governor's ear. Why this occurs to me now, after so much has been explained already, I cannot understand. But I'm not bringing forward any proofs, nor do I assert at all that it is a false document, that it is an invention and a fabrication. Most likely, the truth must be sought somewhere in the middle. . . . However, I have gone too far ahead of my story; it is safer to turn to the document itself. Here is what Tihon read:

From Stavrogin "In the year 186—, I, Nikolay Stavrogin, a retired army officer, was living in Petersburg, indulging in dissipation in which I found no pleasure. In those days, for quite some time I kept three lodgings. I myself was living in a shabby hotel where I got board and service and where Marya Lebyadkin, now my lawful wife, was also staying. The other two places I rented by the month for assignation purposes: in one I received a lady who was in love with me, and in the other, her maid, and for quite a time I was preoccupied with the scheme of bringing the two together, so that mistress and maid would meet in my rooms. Knowing the character of both, I expected to get some entertainment out of this silly joke.

"While I was gradually arranging for that meeting I had to visit one of the two lodgings, which was in a large house on Gorokhovaya Street, more frequently than the other, because it was there that the maid used to come. Here I had a single room on the fourth floor, which I rented from a Russian family of the lower middle class. They occupied the adjacent room, which was smaller, and the door between the two was always open, a fact which fell in with my desires. The husband, who wore a beard and a long coat, was employed in some office and was absent from morning till night. The wife, a woman of forty, was generally busy making over old clothes and she too often went out to dispose of these. I remained all alone with their daughter, who, by the looks of her, was quite a child. Her name was Matryosha. Her mother loved her, but would often beat her, and had a way of screaming at her on every occasion, as is the manner of women of her class. This little girl waited on me, and tidied up behind the screen. I declare that I have forgotten the house-number. On inquiry I found out that the old house has been torn down and where two or three buildings used to stand, there is now one large new one. I have also forgotten the surname of the people from whom I rented the room (perhaps I didn't even know it at the time). I recall that the woman's name was, if I am not mistaken, Stepanida. The husband's I don't remember at all. What has become of the woman I do not know. I fancy that it might be possible to trace them with the aid of the Petersburg police. It was a corner flat, opening onto the courtyard. It all happened in June. The house was painted pale blue.

"One day a penknife which I didn't need and which was just lying around disappeared from my table. I mentioned the matter to the woman, without thinking that she would whip her daughter for it. She had just been screaming at the child on account of the loss of a scrap of cloth, suspecting that she had taken it for her dolls, and had pulled her hair for her. When the scrap was found under the tablecloth the little girl chose not to say a word of reproach for having been unjustly punished, but just looked at her mother silently. I noticed this and fixed it in my memory, and it was now for the first time that I remarked the little girl's face which had been a blank to me before. She was a fair-skinned and freckled little girl, with an ordinary face, but a child's face, and gentle, exceedingly gentle. The mother didn't like the little girl's failure to reproach her for the unmerited beating, and then the matter of the penknife came up. The woman flew into a passion, especially because she had just beaten the child unjustly. She plucked some twigs from the broom, and whipped the girl so that she raised welts on her, before my very eyes, although the child was already in her twelfth year. Matryosha did not scream under the strokes, obviously because I was present, but she gasped strangely at each blow. And afterward she continued to sob gaspingly for a whole hour. As soon as the whipping was over, I suddenly found the penknife on my bed, in the folds of the blanket. Then I quietly put the penknife into my vest pocket, went out, and on the street threw the penknife away, far from the house so that no one should discover it. Immediately I felt that I had done something vile. At the same time I experienced a pleasurable sensation because suddenly a certain desire pierced me like a blade, and I began to busy myself with it. Let me note here that often various base feelings took possession of me to the point of making me utterly unreasonable or, better still, exceedingly stubborn, though they never made me forget myself. Though such a feeling mounted to frenzy in me, I could always overcome it, even stop it at its height, but I very seldom wished to do so. And I declare that I do not wish to claim freedom from responsibility for my crimes on the grounds of either environment or disease.

"Then I waited two days. The little girl, having cried her fill, became even more silent, yet I am convinced that she cherished no ill feeling toward me. However, she certainly felt ashamed because she had been punished in such a way in my presence. But being an obedient child, she undoubtedly blamed herself even for her shame. I note this, because it is important for the story. . . . Then I spent three days in my main apartment.

"These crowded lodgings, reeking of stale food, housed many people, mostly government clerks out of employment or on the lowest possible salary, doctors looking for an out-of-town position, all manner of Poles, who always hung around me. I remember everything clearly. In this hell-hole I lived a lonely life, that is, in the spiritual sense, for all day long I was surrounded by a whole crew of 'pals' who were terribly devoted to me and almost worshipped me for my purse. I believe we did many vile things and the other tenants were afraid of us, that is, they were polite, in spite of the revolting pranks and silly jokes which we perpetrated. I repeat: at that time I was not at all averse to being deported to Siberia. I was so utterly bored that I could have hanged myself, and if I didn't, it was because I was still looking forward to something, as I have all my life. I recall that at that time I was seriously engaged in the study of theology. This somewhat distracted me, but afterwards I grew more bored than ever. I was in a state where I wanted to put powder under the four corners of the earth and blow it all up, but it didn't seem worth the effort. Yet there was no malice in my heart, it was merely that I was bored. I am no Socialist. I fancy it must have been sickness. In jest I once asked the unemployed Dr. Dobrolubov who was starving in the lodgings with his family, 'Are there no drops to stimulate one's civic energy?' 'For civil energy,' he answered, 'maybe not, but for criminal—perhaps, yes!' And he was pleased with his shabby pun, although he and his pregnant wife and his two little girls were without anything to eat. But if people didn't have this capacity for being satisfied with themselves, they wouldn't want to live.

"It was in the course of those two days that I once put to myself the question, as to whether I could give up my intention, and I immediately felt that I could, at any time, even that very minute.

"Three days later I went back to the Gorokhovaya Street place. The mother was getting ready to leave with a bundle; the man, as usual, was not at home, so I remained alone with Matryosha. The windows were open. The house was occupied mostly by artisans and all day long the place was filled with songs and the sound of hammers. An hour passed. Matryosha was sitting in the next room on a little stool, with a bit of sewing, her back turned toward me. After a while she began to hum, softly, very softly. She did that sometimes. I took out my watch; it was two o'clock. My heart began to beat fast. I rose and stole toward her. On their window-sills there were many geranium pots and the sun was shining very brightly. I quietly sat down on the floor beside her. She started, and at first was incredibly frightened and jumped to her feet. I took her hand and kissed it, drew her down to the stool again, and began looking into her eyes. The fact that I kissed her hand, suddenly made her laugh like a baby. But her amusement lasted only an instant: she quickly jumped up again and this time in such fright that her face was convulsed. She stared at me, her eyes motionless with terror, and her lips began to twitch as though she were going to cry, but she did not. I kissed her hand again and seated her on my knees. She suddenly pulled away from me with a jerk of her whole body and smiled as though ashamed, but it was a strangely wry smile: Her whole face reddened with shame. I was whispering to her and laughing. Suddenly something happened that astonished me—a thing so odd that I shall never forget it: the little girl threw her arms around my neck and suddenly began to kiss me violently of her own accord. Her face expressed perfect rapture. I got up, almost indignant—this behavior in so young a creature repelled me, the more so because my repulsion was born of the pity which I suddenly felt . . . ''

Here the sheet ended and the sentence broke off abruptly.

What occurred next cannot be passed over. Of the five sheets of which the document consisted, one, which Tihon had just read and which ended abruptly in mid-sentence, was in his hands, the other four remaining in Stavrogin's hands. As Tihon looked at him inquiringly, Stavrogin, who held himself in readiness, instantly gave him further sheets.

"But there is a gap here," said Tihon, looking closely at the sheet he held. "Bah, this is the third sheet, I need the second."

"Yes, the third, but that sheet . . . the second sheet has been confiscated for the present," Stavrogin answered quickly, with an awkward smile. He was sitting motionless in the corner of the sofa watching Tihon feverishly as he read. "You will get it later when . . . you deserve it," he added, with an unsuccessful gesture of familiarity. He was laughing, but it was pitiful to look at him.

"Well, sheet two or three—it's all the same now," Tihon began.

"What do you mean—all the same? Why?" Stavrogin made a sudden eager movement toward Tihon. "Not at all. Ah, in your monkish way you are ready to suspect the worst. A monk would be the best criminal prosecutor!"

Tihon watched him narrowly in silence.

"Calm down. It's not my fault if the little girl was foolish and misunderstood me. . . . Nothing happened. Nothing."

"Well, God be praised," Tihon crossed himself.

"It would take too long to explain . . . it was . . . simply a psychological misunderstanding. . . ."

He suddenly blushed. An expression of disgust, anxiety, despair, slowly passed over his face. Abruptly he grew silent. For a long time, for more than a minute, the two were silent and avoided looking at each other.

"Well, you had better go on reading," he said mechanically wiping the cold sweat off his forehead with his fingers. "And . . .

better not look at me at all. . . . It seems to me I am dreaming. . . . And . . . do not try my patience. . . ." he added in a whisper.

Tihon quickly looked away, took up the third sheet and continued reading to the end without stopping. In the three sheets handed to him by Stavrogin there were no more gaps. The third sheet also began in mid-sentence. I transcribe verbatim:

". . . for a moment I was really frightened, though not intensely. I was in very good spirits that morning, and awfully kind toward everyone, and the whole crew was very well pleased with me. But I left them all and went to the place on Gorokhovaya Street. I met her downstairs in the hall. She was coming from the grocery where she had been sent for some chicory. Seeing me, she shot up the stairs in a terrible fright. It was not just fright, but a dumb, paralysing terror. When I came in, her mother had already given her a slap because she had entered the room at 'breakneck speed,' and this incident covered the true cause of her fear. And so for the present all was well. She had retired to a corner and did not show herself all the time I was there. I stayed for an hour and then left.

"Toward evening I felt afraid again, but this time the fear was incomparably more intense. The main thing was that I was afraid and that I was so conscious of being afraid. Oh, I know of nothing more absurd and more abominable! I had never experienced fear before, never before and never afterwards, but this one time in my life I was afraid, and in fact, I literally trembled. The intense consciousness of it was a profound humiliation. If I could, I would have killed myself, but I felt myself unworthy of death. However, if I did not kill myself it was not because of that, but again, because I was afraid. People kill themselves out of fear, but out of fear, too, people remain alive: a time comes when a man no longer dares kill himself and the act itself becomes unthinkable. Besides, in the evening, when I was in my lodgings, I began to hate her so that I decided to kill her. At dawn I ran with that purpose to Gorokhovaya Street. On my way I kept imagining myself in the act of killing and defiling her. My hatred rose especially at the memory of her smile: my contempt mixed with measureless disgust as I remembered the way she had thrown herself on my neck with heaven knows what notion. But when I reached Fontanka, I felt ill. Furthermore, I conceived a new and terrible thought, terrible because I was so conscious of my feelings. When I came home I lay down in a fever. But I was so completely overcome by fear that I even stopped hating the little girl. I no longer wanted to kill her, and that was the new thought that occurred to me on Fontanka. I realized that fear at its height banishes hatred, even the desire to avenge an insult.

"I woke up around noon feeling relatively well and I was even astonished at the violence of my sensations the day before. I was ashamed of my desire to kill her. But I was in a bad humor and in spite of my disgust was again compelled to go to Gorokhovaya Street. I remember I had an intense desire at that moment to pick a serious quarrel with somebody on my way there. On reaching my room I found Nina Savelyevna there, the maid. She had been waiting for me for an hour. I didn't care for her at all, so that she came with some fear that I might be angry because of her uninvited presence. She always came that way. But this time I suddenly found myself glad to see her and that made her ecstatic. She was rather pretty, modest, and had the manners which the lower middle class prizes, so that my landlady had for a long time been singing her praises to me. I found the two of them having coffee and my landlady was hugely enjoying the pleasant chat. I noticed Matryosha in a corner of the other room. She stood there without stirring, staring at her mother and the visitor with a frown. When I came in she did not hide as before, nor did she run away. I remember that distinctly—it rather struck me. Only it seemed to me at first blush that she had grown very haggard and that she was feverish. I was very tender to Nina, so that she left in a most contented mood. We went out together, and for two days I did not return to Gorokhovaya Street. I was already fed up with the whole thing.

"Finally I decided to put an end to everything, and leave Petersburg: I'd come to that stage. But when I came there in order to give up the room I found the woman worried and distressed: Matryosha had been ill for three days now, and every night she had been delirious. Of course I immediately asked what she said in her delirium (we talked in whispers in my room), and the woman whispered back that her ravings were terrible; she kept saying: 'I killed God.' I offered to send for the doctor at my expense, but she would not let me. 'With God's mercy it will pass. She isn't in bed all the time. She has just been to the grocer's on an errand.' I decided to find Matryosha alone, and, since the woman let fall that she had to leave the house at five, I made up my mind to come back in the evening.

"I didn't know why, or what I wanted to do when I got there.

"I had dinner at a restaurant. At a quarter past five sharp I returned. I let myself in as usual, with my own key. There was nobody there but Matryosha. She lay in her mother's bed behind the screen, and I noticed that she peeked out, but I pretended that I didn't see her. The windows were open. The air was warm, hot, in fact. I paced up and down for a while and then sat down on the sofa. I remember everything up to the last minute. It positively gave me pleasure—I do not know why—not to say a word to Matryosha and to keep her in suspense. I waited a whole hour, when suddenly she jumped out from behind the screen. I heard her feet strike the floor, the noise as she got out of bed, then her rapid steps, and there she was standing on the threshold of my room. I was so mean that I was glad to know that she was the first to yield. Oh, how base it all was, and how humiliated I was! She stood and looked at me silently.

"In these days when I hadn't seen her at close range she had really grown terribly thin. Her face had shrunk and her head must have been hot with fever. Her eyes had grown big and she stared at me fixedly with dull curiosity, as it seemed to me at first. I sat, looking at her and did not budge. And now suddenly I was moved to hatred again. But very soon I noticed that she was not afraid of me at all, and that she was perhaps delirious. But that was not the case. Suddenly she began to shake her head at me as naïve and ill-mannered people do by way of reproach. And suddenly she raised her little fist at me and began to threaten me from where she stood. For a moment this gesture seemed ridiculous to me, but instantly I could not bear it. I got to my feet and stirred in terror. Her face betrayed such despair as was intolerable to see in a creature so small. She kept on threatening me with her little fist and shaking her head in reproach. I began to talk to her kindly in a low, cautious voice, out of cowardice, but saw immediately that she wouldn't understand me, and my terror increased. Then suddenly she covered her face with her hands as she had done before, moved away and stood at the window with her back turned toward me. I also turned away and sat down by my own window. I cannot possibly understand why I did not leave then and there, but remained. I must have been waiting for something to happen. Perhaps I would have sat a while and then would have gotten up and killed her, to put an end to everything in my despair.

"Soon I heard her quick steps again. She passed through the door on to a wooden gallery which led to the stairs. I hurried to my door and got there just in time to notice that Matryosha had stepped into a tiny cubicle, something like a hen-coop, adjacent to a privy. When I retraced my steps and sat down at the window again, a fateful thought flashed through my mind. Even now I cannot understand why this rather than any thought suddenly occurred to me; things must have led me to it. Of course it was still an incredible thought—nevertheless . . ." (I remember everything perfectly and my heart beat violently.)

"A minute later I looked at my watch again and noted the time with great care. Why I had to be so precise I do not know. Generally at that moment I wanted to notice everything. As a result, I still remember everything and see all that took place as if it were happening before my very eyes. Evening was coming on. A fly was buzzing overhead and kept settling on my face. I caught it, held it awhile in my fingers, and let it fly out of the window. A cart rumbled noisily into the courtyard. In the corner of the courtyard a tailor at his window had been singing a song in a loud voice for some time. He was sitting at his work and I could see him plainly. It occurred to me that since nobody had met me when I was passing through the gates and while I was going upstairs, it would be best if nobody saw me as I went downstairs, and I cautiously moved my chair away from the window so that the tenants could not see me. Oh, how abominable it was! I took up a book, but soon cast it aside and began to look at a tiny red spider on a geranium leaf, and dozed off. I remember everything down to the last moment.

"Suddenly I whipped out my watch. Twenty minutes had passed since she went out. I decided to wait exactly another quarter of an hour. I made up my mind to that. It also occurred to me that perhaps she had returned without my having heard her, but this was impossible: there was a dead silence, and I could hear the buzzing of every fly. Suddenly my heart began to beat violently again. I took out my watch: three minutes more to wait. I sat through them, although my heart beat so violently that it hurt. Then I got up, put on my hat, buttoned my coat, and looked about the room to see if I were leaving any traces of my having been there. I moved the chair nearer to the window, where it had stood before. At last I opened the door, quietly locked it with my key, and went to the cubicle. The door was shut but not locked; I knew that it didn't lock, but I didn't want to open it, so I stood on tiptoe and looked through a crack high up. At the very moment when I was rising on the tips of my toes I recalled that when I was sitting by the window, looking at the little red spider, and was about to doze off, I had thought of how I would lift myself on my toes so that my eye would be on a level with that crack. I insert this detail to prove without fail that I was in full possession of my faculties, and that consequently I was not a madman, and that I am responsible for everything. I stood peering through the crack for a long time, because it was dark inside, yet not altogether, so that at length I saw what I had to see.

"Then I decided that I could leave and I went down the stairs. I did not meet anybody and nobody could offer any evidence against me. About three hours later we were all in our shirt-sleeves, drinking tea and playing with an old pack of cards, while Lebyadkin recited poetry. Many stories were told, and it so happened that they were related well and amusingly, and not stupidly as usual. Kirillov was also there. Nobody drank, except Lebyadkin, although there was a bottle of rum on the table.

"Prokhor Malov said: 'When Nikolay Vsyevolodovitch is contented and doesn't sulk, all of us are in good spirits and talk cleverly.' The phrase stuck in my memory, and so it seems that I was gay and contented then, and did not sulk, and talked cleverly. I remember that I knew perfectly well, however, at the time, that I was a low and vile coward rejoicing in his deliverance, and that I would never be decent again, either here on earth or after my death or ever. And one more thing: I was reminded of the Jewish proverb: 'one's own may be bad, but it does not smell.' For although at heart I felt that I was a scoundrel, I was not ashamed of it and, in general, I was not much distressed. On that occasion, sitting at tea and chatting with the crew, for the first time in my life I clearly formulated the following for myself: I have neither the feeling nor the knowledge of good and evil, and not only have I lost the sense of good and evil, but good and evil really do not exist (and this pleased me) and are but a prejudice; I can be free of all prejudices, but at the very moment when I achieve that freedom I shall perish. For the first time I put it thus clearly to myself, and that happened just then at tea when I was fooling and laughing with my companions. I remember everything clearly. Old, familiar thoughts sometimes take on the appearance of brand-new ones, even after you have lived fifty years.

"All the time I kept waiting for something to happen. Indeed, about eleven o'clock the little daughter of the janitor on Gorokhovaya Street brought me the news from my landlady that Matryosha had hanged herself. I went with the child and discovered that the woman herself did not know why she had sent for me. Of course she screamed and carried on very loudly, as they all do on such occasions. There was a crowd, too, and policemen. I stood about for a while and then left.

"I was hardly disturbed the whole time, except to be asked the usual questions. I said nothing but that the girl had been ill and delirious, and that on my part, I had offered to call a doctor at my own expense. The penknife too was mentioned. I said that my landlady whipped the child but that this was nothing. No one found out about my visit in the evening. That was the end of it.

"For about a week I did not return to the place. I only went there in order to give up the room. My landlady still cried, although she was already busy again with her scraps of cloth and sewing. 'It was because of your penknife that I hurt her feelings so,' she said, but without much bitterness. It was as though she had been waiting for the chance to say that to me. I gave up the room on the pretext that naturally this was now no place in which to receive Nina Savelyevna. When I took leave she again spoke in praise of Nina Savelyevna. I gave her five roubles in addition to what I owed her for the room.

"The main thing was that life bored me to the point of stupefaction. The danger having passed, I would have wholly forgotten the Gorokhovaya Street affair, if it hadn't been that, for some time, I kept remembering the attendant circumstances with vexation. I vented my anger on whomever I could. It was at this time that, for no apparent reason at all, I conceived the idea of somehow crippling my life, in the most repulsive manner possible. The year before I had already had the idea of shooting myself; now something better presented itself.

"One day as I was watching the lame Marya Timofeyevna Lebyadkin, who was more or less of a servant in my lodgings, I suddenly decided to marry her—at that time she was not yet insane, but simply a rapturous idiot, and secretly head over heels in love with me. (The gang found that out.) The thought of Stavrogin's marriage to a creature like that, the lowest of the low, tickled my nerves. It would be impossible to imagine anything more monstrous. But this was in those days, it happened in those days, and so it is intelligible. At any rate, I married her, not solely 'for a bet, after a drunken dinner.' It was in those days, in those days, and I couldn't have known yet—that's the main thing. The ceremony was witnessed by Kirillov and Pyotr Verhovensky, who at that time happened to be in Petersburg; also by Lebyadkin himself and Prokhor Malov (he is dead now). Nobody else ever discovered it, and they promised to keep quiet about it. This secrecy has always seemed abominable to me, but it hasn't been violated even yet, although I had the intention of making the fact public; now I am making it public with the rest.

"After the wedding I went to the provinces to see my mother. I went there to distract myself. In our town I left behind me the reputation of being a madman—a reputation which has endured to this very day and which, no doubt, is harmful to me, as I shall explain below. I mention this merely to make this confession fuller. Then I went abroad and remained there for four years.

"I visited the Orient, at Mt. Athos I stood through night services which lasted for eight hours, I was in Egypt, stayed in Switzerland, travelled as far as Iceland, attended the University of Göttingen for a whole academic year. In the course of the last year I became intimate with a Russian family of high rank that was living in Paris, and with two Russian girls in Switzerland. Some two years ago at Frankfort, passing by a stationery store, I noticed among the photographs on sale a small picture of a little girl elegantly dressed, but very closely resembling Matryosha. I immediately bought the photograph, and coming to the hotel, placed it on the mantelpiece. There it lay for a week, untouched, and I didn't look at it even once, and when I left Frankfort I forgot to take it along.

"I note this precisely in order to show to what extent I was able to master my memories and to what extent I became callous to them. I would spurn the whole lot of them, and they would all vanish obediently every time I so desired. It has always bored me to recall the past, and I could never long for the past as almost everyone else does, the more so because I hated it as I did everything else that was part of me. As for Matryosha, I even forgot her photograph on the mantelpiece.

"About a year ago, in the spring, travelling in Germany, I absent-mindedly passed the railway station at which I had to change for my destination, and so found myself on another line. I got off at the next station; it was between two and three in the afternoon, the day was clear. It was a tiny German town. A hotel was pointed out to me. It was necessary to wait. The next train was due at eleven at night. As a matter of fact, I was rather pleased with this adventure, for I wasn't in a hurry to get anywhere. The hotel proved to be a small, mean place, but with shrubs and flower-beds all about it. I was given a small room. I made a good meal and as I had spent all of the previous night on the road, I fell sound asleep around four o'clock.

"I had a dream which was totally surprising to me because I had never dreamed anything like it before. All my dreams have always been either silly or terrifying. In the Dresden gallery there is a painting by Claude Lorraine, called in the catalogue *Acis and Galatea,* if I am not mistaken, but which I always called *The Golden Age,* I don't know why. I had seen it before and just three days earlier I saw it again in passing. As a matter of fact, I went to the gallery simply in order to look at it and it was perhaps for that reason alone that I stopped at Dresden. It was this picture that appeared to me in a dream, yet not as a picture but as though it were an actual scene.

"I cannot quite tell, however, what I dreamed of. As in the picture, I saw a corner of the Greek archipelago the way it was some three thousand years ago: caressing azure waves, rocks and islands, a shore in blossom, afar a magic panorama, a beckoning sunset — words fail one. European mankind remembers this place as its cradle, and the thought filled my soul with the love that is bred in kinship. Here was mankind's earthly paradise, gods descended from heaven and united with mortals, here occurred the first scenes of mythology. Here lived beautiful men and women! They rose, they went to sleep, happy and innocent; the groves rang with their merry songs, the great overflow of unspent energies poured itself into love and simple-hearted joys, and I sensed all that, and at the same time I envisaged as with second sight, their great future, the three thousand years of life which lay unknown and unguessed before them, and my heart was shaken with these thoughts. Oh, how happy I was that my heart was shaken and that at last I loved! The sun poured its rays upon these isles and this sea, rejoicing in its fair children. Oh, marvellous dream, lofty illusion! The most improbable of all visions, to which mankind throughout its existence has given its best energies, for which it has sacrificed everything, for which it has pined and been tormented, for which its prophets were crucified and killed, without which nations will not desire to live, and without which they cannot even die! All these sensations I lived through, as it were, in this dream; I repeat. I do not know exactly what I dreamed about, my dream was only of sensation, but the cliffs, and the sea, and the slanting rays of the setting sun, all that I still seemed to see when I woke up and opened my eyes, for the first time in my life literally wet with tears. I remember these tears, I remember that I was glad of them, that I was not ashamed of them. A feeling of happiness, hitherto unknown to me, pierced my heart till it ached. Evening had already set in; a sheaf of bright slanting sunrays pierced the green foliage in the window-boxes of my little room and flooded me with light. I quickly closed my eyes again, as if eager to call back the vanished dream, but suddenly I noticed a tiny dot in the centre of bright, bright light. That's exactly how it all was and that's how it started. Suddenly this dot began to assume a shape, and all of a sudden I saw clearly a tiny red spider. I remembered it at once as it had looked on the geranium leaf, when the rays of the setting sun were pouring down in the same way. It was as if something had stabbed me, I sat up in bed. That is the way it all happened!

"I saw before me (O not that I really saw her! If only it had been a genuine apparition! If she had appeared only for an instant, for one instant, in the flesh and alive, so that I could have spoken to her!), I saw Matryosha, grown haggard and with feverish eyes, precisely as she had looked at the moment when she stood on the threshold of my room, and shaking her head, had lifted her tiny fist against me. The pitiful despair of a helpless creature with an immature mind, who threatened me (with what? what could she do to me, O God?) but who, of course, blamed herself alone! Never has anything like that happened to me. I sat until nightfall, motionless, forgetful of time. I should like to explain myself now, and clearly express exactly what went on. Was this what is called remorse or repentance? I do not know and cannot tell even now. But what is intolerable to me is only this image, namely, the little girl on the threshold with her little fist lifted threatening me, only the way she looked then, only that moment, neither before nor after, only that shaking of the head. This threatening gesture of hers no longer seemed ridiculous to me, but terrifying. Pity for her stabbed me, a maddening pity, and I would have given my body to be torn to pieces if that would have erased what had happened. What I regret is not the crime, nor her death. I'm not sorry for her, what I cannot bear is just that one instant, I can't, I can't, because I see her that way every day, and I know for a certainty that I am doomed. It is precisely that which I have not been able to bear since then, and I couldn't bear it before either, but I didn't know it. Since then I see the vision almost every day. It does not appear to me of itself, yet I summon it of my own accord, but I cannot help summoning it, although I cannot live with it. Oh, if I could only see her sometimes in the flesh, even if it were only a hallucination. I wish that she would look at me again at least once, with her eyes big and feverish as they were then, look into my eyes and see. . . . Foolish dream, it will never come true!

"Why does no other memory of mine arouse any such feelings in me? And yet I have memories of deeds which people would condemn as much worse. Such memories arouse only hatred in me, and at that, the feeling is caused by my present condition; formerly, I used to forget them cold-bloodedly, shove them into the background, and remain unnaturally easy in my mind.

"After that I roamed about nearly all that year and tried to divert myself. I know that even now I can get rid of Matryosha if I so desire. I am in complete possession of my will, as before. But the whole point is that I never wanted to do it, that I do not want to do it now and that I never shall. It will continue like this until I go mad.

"In Switzerland two months later I was seized by a fit of passion, accompanied by an impulse toward violence, such as I had experienced only in my early years. It was a kind of contrast, a measure of self-defence, as it were, on the part of the organism. I felt terribly tempted to commit a new crime, namely, bigamy (because I was already married), but I fled on the advice of another girl, to whom I confessed practically everything, even the fact that I did not love the one I desired so much, and that I could never love any one, and that there was nothing here but lust. Besides, this new crime would not by any means have freed me from Matryosha.

"Consequently I have decided to have these sheets printed and to import three hundred copies of them into Russia; when the time comes, I shall send them to the police and to the local authorities; at the same time I shall send them to the editorial offices of all the newspapers with a request to publish them, and also to my many acquaintances in Petersburg and elsewhere in Russia. My confession will also appear in translation abroad. Perhaps this makes no sense, but I will publish it nevertheless. I know that legally I shall probably not get into trouble, at least not to any serious extent: I alone denounce myself, and have no accuser; besides, there is little or no evidence. Finally, there is the generally credited notion of my mental derangement, of which my relatives will surely take advantage and thus stop any legal prosecution that may seriously threaten me. One of my purposes in making this statement is to prove that I am now in full possession of my mental faculties and that I understand my situation. But there will remain those who will know everything and who will look at me, and I will look at them. I wish everyone would look at me. I do not know whether or not this will relieve me. I resort to it as the last measure.

"I repeat: if a thorough search is made in the Petersburg police records, perhaps something may be discovered. The people from whom I rented the room may still be in the capital. Of course, they will remember the house. It was painted a pale blue. As for me, I shall not leave my present place of residence but for some time (a year or two) I shall stay at Skvoreshniki, my mother's estate. If I am summoned, I shall present myself, wherever it may be.

"Nikolay Stavrogin."

III

The reading lasted about an hour. Tihon read slowly and possibly read some passages twice. All the time, ever since the interruption caused by the confiscation of the second sheet, Stavrogin sat silent and motionless in the corner of the sofa, pressed against its back, and in an obviously expectant attitude. Tihon took off his spectacles, paused, and finally looked up at Stavrogin hesitatingly. The latter started and jerked his whole body forward.

"I forgot to warn you," said Stavrogin quickly and sharply, "that all your words will be useless; I will not delay carrying out my intention; do not trouble to dissuade me. I will publish it."

He reddened and grew silent.

"But you didn't forget to warn me just now, even before I began reading."

There was a note of irritation in Tihon's voice. "The document" had apparently made a strong impression on him. His Christian sentiment was wounded, and he was not the man to keep himself always in hand. Let me observe that not for naught did he have the reputation of a man "incapable of cutting a proper figure in public," as the monastery people said of him. In spite of all his Christian meekness, great indignation was heard in his voice.

"It doesn't matter," Stavrogin continued brusquely and without noticing any change in his host's tone. "However strong your objections may be, I won't give up my intention. Note that by this awkward or perhaps shrewd remark, take it as you please, I'm not trying in any way to induce you to start arguing with me and coaxing me," he concluded with a crooked smile.

"I could hardly attempt to argue with you, let alone beg you to give up your intention. Your idea is a lofty idea, and a Christian thought could not express itself more amply. Repentance can go no further than the admirable act, the self-chastisement which you have in mind, if only . . ."

"If only what?"

"If only it is really repentance and really a Christian thought."

"Quibbling," mumbled Stavrogin, pensively and absent-mindedly. He got to his feet and began to pace the floor without noticing what he was doing.

"It is as though you purposely wished to represent yourself as a coarser man than your heart would desire . . . ," Tihon was more and more outspoken.

"'*Represent?*' I repeat, I didn't represent myself, I did not pose. 'Coarser,' what is 'coarser?'" he grew flushed again and got enraged in consequence. "I know that what is described there—" he nodded in the direction of the sheets— "is vile, crawling and abominable, but let its very vileness serve to redouble . . ."

He suddenly broke off, as if he were ashamed to go on and considered it humiliating to enter into explanations. At the same time he was achingly and unconsciously obeying a compulsion to remain, and precisely for the sake of offering explanations. Curiously enough, in all he said then and thereafter not a word was uttered that bore out his explanation of why he had confiscated the second sheet—indeed, what he had said about it seemed to have been forgotten by both of them. Meanwhile, Stavrogin stopped at the writing-table, and taking up a small ivory crucifix, began to turn it about in his fingers, and suddenly broke it in half. Coming to himself, he looked at Tihon in surprise, and suddenly his upper lip trembled as if he were insulted but also proudly defiant.

"I thought that you would really tell me something, that's why

I came," he said in an undertone, as if making every effort to control himself, and he threw the fragments of the crucifix on the table.

Tihon quickly looked down.

"This document is born of the need of a heart wounded unto death. Am I not right?" he asked with insistence and almost with heat. "Yes, it is repentance and the natural need for it which has overcome you. You were pierced to the quick by the suffering of a creature whom you wronged. Therefore there is still hope for you, and you have taken a great road, an unheard of road, that of inflicting upon yourself before the whole people the shameful punishment you so amply deserve. You have appealed to the judgment of the whole Church, although you do not believe in the Church; am I not right? But it is as though you were already hating and despising in advance all those who will read what you have written, and challenging them to an encounter."

"I? Challenging?"

"Since you are not ashamed to confess your crime, why are you ashamed of repentance?"

"I? Ashamed?"

"Yes, you are ashamed and afraid."

"Afraid?" Stavrogin smiled convulsively and again his upper lip trembled, as it were.

"'Let them look at me,' you say; and you, how will you look at them? You are waiting for their malice, to respond with greater malice. Some of the passages in your account are couched in exaggerated language; it is as if you were admiring your own psychologising, and you cling to each detail so as to amaze the reader by a callousness and shamelessness which isn't really in you. On the other hand, evil passions and the habit of idleness render you really callous and stupid."

"Stupidity is no vice," Stavrogin smiled, beginning to blanch.

"Sometimes it is," Tihon continued rigorously and passionately. "Wounded unto death by the vision on the threshold and tormented by it, you do not see, to judge by this document, what your chief crime is, and of what to be most ashamed before the people whose judgment you invoke: whether of the callousness of the act of violence that you committed, or of the cowardice you exhibited. In one place you hasten, as it were, to assure your reader that the maiden's threatening gesture was no longer 'ridiculous' to you, but annihilating. But how, even for a moment, could it have seemed 'ridiculous' to you? And yet it did, I bear witness to it."

Tihon grew silent. He had spoken as a man not wishing to restrain himself.

"Speak, speak," Stavrogin urged him. "You are irritated and you . . . do not choose your words; I like this coming from a monk. But let me ask you one thing: we have been talking for some ten minutes since you read this," he nodded at the sheets, "and although you do scold me, I do not see you showing any particular disgust or shame. . . . Apparently, you are not squeamish and you speak to me as to an equal."

He added this in a very low voice, and the phrase "as to an equal" escaped him quite unexpectedly, as a surprise to himself. Tihon looked at him closely.

"You astonish me," he said after a pause, "for your words are unfeigned, I see, and if such is the case . . . I am guilty before you. Be advised then, that I was uncivil to you, as well as squeamish, and you, in your passion for self-punishment, did not even notice it, although you did become aware of my impatience and called it 'scolding.' You believe that you deserve incomparably greater contempt, and your remark that I speak to you 'as to an equal' is an admirable, if involuntary, phrase. I shall conceal nothing from you: I was horrified at so much idle power deliberately spent on abominations. Apparently one does not become a foreigner in one's own country with impunity. There is one punishment that falls upon those who divorce themselves from their native soil: boredom and a tendency toward idleness even where there is a desire for work. But Christianity insists upon responsibility irrespective of the environment. The Lord has not deprived you of intelligence. Judge for yourself; if you can put the question: am I or am I not responsible for my acts? then you are unquestionably responsible. It is written: 'Temptation cannot but enter the world, but woe unto him through whom temptation cometh.' As for your . . . transgression itself, many sin in like fashion, but live in peace and quiet with their conscience, even considering what they have done an inevitable sin of youth. There are old men who smell of the grave who sin likewise, and even playfully and with comfort. The world is full of such horrors. You at least have felt the enormity of it to a degree which is very rare."

"Is it possible that you have begun to respect me after reading these sheets?" Stavrogin grinned crookedly. "No, Reverend Father Tihon, you are not, as I have heard said, you are not fit to be a spiritual guide," he added, continuing to smile with an even more forced and inappropriate smile. "You are severely criticized here in the monastery. They say that as soon as you see a sign of sincerity and humility in a sinner, you break into ecstasies, you repent and humble yourself and fawn upon and flatter the sinner."

"I shall not answer your question directly. But of course it is true that I do not know how to approach people. I have always been aware of that great defect," Tihon said with a sigh, and so simply that Stavrogin looked at him with a smile. "As for this," he continued, glancing at the sheets, "of course there is not and there cannot be, a greater and more fearful crime than your sin against the little girl."

"Let's give up this measuring by the yard-stick," said Stavrogin with some annoyance, after a pause. "Perhaps I do not suffer as much as I set down here. And perhaps I lied a lot about myself," he added unexpectedly.

Tihon passed this over in silence. Stavrogin was pacing the room, deep in thought and with his head down.

"And this young lady," Tihon asked suddenly, "with whom you broke off in Switzerland, where is she at present?"

"Here."

Another pause.

"Perhaps I lied to you a good deal about myself," Stavrogin repeated insistently. "I myself do not know even yet. Well, what if I have defied them by the crudeness of my confession, if you *did* notice the challenge? That's the right way. They deserve it. I will only force them to hate me more, that's all. It will only make it easier for me."

"That is, hating them, you will feel more comfortable than if you had to accept pity from them."

"You're right; I am not in the habit of being frank, but since I have started . . . with you . . . know that I despise them all, just as much as I do myself, as much if not more, infinitely more. No one can be my judge . . . I wrote this nonsense," he nodded at the sheets, "just so, because the thought popped into my head, just to be shameless . . . perhaps I simply made up a story, I exaggerated in a fanatical moment . . . ," he broke off angrily and again reddened as before because of what he had said against his will. He turned to the table, and, with his back to Tihon, again took up a piece of the crucifix.

"Answer a question, but sincerely, speak to me alone, as you would speak to yourself in the darkness of night," Tihon began in a poignant voice. "If someone were to forgive you for this" (Tihon pointed to the pamphlet), "and not any one whom you respect or fear, but a stranger, a man whom you will never know, who would forgive you mutely, in his own heart, while reading your terrible confession, would the thought of this make it easier for you, or would it be all the same to you? If it would injure your amour-propre to answer, do not speak, but only think to yourself."

"It would be easier," answered Stavrogin under his breath. "If you were to forgive me, it would make it much easier for me," he added quickly and in a half-whisper, with his back still toward Tihon.

"I will forgive you, if you forgive me also," said Tihon, in a voice betraying deep emotion.

"What shall I forgive you for?" Stavrogin faced him, "what have you done to me? Oh, yes, that is your monastic formula. Bad humility. Do you know, these ancient monkish formulae of yours are quite inelegant. Do you really think they are elegant?" he grumbled irritably. "I do not know why I am here," he added, suddenly looking around. "Bah, I have broken this thing. Is it worth about twenty-five roubles?"

"Never mind," said Tihon.

"Or fifty? Why shouldn't I mind? Why should I break your things, and you forgive me the damage? Here, take these fifty roubles." He produced money and placed it on the table. "If you do not wish to take it for yourself, take it for the poor, for the Church. . . ." He grew more and more irritable. "Listen, I will tell you the whole truth: I want to have you forgive me. And perhaps to have another man, and even a third, do so too, but by all means let everybody else hate me!" His eyes flashed.

"And universal pity, couldn't you bear that with humility?"

"I couldn't. I do not want universal pity; besides, there can be no universal pity, it is an idle question. Listen, I do not want to wait, I will publish the statement without fail . . . do not try to dissuade me . . . I cannot wait, I cannot . . ." he added fiercely.

"I fear for you," Tihon said, almost timidly.

"You are afraid that I shan't be able to endure it, to endure their hatred?"

"Not hatred alone."

"What else?"

"Their . . . laughter," the words escaped from Tihon as though with difficulty, in a half-whisper.

The poor man could not control himself and broached a subject which he knew it would have been better to pass over in silence.

Stavrogin was taken aback. His face betrayed uneasiness.

"I had a foreboding of it. Do you too find me very ridiculous, after having read my document? Don't let it trouble you, don't be embarrassed. I expected it."

Tihon really seemed embarrassed and hastened to offer explanations, which of course merely made matters worse.

"For such heroic acts one needs moral serenity, even in suffering one needs spiritual enlightenment . . . but nowadays moral serenity is nowhere to be had. A great conflict is going on everywhere. Men do not understand each other as in the time of the confusion of Babel."

"This is all very dull, I know it, it has been said a thousand times . . ." Stravrogin interrupted.

"But consider that you will not achieve your purpose," Tihon began, coming straight to the point; "legally you are well-nigh invulnerable—that is what people will say first of all—with sarcasm. Some will be puzzled. Who will understand the true reasons for the confession? Indeed, people will purposely refuse to understand it, for such unconventional acts are feared; they rouse alarm, people hate one and take revenge on one for them, for the world loves its abomination and does not wish to see it threatened; for that reason people will turn it to ridicule, for ridicule is the world's strongest weapon."

"Speak more precisely, say everything," Stavrogin urged him.

"At first, of course, people will express horror, but it will be more sham than real, just to save appearances. I do not speak of the pure souls: they will be horrified privately and will blame themselves, but they will not be noticed, because they will keep silent. The rest, the worldlings, fear only what directly threatens their personal interests. After the first puzzlement and feigned horror, they will soon begin to laugh. There will be curiosity about this madman, for you will be considered a madman, that is, not quite a madman, one sufficiently responsible for his actions to allow them to smile at him. Will you be able to bear it? Will not your heart be filled with such hatred that you will inevitably end by blaspheming and so perish. . . . That is what I fear!"

"But you . . . you yourself . . . I am surprised to see what a low opinion you have of people, how much they disgust you," Stavrogin dropped, in a somewhat embittered tone.

"And will you believe me, I judged more by myself than by what I know of others," exclaimed Tihon.

"Really? Is it possible that there is that in your soul which rejoices in my misfortune?"

"Who knows? Perhaps there is. Oh, yes, perhaps there is."

"Enough. Tell me then, exactly what is there in my manuscript that is ridiculous? I know it myself, but I want your finger to point it out. And say it as cynically as possible, because you are a great cynic . . . you holy men are terrible cynics; you do not suspect to what extent you despise people! Speak with all the frankness of which you are capable. And let me tell you again that you are an awfully queer fellow."

"Even in the very intention of this great penitence there is something ridiculous, something false, as it were . . . not to speak of the form, which is loose, vague, unsustained because it is weakened by fear, as it were. Oh, don't doubt but that you'll conquer,'' he suddenly exclaimed, almost rapturously. ''Even this form,'' he pointed to the pamphlet again, ''will avail, if only you will sincerely accept the blows and the spittle, if you will endure it! It was always thus, that the most degrading cross became a great glory and a great power, if only the humility of the act was sincere. But is it? Is it? Will it be sincere? Oh, what you should have is not a challenging attitude, but measureless humility and self-abasement! What you should do is not despise your judges, but sincerely believe in them, as in a great Church, then you would conquer them and draw men to you and unite them in love. . . . Oh, if only you could endure it!''

''Tell me, what, in your opinion, is the most ridiculous thing in these sheets?''

''Why this concern about the ridiculous, why such morbid curiosity?'' exclaimed Tihon sorrowfully, shaking his head.

''Never mind. Just tell me what's laughable.''

''The ugliness of it will kill it,'' whispered Tihon, lowering his eyes.

''The ugliness? What ugliness?''

''Of the crime. It is a truly unbeautiful crime. Crimes, no matter what they are, are the more imposing, the more picturesque, so to speak, the more blood, the more horror there is; but there are truly shameful, disgraceful crimes which are not redeemed by horror . . .''

Tihon did not finish his sentence.

''That is, you find I cut a very ridiculous figure when I kissed the nasty little girl's hand . . . and then trembled with fear . . . and . . . and all the rest . . . I understand. I understand you very well. And you fear that I shall not be able to bear it?''

Tihon was silent. Stavrogin's face blanched and something like a spasm passed over it.

''Now I think I know why you asked whether the young lady from Switzerland was here,'' he said quietly, as if to himself.

''You aren't prepared, you are not steeled,'' added Tihon.

''Listen to me, Father Tihon: I want to forgive myself. That's my chief object, that's my whole aim!'' Stavrogin said suddenly, with gloomy rapture in his eyes. ''This is my entire confession, the whole truth; all the rest is a lie. I know that only then will the apparition vanish. That is why I seek measureless suffering, I seek it myself. So, do not frighten me, or I shall perish in my viciousness,'' he added, as if the words had again issued from his mouth against his will.

These words so surprised Tihon that in his amazement he rose to his feet.

"If you believe that you can forgive yourself, and if you seek to attain to that forgiveness in this world by your suffering, then you have complete faith!" exclaimed Tihon rapturously. "How then could you have said that you didn't believe in God?"

Stavrogin did not answer.

"God will forgive your unfaith, for in truth even in ignorance of the Holy Ghost, you honour it."

"There is no forgiveness for me," Stavrogin said gloomily; "in your book it is written that there is and can be no greater crime than to offend 'one of these little ones.' In this book here!"

He pointed to the Gospels.

"As to that, I will give you joyous tidings," said Tihon with emotion; "Christ too will forgive you if you reach the point where you can forgive yourself. . . . Oh, no, no, do not believe I am uttering blasphemy: even if you do not achieve reconciliation with yourself and self-forgiveness, even then He will forgive you for your intention and your great suffering . . . for there are no words in the human language, no thoughts in the mind to express all the ways and purposes of the Lamb, 'until His ways are revealed unto us?' Who can fathom Him who is infinite, who can grasp the incomprehensible?"

Again the corners of his mouth twitched and a scarcely perceptible spasm passed over his face. He kept a grip on himself for awhile, then broke down and quickly lowered his eyes.

Stavrogin took his hat from the sofa.

"I will come again some time," he said with an air of extreme fatigue, "we will . . . I appreciate very much both the pleasure of the talk and the honour . . . and your sentiments. Believe me, I understand why some people love you so. Please pray for me to Him whom you so love . . ."

"You are going already?" Tihon quickly rose to his feet, as if he did not expect such a speedy departure. "And I," he seemed lost, "I was thinking of making a request . . . but now I don't know . . . I am afraid . . ."

"Oh, please do," Stavrogin immediately sat down, hat in hand. Tihon looked at this hat, at this pose, the pose of a man excited and half crazy, who suddenly put on his society manners, and was allowing him five minutes to complete the business at hand — and grew even more confused.

"My request is merely this, that you . . . you realise, Nikolay Vsyevolodovitch (that is the name, I believe), that if you publish these sheets, you will ruin your prospects . . . as regards your career, for example . . . and in other respects."

"Career?" Stavrogin frowned with displeasure.

"Why ruin it? Why be so inflexible?" Tihon concluded almost

pleadingly, and obviously aware of his own awkwardness. Stavrogin looked sickened.

"I have already said, and I repeat; all your words will be futile . . . and in general our conversation is becoming intolerable . . ."

He turned significantly in his armchair.

"You don't understand me. Listen to me and do not get irritated. You know my opinion: what you intend to do, if it really is the result of humility, would be a deed of the highest Christian heroism, provided you hold out. Even if you don't, the Lord will take account of your original sacrifice. Everything will be taken into account; not a word, not a movement of the spirit, not a half-thought will be lost. But I offer you instead an even higher deed, something great beyond question."

Stavrogin was silent.

"You are possessed by a desire for martyrdom and self-sacrifice; overcome this desire, too, put aside these sheets and your intention, and then you will overcome everything. You will put to shame your pride and your demon. You will end as a victor, and achieve freedom . . ."

His eyes kindled; he clasped his hands beseechingly.

"How morbidly you react to all this, and how highly you prize it all. . . . Believe me, however, that I appreciate it all," Stavrogin said politely, but not without disgust, as it were. "I observe that you are eager to lay a trap for me — unquestionably with the noblest purpose, out of a desire for good and out of love for mankind. What you want is to have me settle down, to have me marry, perhaps, and end my life as a member of the local club, visiting the monastery on holidays. Isn't that so? However, as a reader of hearts and a cynic, perhaps you have a foreboding that, no doubt, that's how it will all end, and it's all a question of having you plead with me insistently for the sake of appearances, because all that I'm after is to be coaxed, isn't that so? I wager that you are also thinking of my mother and her peace of mind . . ."

He smiled wryly.

"No, not that penance, I'm preparing another one," continued Tihon with fire, without paying the slightest attention to Stavrogin's remark and his laughter. "I know an old man, not far from here, a monk and a hermit, and of such Christian wisdom that you and I could hardly understand it. He will heed my entreaties. I will tell him everything about you. Will you permit me? Go to him, and become a novice under him for some five or seven years, for as long as you find it necessary. Take a vow, and with this great sacrifice you will purchase all that you desire, and even more than you expect, for you cannot understand now what you will receive."

Stavrogin listened earnestly. His pale cheeks flushed.

"You bid me become a monk and enter a monastery?" he asked.

"You do not have to enter a monastery. You do not have to take orders. Simply be a novice, secretly. You can do this, living in the world."

"Quit it, Father Tihon," Stavrogin interrupted disgustedly and rose from his chair. Tihon rose also.

"What is the matter with you?" he exclaimed suddenly, staring almost fearfully at Tihon.

Tihon stood before him, his palms pressed together and thrust forward, and a morbid convulsion, apparently caused by an overwhelming fear, momentarily contorted his features.

"What is the matter with you? What is the matter with you?" repeated Stavrogin, running toward him to support him. It seemed to Stavrogin that the man was going to drop.

"I see . . . I see clearly," exclaimed Tihon in a penetrating voice and with an expression of most intense grief, "that never, poor lost youth, have you stood nearer to a new and more terrible crime than at this moment."

"Calm yourself," Stavrogin begged him, positively alarmed for him. "Perhaps I will postpone. . . . You're right . . . I will not publish the sheets. Compose yourself."

"No, not after the publication, but even before it, a day, an hour perhaps, before the great step, you will plunge into a new crime as a way out, and you will commit it solely to avoid the publication of these sheets, upon which you now insist."

Stavrogin veritably shook with anger and almost with fear.

"Cursed psychologist!" he suddenly cut the conversation short in a rage, and, without looking back, left the cell.

Karl Jaspers

Differentiation of German Guilt

Political Guilt

40   For crimes the criminal is punished. The restriction of the Nuremberg trial to criminals serves to exonerate the German people. Not, however, so as to free them of all guilt — on the contrary. The nature of our real guilt only appears the more clearly.

We were German nationals at the time when the crimes were committed by the régime which called itself German, which claimed to be Germany and seemed to have the right to do so, since the power of the state was in its hands and until 1943 it found no dangerous opposition.

The destruction of any decent, truthful German polity must have its roots also in modes of conduct of the majority of the German population. A people answers for its polity.

Every German is made to share the blame for the crimes committed in the name of the Reich. We are collectively liable. The question is in what sense each of us must feel co-responsible. Certainly in the political sense of the joint liability of all citizens for acts committed by their state — but for that reason not necessarily also in the moral sense of actual or intellectual participation in crime. Are we Germans to be held liable for outrages which Germans inflicted on us, or from which we were saved as by a miracle? Yes — inasmuch as we let such a régime rise among us. No — insofar as many of us in our deepest hearts opposed all this evil and have no morally guilty acts or inner motivations to admit. To hold liable does not mean to hold morally guilty.

Guilt, therefore, is necessarily collective as the political liability of nationals, but not in the same sense as moral and metaphysical, and never as criminal guilt. True, the acceptance of political liability with its fearful consequences is hard on every individual. What it means to us is political impotence and a poverty which will compel us for long times to live in or on the fringes of hunger and cold and to struggle vainly. Yet this liability as such leaves the soul untouched.

Politically everyone acts in the modern state, at least by voting, or failing to vote, in elections. The sense of political liability lets no man dodge.

If things go wrong the politically active tend to justify them-selves; but such defenses carry no weight in politics. For instance, they meant well and had the best intentions—Hindenburg, for one, did surely not mean to ruin Germany or hand it over to Hitler. That does not help him; he did—and that is what counts. Or they foresaw the disaster, said so, and warned; but that does not count politically, either, if no action followed or if it had no effect.

One might think of cases of wholly non-political persons who live aloof of all politics, like monks, hermits, scholars, artists—if really quite non-political, those might possibly be excused from all guilt. Yet they, too, are included among the politically liable, because they, too, live by the order of the state. There is no such aloofness in modern states.

One may wish to make such aloofness possible, yet one cannot help admit to this limitation. We should like to respect and love a non-political life, but the end of political participation would also end the right of the non-political ones to judge concrete political acts of the day and thus to play riskless politics. A non-political zone demands withdrawal from any kind of political activity—and still does not exempt from joint political liability in every sense.

Moral Guilt

Every German asks himself: how am I guilty?

The question of the guilt of the individual analyzing himself is what we call the moral one. Here we Germans are divided by the greatest differences.

While the decision in self-judgment is up to the individual alone, we are free to talk with one another, insofar as we are in communication, and morally to help each other achieve clarity. The moral sentence on the other is suspended, however—neither the criminal nor the political one.

There is a line at which even the possibility of moral judgment ceases. It can be drawn where we feel the other not even trying for a moral self-analysis—where we perceive mere sophistry in his argument, where he seems not to hear at all. Hitler and his accomplices, that small minority of tens of thousands, are beyond moral guilt for as long as they do not feel it. They seem incapable of repentance and change. They are what they are. Force alone can deal with such men who live by force alone.

But the moral guilt exists for all those who give room to conscience and repentance. The morally guilty are those who are capable of penance, the ones who knew, or could know, and yet walked in ways which self-analysis reveals to them as culpable error—whether conveniently closing their eyes to events, or permitting themselves to be intoxicated, seduced or bought with personal advantages, or obeying from fear. Let us look at some of these possibilities.

1. By *living in disguise*—unavoidable for anyone who wanted to survive—moral guilt was incurred. Mendacious avowals of loyalty to threatening bodies like the Gestapo, gestures like the Hitler salute, attendance at meetings, and many other things causing a semblance of participation—who among us in Germany was not guilty of that, at one time or another? Only the forgetful can deceive themselves about it, since they want to deceive themselves. Camouflage had become a basic trait of our existence. It weighs on our moral conscience.

2. More deeply stirring at the instant of cognition is guilt incurred by a *false conscience.* Many a young man or woman nowadays awakens with a horrible feeling: my conscience has betrayed me. I thought I was living in idealism and self-sacrifice for the noblest goal, with the best intentions—what can I still rely on? Everyone awakening like this will ask himself how he became guilty, by haziness, by unwillingness to see, by conscious seclusion, isolation of his own life in a "decent" sphere.

Here we first have to distinguish between military honor and political sense. For whatever is said about guilt cannot affect the consciousness of military honor. If a soldier kept faith with his comrades, did not flinch in danger and proved himself calm and courageous, he may preserve something inviolate in his self-respect. These purely soldierly, and at the same time human, values are common to all peoples. No guilt is incurred by having stood this test; in fact, if probation here was real, unstained by evil acts or execution of patently evil commands, it is a foundation of the sense of life.

But a soldier's probation must not be identified with the cause he fought for. To have been a good soldier does not absolve from all other guilt.

The unconditional identification of the actual state with the German nation and army constitutes guilt incurred through false conscience. A first-class soldier may have succumbed to the falsification of his conscience which enabled him to do and permit obviously evil things because of patriotism. Hence the good conscience in evil deeds.

Yet our duty to the fatherland goes far beneath blind obedience to its rulers of the day. The fatherland ceases to be a fatherland when its soul is destroyed. The power of the state is not an end in itself; rather, it is pernicious if this state destroys the German character. Therefore, duty to the fatherland did not by any means lead consistently to obedience to Hitler and to the assumption that even as a Hitler state Germany must, of course, win the war at all costs. Herein lies the false conscience. It is no simple guilt. It is at the same time a tragic confusion, notably of a large part of our unwitting youth. To do one's duty to the fatherland means to commit one's whole person to the highest demands made on us by the best of our ancestors, not by the idols of a false tradition.

It was amazing to see the complete self-identification with army and state, in spite of all evil. For this unconditionality of a blind nationalism — only conceivable as the last crumbling ground in a world about to lose all faith — was moral guilt.

It was made possible, furthermore, by a misinterpretation of the Biblical warning: "Let every soul be subject unto the higher powers" — a warning completely perverted by the curious sanctity appertaining to orders in military tradition. "This is an order" — in the ears of many these words had and still have a ring of pathos as if voicing the highest duty. But simultaneously, by shrugging off stupidity and evil as inevitable, they furnished an excuse. What finally turned this conduct into full-fledged moral guilt was the eagerness to obey — that compulsive conduct, feeling itself conscientious and, in fact, forsaking all conscience.

Many a youth nauseated by Nazi rule in the years after 1933 chose the military career because it seemed to offer the only decent atmosphere uninfluenced by the Party. The army, mentally against the Party, seemed to exist outside and without the Party as though it were a power of its own. It was another error of conscience; eventually, with all the independent generals in the old tradition eliminated, the consequences appeared as moral decay of the German officer in all positions of leadership — notwithstanding the many likable and even noble soldierly personalities who had sought salvation in vain, misled by a betraying conscience.

The very fact that honest consciousness and good-will were our initial guides is bound to deepen our later disillusionment and disappointment in ourselves. It leads us to question even our best faith; for we are responsible for our delusions — for every delusion to which we succumb.

Awakening and self-analysis of this delusion are indispensable. They turn idealistic youths into upright, morally reliable, politically lucid German men acquiescing in their lot as now cast.

3. By partial approval of National-Socialism, by *straddling* and occasional *inner assimilation* and accommodation, moral guilt was incurred without any of the tragic aspects of the previous types.

The argument that there was some good to it, after all—this readiness to a supposedly unbiased appraisal—was widespread among us. Yet the truth could be only a radical "either-or": if I recognize the principle as evil, everything is evil and any seemingly good consequences are not what they seem to be. It was this erring objectiveness, ready to grant something good in National-Socialism, which estranged close friends so they could no longer talk frankly. The same man who had just lamented the failure of a martyr to appear and sacrifice himself for the old freedom and against injustice was apt to praise the abolition of unemployment (by means of armament and fraudulent financial policies), apt to hail the absorption of Austria in 1938 as the fulfillment of the old ideal of a united Reich, apt to cast doubts on Dutch neutrality in 1940 and to justify Hitler's attack, and apt, above all, to rejoice in the victories.

4. Many engaged in convenient *self-deception*. In due time they were going to change this evil government. The Party would disappear again—with the Fuehrer's death at the latest. For the present one had to belong, to right things from within. The following conversations were typical:

An officer speaks: "After the war we'll finish National-Socialism on the very basis of our victory; but now we must stick together and lead Germany to that victory—when the house burns down you pour water and don't stop to ask what caused the fire."—Answer: "After victory you'll be discharged and glad to go home. The SS alone will stay armed, and the reign of terror will grow into a slave state. No individual human life will be possible; pyramids will rise; highways and towns will be built and changed at the Fuehrer's whim. A giant arms machine will be developed for the final conquest of the world."

A professor speaks: "We are the Fronde within the Party. We dare frank discussion. We achieve spiritual realizations. We shall slowly turn all of it back into the old German spirituality."—Answer: "You are deceiving yourselves. Allowed a fool's freedom, on condition of instant obedience, you shut up and give in. Your fight is a mirage, desired by the leaders. You only help to entomb the German spirit."

Many intellectuals went along in 1933, sought leading positions and publicly upheld the ideology of the new power, only to become resentful later when they personally were shunted aside. These — although mostly continuing positive until about 1942, when the course of the war made an unfavorable outcome certain and sent them into the oppositionist ranks — now feel that they suffered under the Nazis and are therefore called for what follows. They regard themselves as anti-Nazis. In all these years, according to their self-proclaimed ideology, these intellectual Nazis were frankly speaking truth in spiritual matters, guarding the tradition of the German spirit, preventing destructions, doing good in individual cases.

Many of these may be guilty of persisting in a mentality which, while not identical with Party tenets and even disguised as metamorphosis and opposition, still clings in fact to the mental attitude of National-Socialism and fails to clear itself. Through this mentality they may be actually akin to National-Socialism's inhuman, dictatorial, unexistentially nihilistic essence. If a mature person in 1933 had the certainty of inner conviction — due not merely to political error but to a sense of existence heightened by National-Socialism — he will be purified only by a transmutation which may have to be more thorough than any other. Whoever behaved like that in 1933 would remain inwardly brittle otherwise, and inclined to further fanaticism. Whoever took part in the race mania, whoever had delusions of a revival based on fraud, whoever winked at the crimes then already committed is not merely liable but must renew himself morally. Whether and how he can do it is up to him alone, and scarcely open to any outside scrutiny.

5. There is a difference between *activity* and *passivity.* The political performers and executors, the leaders and the propagandists are guilty. If they did not become criminals, they still have, by their activity, incurred a positively determinable guilt.

But each one of us is guilty insofar as he remained inactive. The guilt of passivity is different. Impotence excuses; no moral law demands a spectacular death. Plato already deemed it a matter of course to go into hiding in desperate times of calamity, and to survive. But passivity knows itself morally guilty of every failure, every neglect to act whenever possible, to shield the imperiled, to relieve wrong, to countervail. Impotent submission always left a margin of activity which, though not without risk, could still be cautiously effective. Its anxious omission weighs upon the individual as moral guilt. Blindness for the misfortune of others, lack of imagination of the heart, inner indifference toward the witnessed evil — that is moral guilt.

6. The moral guilt of outward compliance, of *running with the*

pack, is shared to some extent by a great many of us. To maintain his existence, to keep his job, to protect his chances a man would join the Party and carry out other nominal acts of conformism.

Nobody will find an absolute excuse for doing so—notably in view of the many Germans who, in fact, did not conform, and bore the disadvantages.

Yet we must remember what the situation looked like in, say, 1936 or '37. The Party was the state. Conditions seemed incalculably permanent. Nothing short of a war could upset the régime. All the powers were appeasing Hitler. All wanted peace. A German who did not want to be out of everything, lose his profession, injure his business, was obliged to go along—the younger ones in particular. Now, membership in the Party or its professional organizations was no longer a political act; rather, it was a favor granted by the state which allowed the individual to join. A "badge" was needed, an external token without inner assent. A man asked to join in those days could hardly refuse. It is decisive for the meaning of compliance in what connection and from what motives he acquired his membership in the Party; each year and every situation has its own mitigating and aggravating circumstances, to be distinguished only in each individual case.

Metaphysical Guilt

Morality is always influenced by mundane purposes. I may be morally bound to risk my life, if a realization is at stake; but there is no moral obligation to sacrifice one's life in the sure knowledge that nothing will have been gained. Morally we have a duty to dare, not a duty to choose certain doom. Morally, in either case, we rather have the contrary duty, not to do what cannot serve the mundane purpose but to save ourselves for realizations in the world.

But there is within us a guilt consciousness which springs from another source. Metaphysical guilt is the lack of absolute solidarity with the human being as such—an indelible claim beyond morally meaningful duty. This solidarity is violated by my presence at a wrong or a crime. It is not enough that I cautiously risk my life to prevent it; if it happens, and if I was there, and if I survive where the other is killed, I know from a voice within myself: I am guilty of still being alive.

I quote from an address I gave in August 1945: "We ourselves have changed since 1933. It was possible for us to seek death in humiliation—in 1933 when the Constitution was torn up, the dictatorship established in sham legality and all resistance swept away in the intoxication of a large part of our people. We could seek death when the crimes of the régime became publicly apparent on June 30, 1934, or with the lootings, deportations and murders of our Jewish friends and fellow-citizens in 1938, when to our ineradicable shame and disgrace the synagogues, houses of God, went up in flames throughout Germany. We could seek death when from the start of the war the régime acted against the words of Kant, our greatest philosopher, who called it a premise of international law that nothing must occur in war which would make a later reconcilement of the belligerents impossible. Thousands in Germany sought, or at least found death in battling the régime, most of them anonymously. We survivors did not seek it. We did not go into the streets when our Jewish friends were led away; we did not scream until we too were destroyed. We preferred to stay alive, on the feeble, if logical, ground that our death could not have helped anyone. We are guilty of being alive. We know before God which deeply humiliates us, What happened to us in these twelve years is like a transmutation of our being.''

In November 1938, when the synagogues burned and Jews were deported for the first time, the guilt incurred was chiefly moral and political. In either sense, the guilty were those still in power. The generals stood by. In every town the commander could act against crime, for the soldier is there to protect all, if crime occurs on such a scale that the police cannot or fail to stop it. They did nothing. At that moment they forsook the once glorious ethical tradition of the German Army. It was not their business. They had dissociated themselves from the soul of the German people, in favor of an absolute military machine that was a law unto itself and took orders.

True, among our people many were outraged and many deeply moved by a horror containing a presentiment of coming calamity. But even more went right on with their activities, undisturbed in their social life and amusements, as if nothing had happened. That is moral guilt.

But the ones who in utter impotence, outraged and despairing, were unable to prevent the crimes took another step in their metamorphosis by a growing consciousness of metaphysical guilt.

Recapitulation

Consequences of guilt   If everything said before was not wholly unfounded, there can be no doubt that we Germans, every one of us, are guilty in some way. Hence there occur the consequences of guilt.

1. All Germans without exception share in the political lia-

bility. All must cooperate in making amends to be brought into legal form. All must jointly suffer the effects of the acts of the victors, of their decisions, of their disunity. We are unable here to exert any influence as a factor of power.

Only by striving constantly for a sensible presentation of the facts, opportunities and dangers can we—unless everyone already knows what we say—collaborate on the premises of the decisions. In the proper form, and with reason, we may appeal to the victors.

2. Not every German—indeed only a very small minority of Germans—will be punished for crimes. Another minority has to atone for National-Socialist activities. All may defend themselves. They will be judged by the courts of the victors, or by German courts established by the victors.

3. Probably every German—though in greatly diverse forms—will have reasons morally to analyze himself. Here, however, he need not recognize any authority other than his own conscience.

4. And probably every German capable of understanding will transform his approach to the world and himself in the metaphysical experiences of such a disaster. How that happens none can prescribe, and none anticipate. It is a matter of individual solitude. What comes out of it has to create the essential basis of what will in future be the German soul.

Such distinctions can be speciously used to get rid of the whole guilt question, for instance like this:

Political liability—all right, but it curtails only my material possibilities; I myself, my inner self is not affected by that at all.

Criminal guilt—that affects just a few, not me; it does not concern me.

Moral guilt—I hear that my conscience alone has jurisdiction, others have no right to accuse me. Well, my conscience is not going to be too hard on me. It wasn't really so bad; let's forget about it, and make a fresh start.

Metaphysical guilt—of that, finally, I was expressly told that none can charge it to another. I am supposed to perceive that in a transmutation. That's a crazy idea of some philosopher. There is no such thing. And if there were, I wouldn't notice it. That I needn't bother with.

Our dissection of the guilt concepts can be turned into a trick, for getting rid of guilt. The distinctions are in the foreground. They can hide the source and the unity. Distinctions enable us to spirit away what does not suit us.

Collective guilt   Having separated the elements of guilt, we return in the end to the question of collective guilt.

Though correct and meaningful everywhere, the separation carries with it the indicated temptation — as though by such distinctions we had dodged the charges and eased our burden. Something has been lost in the process — something which in collective guilt is always audible in spite of everything. For all the crudeness of collective thinking and collective condemnation we feel that we belong together.

In the end, of course, the true collective is the solidarity of all men before God. Somewhere, everyone may free himself from the bonds of state or people or group and break through to the invisible solidarity of men — as men of goodwill and as men sharing the common guilt of being human.

But historically we remain bound to the closer, narrower communities, and we should lose the ground under our feet without them.

Political Liability and Collective Guilt

First to restate the fact that all over the world collective concepts largely guide the judgment and feelings of men. This is undeniable. In the world today the German — whatever the German may be — is regarded as something one would rather not have to do with. German Jews abroad are undesirable as Germans; they are essentially deemed Germans, not Jews. In this collective way of thought political liability is simultaneously justified as punishment of moral guilt. Historically such collective thought is not infrequent; the barbarism of war has seized whole populations and delivered them to pillage, rape and sale into slavery. And on top of it comes moral annihilation of the unfortunates in the judgment of the victor. They shall not only submit but confess and do penance. Whoever is German, whether Christian or Jew, is evil in spirit.

This fact of a widespread, though not universal, world opinion keeps challenging us, not only to defend ourselves with our simple distinction of political liability and moral guilt but to examine what truth may possibly lie in collective thinking. We do not drop the distinction, but we have to narrow it by saying that the conduct which made us liable rests on a sum of political conditions whose nature is moral, as it were, because they help to determine individual morality. The individual cannot wholly detach himself from these conditions, for — consciously or unconsciously — he lives as a link in their chain and cannot escape from their influence even if he was in opposition. There is a sort of collective moral guilt in a people's way of life which I share as an individual, and from which grow political realities.

For political conditions are inseparable from a people's whole way of life. There is no absolute division of politics and human existence as long as man is still realizing an existence rather than perishing in eremitical seclusion.

By political conditions the Swiss, the Dutch have been formed, and all of us in Germany have been brought up for ages—we to obey, to feel dynastically, to be indifferent and irresponsible toward political reality—and these conditions are part of us even if we oppose them.

The way of life effects political events, and the resulting political conditions in turn place their imprint on the way of life. This is why there can be no radical separation of moral and political guilt. This is why every enlightenment of our political consciousness proportionately burdens our conscience. Political liberty has its moral aspects.

Thus, actual political liability is augmented by knowledge and then by a different self-esteem. That in fact all the people pay for all the acts of their government—*quidquid delirant reges plectuntur Achivi*—is a mere empirical fact; that they know themselves liable is the first indication of their dawning political liberty. It is to the extent of the existence and recognition of this knowledge that freedom is real, not a mere outward claim put forth by unfree men.

The inner political unfreedom has the opposite feeling. It obeys on the one hand, and feels not guilty on the other. The feeling of guilt, which makes us accept liability, is the beginning of the inner upheaval which seeks to realize political liberty.

The contrast of the free and the unfree mental attitude appears, for instance, in the two concepts of a statesman. The question has been raised whether nations are to blame for the leaders they put up with—for example, France for Napoleon. The idea is that the vast majority did go along and desired the power and the glory which Napoleon procured. In this view Napoleon was possible only because the French would have him; his greatness was the precision with which he understood what the mass of the people expected, what they wanted to hear, what illusions they wanted, what material realities they wanted. Could Lenz have been right in saying, "The state was born which suited the genius of France"? A part, a situation, yes—but not the genius of a nation as such! Who can define a national genius? The same genius has spawned very different realities.

One might think that, as a man must answer for his choice of the beloved to whom marriage binds him in a lifelong community of fate, a people answers for whomever it meekly obeys. Error is culpable; there is no escape from its consequences.

Precisely this, however, would be the wrong approach. The unconditional attachment to one person which is possible and proper in a marriage is pernicious on principle in a state. The loyalty of followers is a non-political relationship limited to narrow circles and primitive circumstances. In a free state all men are subject to control and change.

Hence there is twofold guilt—first, in the unconditional political surrender to a leader as such, and second, in the kind of leader submitted to. The atmosphere of submission is a sort of collective guilt.

All the restrictions concerning our liberation from moral guilt—in favor of mere political liability—do not affect what we established at the beginning and shall now restate:

We are politically responsible for our régime, for the acts of the régime, for the start of the war in this world-historical situation, and for the kind of leaders we allowed to rise among us. For that we answer to the victors, with our labor and with our working faculties, and must make such amends as are exacted from the vanquished.

In addition there is our moral guilt: Although this always burdens only the individual who must get along with himself, there still is a sort of collective morality contained in the ways of life and feeling, from which no individual can altogether escape and which have political significance as well. Here is the key to self-improvement; its use is up to us.

**Individual Awareness of
Collective Guilt**

We feel something like a co-responsibility for the acts of members of our families. This co-responsibility cannot be objectivized. We should reject any manner of tribal liability. And yet, because of our consanguinity we are inclined to feel concerned whenever wrong is done by someone in the family—and also inclined, therefore, depending on the type and circumstances of the wrong and its victims, to make it up to them even if we are not morally and legally accountable.

Thus the German—that is, the German-speaking individual—feels concerned by everything growing from German roots. It is not the liability of a national but the concern of one who shares the life of the German spirit and soul—who is of one tongue, one stock, one fate with all the others—which here comes to cause, not as tangible guilt, but somehow analogous to co-responsibility.

We further feel that we not only share in what is done at present—thus being co-responsible for the deeds of our contemporaries—but in the links of tradition. We have to bear the guilt of our fathers. That the spiritual conditions of German life provided an opportunity for such a régime is a fact for which all of us are co-responsible. Of course this does not mean that we must acknowledge "the world of German ideas" or "German thought of the past" in general as the sources of the National-Socialist misdeeds. But it does mean that our national tradition contains something, mighty and threatening, which is our moral ruin.

We feel ourselves not only as individuals but as Germans. Every one, in his real being, is the German people. Who does not remember moments in his life when he said to himself, in opposition and in despair of his nation, "I am Germany"—or, in jubilant harmony with it, "I, too, am Germany!" The German character has no other form than these individuals. Hence the demands of transmutation, of rebirth, of rejection of evil are made of the nation in the form of demands from each individual.

Because in my innermost soul I cannot help feeling collectively, being German is to me—is to everyone—not a condition but a task. This is altogether different from making the nation absolute. I am a human being first of all; in particular I am a Frisian, a professor, a German, linked closely enough for a fusion of souls with other collective groups, and more or less closely with all groups I have come in touch with. For moments this proximity enables me to feel almost like a Jew or Dutchman or Englishman. Throughout it, however, the fact of my being German—that is, essentially, of life in the mother tongue—is so emphatic that in a way which is rationally not conceivable, which is even rationally refutable, I feel co-responsible for what Germans do and have done.

I feel closer to those Germans who feel likewise—without becoming melodramatic about it—and farther from the ones whose soul seems to deny this link. And this proximity means, above all, a common inspiring task—of not being German as we happen to be, but becoming German as we are not yet but ought to be, and as we hear it in the call of our ancestors rather than in the history of national idols.

By our feeling of collective guilt we feel the entire task of renewing human existence from its origin—the task which is given to all men on earth but which appears more urgently, more perceptibly, as decisively as all existence, when its own guilt brings a people face to face with nothingness.

As a philosopher I now seem to have strayed completely into the realm of feeling and to have abandoned conception. Indeed language fails at this point, and only negatively we may recall that all our distinctions — notwithstanding the fact that we hold them to be true and are by no means rescinding them — must not become resting places. We must not use them to let matters drop and free ourselves from the pressure under which we continue on our path, and which is to ripen what we hold most precious, the eternal essence of our soul.

Sigmund Freud

Origin of the Sense of Guilt

54 What means does civilization employ in order to inhibit the aggressiveness which opposes it, to make it harmless, to get rid of it, perhaps? We have already become acquainted with a few of these methods, but not yet with the one that appears to be the most important. This we can study in the history of the development of the individual. What happens in him to render his desire for aggression innocuous? Something very remarkable, which we should never have guessed and which is nevertheless quite obvious. His aggressiveness is introjected, internalized; it is, in point of fact, sent back to where it came from—that is, it is directed towards his own ego. There it is taken over by a portion of the ego, which sets itself over against the rest of the ego as super-ego, and which now, in the form of 'conscience', is ready to put into action against the ego the same harsh aggressiveness that the ego would have liked to satisfy upon other, extraneous individuals. The tension between the harsh super-ego and the ego that is subjected to it, is called by us the sense of guilt; it expresses itself as a need for punishment. Civilization, therefore, obtains mastery over the individual's dangerous desire for aggression by weakening and disarming it and by setting up an agency within him to watch over it, like a garrison in a conquered city.

As to the origin of the sense of guilt, the analyst has different views from other psychologists; but even he does not find it easy to give an account of it. To begin with, if we ask how a person comes to have a sense of guilt, we arrive at an answer which cannot be disputed: a person feels guilty (devout people would say 'sinful') when he has done something which he knows to be 'bad'. But then we notice how little this answer tells us. Perhaps, after some hesitation, we shall add that even when a person has

Reprinted from *Civilization and Its Discontents* by Sigmund Freud. Translated from the German and edited by James Strachey. Copyright © 1961 by James Strachey. By permission of W. W. Norton & Company, Inc, The Hogarth Press, Ltd., and Sigmund Freud Copyrights Limited, and The Institute of Psycho-Analysis.

not actually *done* the bad thing but has only recognized in himself an *intention* to do it, he may regard himself as guilty; and the question then arises of why the intention is regarded as equal to the deed. Both cases, however, presuppose that one had already recognized that what is bad is reprehensible, is something that must not be carried out. How is this judgement arrived at? We may reject the existence of an original, as it were natural, capacity to distinguish good from bad. What is bad is often not at all what is injurious or dangerous to the ego; on the contrary, it may be something which is desirable and enjoyable to the ego. Here, therefore, there is an extraneous influence at work, and it is this that decides what is to be called good or bad. Since a person's own feelings would not have led him along this path, he must have had a motive for submitting to this extraneous influence. Such a motive is easily discovered in his helplessness and his dependence on other people, and it can best be designated as fear of loss of love. If he loses the love of another person upon whom he is dependent, he also ceases to be protected from a variety of dangers. Above all, he is exposed to the danger that this stronger person will show his superiority in the form of punishment. At the beginning, therefore, what is bad is whatever causes one to be threatened with loss of love. For fear of that loss, one must avoid it. This, too, is the reason why it makes little difference whether one has already done the bad thing or only intends to do it. In either case the danger only sets in if and when the authority discovers it, and in either case the authority would behave in the same way.

This state of mind is called a 'bad conscience'; but actually it does not deserve this name, for at this stage the sense of guilt is clearly only a fear of loss of love, 'social' anxiety. In small children it can never be anything else, but in many adults, too, it has only changed to the extent that the place of the father or the two parents is taken by the larger human community. Consequently, such people habitually allow themselves to do any bad thing which promises them enjoyment, so long as they are sure that the authority will not know anything about it or cannot blame them for it; they are afraid only of being found out. Present-day society has to reckon in general with this state of mind.

A great change takes place only when the authority is internalized through the establishment of a super-ego. The phenomena of conscience then reach a higher stage. Actually, it is not until now that we should speak of conscience or a sense of guilt. At this point, too, the fear of being found out comes to an end; the distinction, moreover, between doing something bad and wishing to do it disappears entirely, since nothing can be hidden from the super-ego, not even thoughts. It is true that the seriousness of the situation from a real point of view has passed away, for the new authority, the super-ego, has no motive that we know of for ill-treating the ego, with which it is intimately bound up; but genetic influence, which leads to the survival of what is past and has been surmounted, makes itself felt in the fact that fundamentally things remain as they were at the beginning. The super-ego torments the sinful ego with the same feeling of anxiety and is on the watch for opportunities of getting it punished by the external world.

At this second stage of development, the conscience exhibits a peculiarity which was absent from the first stage and which is no longer easy to account for. For the more virtuous a man is, the more severe and distrustful is its behaviour, so that ultimately it is precisely those people who have carried saintliness furthest who reproach themselves with the worst sinfulness. This means that virtue forfeits some part of its promised reward; the docile and continent ego does not enjoy the trust of its mentor, and strives in vain, it would seem, to acquire it. The objection will at once be made that these difficulties are artificial ones, and it will be said that a stricter and more vigilant conscience is precisely the hallmark of a moral man. Moreover, when saints call themselves sinners, they are not so wrong, considering the temptations to instinctual satisfaction to which they are exposed in a specially high degree — since, as is well known, temptations are merely increased by constant frustration, whereas an occasional satisfaction of them causes them to diminish, at least for the time being. The field of ethics, which is so full of problems, presents us with another fact: namely that ill-luck — that is, external frustration — so greatly enhances the power of the conscience in the super-ego. As long as things go well with a man, his conscience is lenient and lets the ego do all sorts of things; but when misfortune befalls him, he searches his soul, acknowledges his sinfulness, heightens the demands of his conscience, imposes abstinences on himself and punishes himself with penances. Whole peoples have behaved in this way, and still do. This, however, is easily explained by the original infantile stage of conscience, which, as we see, is not given up after the introjection into the super-ego, but persists alongside of it and behind it. Fate is regarded as a substitute for the parental agency. If a man is unfortunate it means that he is no longer loved by this highest power; and, threatened by such a loss of love, he once more bows to the parental representative in his super-ego — a representative whom, in his days of good fortune, he was ready to neglect. This becomes especially clear where Fate is looked upon in the strictly religious sense of being nothing else than an expression of the Divine Will. The people of Israel had believed themselves to be the favourite child of God, and when the great Father caused misfortune after misfortune to rain down upon this people of his, they were never shaken in their belief in his relationship to them or questioned his power or righteousness. Instead, they produced the prophets, who held up their sinfulness before them; and out of their sense of guilt they created the over-strict commandments of their priestly religion. It is remarkable how differently a primitive man behaves. If he has met with a misfortune, he does not throw the blame on himself but on his fetish, which has obviously not done its duty, and he gives it a thrashing instead of punishing himself.

Thus we know of two origins of the sense of guilt: one arising from fear of an authority, and the other, later on, arising from fear of the super-ego.

Martin Buber

Guilt and Guilt Feelings

I

58 At the London International Conference for Medical Psychotherapy of 1948,[1] "The Genesis of Guilt" was fixed as the theme of the first plenary session. The first speaker, a Hollander, began with the announcement that in his special group the question had been discussed as to whether the genesis of guilt or the genesis of guilt feelings was meant. The question remained unclarified. But in the course of the discussion it was left to the theologians to speak of guilt itself (by which, indeed, they did not actually mean personal guilt, but the original sin of the human race). The psychologists concerned themselves merely with guilt feelings.

This distribution of themes, through which the factual occurrences of guilt in the lives of "patients," of suffering men, hardly enters into view, is characteristic of most of what one calls the psychotherapeutic discipline. Only in the most recent period have some begun to complain that both in the theory and in the practice of this science only the psychic "projection" of guilt, but not the real events of guilt, is afforded room. But this omission has not been presented and methodologically grounded as such. It has been treated as a limitation that follows as a matter of course from the nature of psychology.

Nothing of the kind is self-evident, however; indeed, nothing of the kind by right exists. Certainly, in the course of the history of the spirit each science that has detached itself from a comprehensive context and insured for itself the independence of its

From *The Knowledge of Man* by Martin Buber, translated and edited by Maurice Friedman. Copyright © 1965 by Martin Buber and Maurice Friedman. Reprinted by permission of Harper & Row Publishers, Inc., and George Allen & Unwin Ltd.

[1] *Proceedings of the International Conference on Medical Psychotherapy,* Vol. III; International Conference of Mental Health, London, 1948; New York, Columbia Univ. Press, 1948.

realm has just thereby severely and ever more severely limited its subject and the manner of its working. But the investigator cannot truthfully maintain his relationship with reality — a relationship without which all his work becomes a well-regulated game — if he does not again and again, whenever it is necessary, gaze beyond the limits into a sphere which is not his sphere of work, yet which he must contemplate with all his power of research in order to do justice to his own task. For the psychotherapist this sphere is formed from the factual course of the so-called external life of his patient and especially the actions and attitudes therein, and again especially the patient's active share in the manifold relation between him and the human world. And not only his decisions are included in this share, but also his failures to come to a decision when, in a manner perceptible to him, they operate as decisions.

To the valid scientific realm of psychotherapy belong the "inner" reactions of the individual to his passive and active life experience, the psychic elaboration of the biographical events, whether it takes place in conscious or in unconscious processes. The relationship of the patient to a man with whom he stands in a contact that strongly affects his own life is for the psychologist only important as such in so far as its effects on the psyche of the patient can serve the understanding of his illness. The relationship itself in its reciprocal reality, the significant actuality of what is happening and has happened between the two men, transcends his task as it transcends his method. He limits himself to those of its inner connections that his work of exploring the mind of the patient makes accessible to him. And yet, if he wishes to satisfy not merely what he owes to the laws of his discipline and their application, but also what he owes to the existence and the need of man, he may — in fact, he must — go beyond that realm where an existing person merely relates to himself. He must cast his glance again and again to where existing person relates to existing person — this person here, the "patient," to another living being who is not "given" to the doctor and who may be completely unknown to him. The psychotherapist cannot include this other person, these other persons in his work. It is not for him to concern himself with them. And yet he may not neglect them in their reality; he must succeed in grasping their reality as adequately as possible in so far as it enters into the relationship between them and his patient.

This state of affairs manifests itself with the greatest intensity in the problem that occupies us here. Within his methods the psychotherapist has to do only with guilt feelings, conscious and unconscious (Freud was already aware of the contradiction that lies in the concept of unconscious feelings). But within a comprehensive service to knowledge and help, he must himself encounter guilt as something of an ontic character whose place is not the soul but being. He will do this, to be sure, with the danger that through his new knowledge the help which he is obliged to give might also be modified so that something uncustomary will be demanded of his method; indeed, he must be ready even to step out of the established rules of his school. But a "doctor of souls" who really is one — that is, who does not merely carry on the work of healing but enters into it at times as a partner — is precisely one who dares.

II

The boundaries set by the psychotherapists' method do not, in any case, suffice to explain the negative or indifferent attitude that psychotherapy has so long taken toward the ontic character of guilt. The history of modern psychology shows us that here deeper motives are at work that have also contributed to the genesis and development of the methods. The two clearest examples of it are provided us by the two most noteworthy representatives of this intellectual tendency, Freud and Jung.

Freud, a great, late-born apostle of the enlightenment, presented the naturalism[2] of the enlightenment with a scientific system and thereby with a second flowering. As Freud himself recognized with all clarity,[3] the struggle against all metaphysical and religious teachings of the existence of an absolute and of the possibility of a relation of the human person to it had a great share in the development of psychoanalytic theory. As a result of this basic attitude, guilt was simply not allowed to acquire an ontic character; it had to be derived from the transgression against ancient and modern taboos, against parental and social tribunals. The feeling of guilt was now to be understood as essentially only the consequence of dread of punishment and censure by this tribunal, as the consequence of the child's fear of "loss of love" or, at times when it was a question of imaginary guilt, as a "need for punishment" of a libidinal nature, as "moral masochism"[4] which is complemented by the sadism of

[2] Freud himself described psychoanalysts as "incorrigible mechanists and materialists". (Sigmund Freud, "Psycho-analysis and Telepathy," in *The Standard Edition of the Complete Psychological Works of Sigmund Freud* 18:177–193; London, Hogarth Press, 1955).

[3] See, for example, "A Philosophy of Life," Ch. 7 in Freud, *New Introductory Lectures on Psycho-Analysis,* New York, Norton, 1933.

[4] Freud, "The Economic Problem in Masochism," in *Collected Papers* 2:255–268; London, Hogarth Press, 1948.

the "superego." "The first renunciation of instinctual gratification," Freud stated in 1924, "is enforced by external powers, and it is this that creates morality which expresses itself in conscience and exacts a further renunciation of instinct."[5]

Of an entirely different, indeed diametrically opposed, nature is the teaching of Carl Jung, whom one can describe as a mystic of a modern, psychological type of solipsism. The mystical and religio-mystical conceptions that Freud despised are for Jung the most important subject of his study; but they are such merely as "projections" of the psyche, not as indications of something extrapsychic that the psyche meets. For Freud the structure of the psyche culminates in the "superego," which represents, with its censory function, only the authoritative tribunals of family and society; for Jung it culminates, or rather is grounded in, the "self" which is "individuality in its highest meaning"[6] and forms "the most immediate experience of the divine which can be grasped at all psychologically."[7] Jung does not recognize at all any relationship between the individual soul and another existing being which oversteps the limits of the psychic. But to this must be added the fact that the integration of evil as the unification of the opposites in the psyche is put forward as a central motif in the process of "individuation," of the "realization of self."[8] Seen from this vantage point, there is in Jung's panpsychism, as in Freud's materialism, no place for guilt in the ontological sense, unless it be in the relationship of man to himself — that is, as failure in the process of individuation. In fact, in the whole great work of Jung's we learn nothing of guilt as a reality in the relation between the human person and the world entrusted to him in his life.

With the other psychoanalytic doctrines it stands, in general, much the same. Almost everyone who seriously concerns himself with the problem of guilt proceeds to derive the guilt feelings that are met with in analysis from hidden elements, to trace them back to such elements, to unmask them as such. One seeks the powerful repressions in the unconscious as those that hide behind the phenomena of illness, but not also the live connection the image of which has remained in the living memory, time and again admonishing, attacking, tormenting, and, after each sub-

[5] Reference footnote 4; p. 267.

[6] Carl Jung, *Von den Wurzeln des Bewusstseins,* Psychologische Abhandlungen, Vol. 9; Zurich, Rascher, 1954; p. 296 f.

[7] Reference footnote 6; p. 300.

[8] For a fuller analysis of Jung, see Martin Buber, *Eclipse of God,* Section 2, "Religion and Modern Thinking," and "Supplement: Reply to C. G. Jung," translated by Maurice S. Friedman; New York, Harper, 1952.

mersion in the river of no-longer-thinking-about-that, returning and taking up its work anew.

A man stands before us who, through acting or failing to act, has burdened himself with a guilt or has taken part in a community guilt, and now, after years or decades, is again and again visited by the memory of his guilt. Nothing of the genesis of his illness is concealed from him if he is only willing no longer to conceal from himself the guilt character of that active or passive occurrence. What takes possession of him ever again has nothing to do with any parental or social reprimand, and if he does not have to fear an earthly retribution and does not believe in a heavenly one, no court, no punishing power exists that can make him anxious. Here there rules the one penetrating insight—the one insight capable of penetrating into the impossibility of recovering the original point of departure and the irreparability of what has been done, and that means the real insight into the irreversibility of lived time, a fact that shows itself unmistakably in the starkest of all human perspectives, that concerning one's own death. From no standpoint is time so perceived as a torrent as from the vision of the self in guilt. Swept along in this torrent, the bearer of guilt is visited by the shudder of identity with himself. I, he comes to know, I, who have become another, am the same.

I have seen three important and, to me, dear men fall into long illnesses from their failing to stand the test in the days of an acute community guilt. The share of the psychogenic element in the illness could hardly be estimated, but its action was unmistakable. One of them refused to acknowledge his self-contradiction before the court of his spirit. The second resisted recognizing as serious a slight error he remembered that was attached to a very serious chain of circumstances. The third, however, would not let himself be forgiven by God for the blunder of a moment because he did not forgive himself. It now seems to me that all three needed and lacked competent helpers.

The psychotherapist into whose field of vision such manifestations of guilt enter in all their forcefulness can no longer imagine that he is able to do justice to his task as doctor of guilt-ridden men merely through the removal of guilt feelings. Here a limit is set to the tendency to derive guilt from the taboos of primeval society. The psychologist who sees what is here to be seen must be struck by the idea that guilt does not exist because a taboo exists to which one fails to give obedience, but rather that taboo and the placing of taboo have been made possible only through the fact that the leaders of early communities knew and made use of a primal fact of man as man — the fact that man can become guilty and know it.

Existential guilt — that is, guilt that a person has taken on himself as a person and in a personal situation — cannot be comprehended through such categories of analytical science as "repression" and "becoming-conscious." The bearer of guilt of whom I speak remembers it again and again by himself and in sufficient measure. Not seldom, certainly, he attempts to evade it — not the remembered fact, however, but its depths as existential guilt — until the truth of this depth overwhelms him and time is now perceived by him as a torrent.

Can the doctor of souls function here as helper, beyond professional custom and correct methods? May he do so? Is he shown at times another and higher therapeutic goal than the familiar one? Can and may he try his strength, not with conscious or unconscious, founded or unfounded guilt feelings, but with the self-manifesting existential guilt itself? Can he allow himself to recognize, from this standpoint, that healing in this case means something other than the customary, and what it means in this case?

The doctor who confronts the effects on the guilty man of an existential guilt must proceed in all seriousness from the situation in which the act of guilt has taken place. Existential guilt occurs when someone injures an order of the human world whose foundations he knows and recognizes as those of his own existence and of a common human existence. The doctor who confronts such a guilt in the living memory of his patient must enter into that situation; he must lay his hand in the ground of the order and learn: this concerns you. But then it may strike him that the orientation of the psychologist and the treatment of the therapist have changed unawares and that, if he wishes to persist as a healer, he must take upon himself a burden he had not expected to bear.

One could protest that an existential guilt is only the exception and that it is not proper to frighten the already over-burdened therapist with the image of such borderline cases. But what I call existential guilt is only an intensification of what is found in some measure wherever an authentic guilt feeling burns, and the authentic guilt feeling is very often inextricably mingled with the problematic, the "neurotic," the "groundless." The therapist's methods, naturally, do not willingly concern themselves with the authentic guilt feeling which, in general, is of a strictly personal character and does not easily allow itself to be imprisoned in general propositions. It lies essentially nearer to the doctrine and practice to occupy itself with the effects of repressed childhood wishes or youthful lusts gone astray, than with the inner consequences of a man's betrayal of his friend or his cause. And for the patient it is a great relief to be diverted from his authentic guilt feeling to an unambiguous neurotic one that, favored within this category by the school of his doctor, allows itself to be discovered in the microcosmos of his dreams or in the stream of his free associations. To all this the genuine doctor of souls stands opposed with the postulative awareness that he should act here as at once bound and unbound. He does not, of course, desist from any of his methods, which have, in fact, become adaptable. But where, as here, he becomes aware of a reality between man and man, between man and the world, a reality inaccessible to any of the psychological categories, he recognizes the limits that are set here for his methods and recognizes that the goal of healing has been transformed in this case because the context of the sickness, the place of the sickness in being, has been transformed. If the therapist recognizes this, then all that he is obliged to do becomes more difficult, much more difficult — and all becomes more real, radically real.

III

I shall clarify this statement through the example of a life history that I have already made use of before, although all too briefly.[9] I select it from among those at my disposal because I was a witness, sometimes more distant, sometimes nearer, to the happenings, and I have followed their sequence. The life course I have in mind is that of a woman — let us call her Melanie — of more intellectual than truly spiritual gifts, with a scientific education, but without the capacity for independent mastery of her knowledge. Melanie possessed a remarkable talent for good comradeship which expressed itself, at least from her side, in more or less erotically tinged friendships that left unsatisfied her more impetuous than passionate need for love. She made the acquaintance of a man who was on the point of marriage with another, strikingly ugly, but remarkable woman. Melanie succeeded without difficulty in breaking up the engagement and marrying the man. Her rival tried to kill herself. Melanie soon afterwards ac-

---

[9]See my Preface to Hans Trüb's posthumous work, *Heilung aus der Begegnung: Eine Auseinandersetzung mit der Psychologie C. G. Jungs,* edited by Ernst Michel and Arie Sborowitz; Stuttgart, Ernst Klett Verlag, 1952. This Preface will appear in English as "Healing Through Meeting" in Martin Buber, *Pointing the Way: Collected Essays,* edited and translated by Maurice S. Friedman; New York, Harper & Brothers, to be published in 1957.

cused her, certainly unjustly, of feigning her attempt at suicide. After a few years Melanie herself was supplanted by another woman. Soon afterwards she fell ill with a neurosis linked with disturbances of the vision. To friends who took her in at the time, she confessed her guilt without glossing over the fact that it had arisen not out of a passion, but out of a fixed will.

Later she gave herself into the care of a well-known psycho-analyst. This man was able to liberate her in a short while from both her feelings of disappointment and of guilt and to bring her to the conviction that she was a "genius of friendship" and would find in this sphere the compensation that was due her. The con-version succeeded, and Melanie devoted herself to a rich sociality which she experienced as a world of friendship. In contrast to this, she associated in general with the men with whom she had to deal in her professional "welfare work" not as persons needing her understanding and even her consolation, but as objects to be seen through and directed by her. The guilt feelings were no longer in evidence; the apparatus that had been installed in place of the paining and admonishing heart functioned in model fashion.

Now that is certainly no extraordinary fate. We recognize again the all too usual distress of human action and suffering, and there can be no talk here of existential guilt in the great sense of the term. And yet, the guilt feeling that grew up at that time in the illness and that so fused with the illness that no one could say which of the two was the cause and which the effect, had through-out an authentic character. With the silencing of the guilt feeling there disappeared for Melanie the possibility of reconciliation through a newly won genuine relationship to her environment in which her best qualities could at the same time unfold. The price paid for the annihilation of the sting was the final annihilation of the chance to become the being that this created person was destined to become through her highest disposition.

Again one may raise the objection that it cannot be the affair of the psychotherapist to concern himself about this kind of thing. His task is to investigate malady and to heal it, or rather to help it toward healing, and it is just this that the doctor who had been called in had done. But here lies an important problem. Stated generally, one can formulate it somewhat as follows: Shall a man who is called upon to help another in a specific manner merely give the help for which he is summoned or shall he also give the other help that, according to the doctor's knowl-edge of him, this man objectively needs?

However, what is the meaning here of the help that one objec-tively needs? Clearly this, that his being follows other laws than his consciousness. But also quite other ones than his "unconscious." The unconscious is still far less concerned than the conscious about whether the essence of this man thrives. Essence—by this I mean that for which a person is peculiarly intended, what he is called to become. The conscious, with its planning and its weighing, concerns itself with it only occasionally; the unconscious, with its wishes and contradictions, hardly ever. Those are great moments of existence when a man discovers his essence or rediscovers it on a higher plane; when he decides and decides anew to become what he is and, as one who is becoming this, to establish a genuine relation to the world; when he heroically maintains his discovery and decision against his everyday consciousness and against his unconscious. Should the helper, can the helper, may the helper now enter into an alliance with the essence of him who summoned him, across this person's conscious and unconscious will, provided that he has really reliably recognized the need of this essence? Is something of this sort at all his office? Can it be his office? Particularly where the helping profession is so exactly circumscribed by principles and methods as in modern psychotherapy? Does not the danger threaten here of a pseudointuitive dilettantism that dissolves all fixed norms?

An important psychologist and doctor of our time, the late Viktor von Weizsaecker, laid down, in very precise language, a sober admonition on this point. There the "treatment of the essential in man" is simply excluded from the realm of psychotherapy. "Just the final destiny of man," he writes, "must not be the subject of therapy."[10] And my lay insight must concur with this declaration. But there is an exceptional case—the case where the glance of the doctor, the perceiving glance that makes him a doctor and to which all his methods stand in a serving relation, extends into the sphere of the essence, where he perceives essential lapse and essential need. There, to be sure, it is still denied him to treat "the essential" in his patients, but he may and should guide it to where an essential help of the self, a help till now neither willed nor anticipated, can begin. It is neither given the therapist nor allowed to him to indicate a way that leads onward from here. But from the watchtower to which the patient has been conducted, he can manage to see a way that is right for him and that he can walk, a way that it is not granted the doctor to see. For at this high station all becomes personal in the strictest sense.

The psychotherapist is no pastor of souls and no substitute for

---

[10]Viktor von Weizsaecker, *Herztliche Fragen;* 1934; p. 9.

one. It is never his task to mediate a salvation; his task is always only to further a healing. But it is not merely incumbent upon him to interest himself in that need of the patient that has become symptomatically manifest in his sickness—to interest himself in it as far as the analysis conducted according to the therapist's method discloses to him the genesis of this illness. That need is also confided to him that first allows itself to be recognized in the immediacy of the partnership between the patient who is having recourse to the doctor and the doctor who is concerned about the recovery of the patient—although occasionally this need remains veiled, even then.

I have already pointed to the fact that the doctor, in order to be able to do this adequately, must for the time being lift himself off the firm ground of principles and methods on which he has learned to walk. One must not, of course, understand this to mean that he now soars in the free ether of an unrestrained "intuition." Now too, and only now really, he is obliged to think consistently and to work exactly. And if he may now surrender himself to a more direct vision, it can still only be one that realizes its individual norms in each of its insights—norms that cannot be translated into general propositions. In this sphere of action, too, even though it seems left to his independent direction, the man of the intellectual profession learns that a true work is an affair of a listening obedience.

But in order that the therapist be able to do this, he must recognize just one thing steadfastly and recognize it ever again: there exists real guilt, fundamentally different from all the anxiety-induced bugbears that are generated in the cavern of the unconscious. Personal guilt, whose reality some schools of psychoanalysis contest and others ignore, does not permit itself to be reduced to the trespass against a powerful taboo.

We cannot now content ourselves, however, with allowing this knowledge, which was long under a ban, to be conveyed to us by this or that tradition which is holy to us. It must arise anew from the historical and biographical self-experience of the generation living today. We who are living today know in what measure we have become historically and biographically guilty. That is no feeling and no sum of feelings. It is, no matter how manifoldly concealed and denied, a real knowledge about a reality. Under the schooling of this knowledge, which is becoming ever more irresistible, we learn anew that guilt exists.

In order to understand this properly we must call to mind one fact, no accessory fact but a basic one. Each man stands in an objective relationship to others; the totality of this relationship constitutes his life as one that factually participates in the being of the world. It is this relationship, in fact, that first makes it at all possible for him to expand his environment (*Umwelt*) into a world (*Welt*). It is his share in the human order of being, the share for which he bears responsibility. An objective relationship in which two men stand to one another can rise, by means of the existential participation of the two, to a personal relation; it can be merely tolerated; it can be neglected; it can be injured. Injuring a relationship means that at this place the human order of being is injured. No one other than he who inflicted the wound can heal it. He who knows the fact of his guilt and is a helper can help him try to heal the wound.

IV

One last clarification is still necessary. When the therapist recognizes an existential guilt of his patient, he cannot—that we have seen—show him the way to the world, which the latter must rather seek and find as his own personal law. The doctor can only conduct him to the point from which he can glimpse his personal way or at least its beginning. But in order that the doctor shall be able to do this, he must also know about the general nature of the way, common to all great acts of conscience, and about the connection that exists between the nature of existential guilt and the nature of this way.

In order not to fall into any error here, however, we must bear in mind that there are three different spheres in which the reconciliation of guilt can fulfill itself and between which noteworthy relations often establish themselves. Only one of these spheres, that which we shall designate as the middle one, directly concerns the therapist whom I have in mind.

The first sphere is that of the law of the society. The action begins here with the demand, actually made or latent, which society places on the guilty man according to its laws. The event of fulfillment is called confession of guilt. It is followed by penalty and indemnification. With this sphere the therapist, naturally, has nothing to do. As doctor, an opinion is not even accorded him as to whether the demand of the society is right or not. His patient, the guilty man, may be guilty toward the society or he may not be; its judgment over him may be just or it may not be. This does not concern the doctor as doctor; he is incompetent here. In his relation to the patient this problematic theme can find no admission, with the exception of the unavoidable occupation with the anxiety of the patient in the face of the punishments, the censure, the boycotts of society.

But the third and highest sphere, that of faith, also cannot be his affair. Here the action commences within the relation between the guilty man and his God and remains therein. It is likewise consummated in three events which correspond to the three of the first sphere, but are connected with each other in an entirely different manner. These are the confession of sin, repentance, and penance in its various forms. The doctor as such may not touch on this sphere even when he and the patient stand in the same community of faith. Here no man can speak, unless it be one whom the guilty man acknowledges as a hearer and speaker who represents the transcendence believed in by the guilty man. Also when the therapist encounters the problem of faith in the anxiety concerning divine punishment that is disclosed in the patient's analysis, he cannot interfere here — even if he possesses great spiritual gifts — without falling into a dangerous dilettantism.

The middle sphere, as we have said, is the one to the sight of which the therapist may lead — up to it, but no farther. This sphere, about which he must *know* for this purpose, we may call that of conscience, with a qualification which I shall shortly discuss. The action demanded by the conscience also fulfills itself in three events, which I call self-illumination, perseverance, and reconciliation, and which I shall define more exactly still.

Conscience means to us the capacity and tendency of man radically to distinguish between those of his past and future actions which should be approved and those which should be disapproved. The disapproval, in general, receives far stronger emotional stress, whereas the approval of past actions at times passes over with shocking ease into a most questionable self-satisfaction. Conscience can, naturally, distinguish and, if necessary, condemn in such a manner not merely deeds but also omissions, not merely decisions but also failures to decide, indeed even images and wishes that have just arisen or are remembered.

In order to understand this capacity and tendency more exactly, one must bear in mind that among all living beings known to us man alone is able to set at a distance not only his environment,[11] but also himself. As a result, he becomes for himself a detached object about which he can not only "reflect," but which he can, from time to time, confirm as well as condemn. The content of conscience is in many ways determined, of course, by the commands and prohibitions of the society to which its bearer belongs or those of the tradition of faith to which he is bound. But conscience itself cannot be understood as an introjection of either the one authority or the other, neither ontogenetically

---

[11] See "Distance and Relation," pp. 97–104 in this issue of *Psychiatry*.

nor phylogenetically. The table of shalts and shalt-nots under which this man has grown up and lives determines only the conceptions which prevail in the realm of the conscience, but not its existence itself, which is grounded in just that distancing and distinguishing — primal qualities of the human race. The more or less hidden criteria that the conscience employs in its acceptances and rejections only rarely fully coincide with a standard received from the society or community. Connected with that is the fact that the guilt feeling can hardly ever be wholly traced to a transgression against a taboo of a family or of society. The totality of the order that a man knows to be injured or injurable by him transcends to some degree the totality of the parental and social taboos that bind him. The depth of the guilt feeling is not seldom connected with just that part of the guilt that cannot be ascribed to the taboo-offense, hence with the existential guilt.

The qualification of which I spoke, accordingly, is that our subject is the relation of the conscience to existential guilt. Its relation to the trespassing of taboos concerns us here only in so far as a guilty man understands this trespassing more strongly or weakly as real existential guilt which arises out of his being and for which he cannot take responsibility without being responsible to his relationship to his own being.

The vulgar conscience that knows admirably well how to torment and harass, but cannot arrive at the ground and abyss of guilt, is incapable, to be sure, of summoning to such responsibility. For this summoning a greater conscience is needed, one that has become wholly personal, one that does not shy away from the glance into the depths and that already in admonishing envisages the way that leads across it. But this in no way means that this personal conscience is reserved for some type of "higher" man. This conscience is possessed by every simple man who gathers himself into himself in order to venture the breakthrough out of the entanglement in guilt. And it is a great, not yet sufficiently recognized, task of education to elevate the conscience from its lower common form to conscience-vision and conscience-courage. For it is innate to the conscience of man that it can elevate itself.

From what has been said it already follows with sufficient clarity that the primeval concept of conscience, if only it is understood as a dynamic one rather than as a static, judging one, is more realistic than the modern structural concept of the superego. The concept of the superego attains only an orienting significance and one, moreover, which easily orients the novice falsely.

If we now wish to speak of actions in the sphere of conscience in this high and strict sense, we do not mean thereby the well-known synthesis out of the internalization of censure, torment, and punishment that one customarily regards as the proper factual content of conscience—that pressuring and oppressing influence of an inner high court on an "ego" that is more or less subject to it. Rather this tormenting complex has, for our consideration, only the character of an angelic-demonic intermezzo on which the high dramatic or tragicomic act of neurosis may follow, and the whole affair may end with a therapy that passes for successful. What concerns us here is another possibility, whether it be the true process of healing after the neurosis, or whether it be without a neurosis preceding it. It is that possible moment when the whole person who has become awake and unafraid ascends from the anguishing lowland of the conscience to its heights and independently masters the material delivered to him by it.

From this position a man can undertake the threefold action to which I have referred: first, to illuminate the darkness that still weaves itself about the guilt despite all previous action of the conscience—not to illuminate it with spotlights but with a broad and enduring wave of light; second, to persevere, no matter how high he may have ascended in his present life above that station of guilt—to persevere in that newly won humble knowledge of the identity of the present person with the person of that time; and third, in his place and according to his capacity, in the given historical and biographical situations, to restore the order-of-being injured by him through the relation of an active devotion to the world—for the wounds of the order-of-being can be healed in infinitely many other places than those at which they were inflicted.

In order that this may succeed in that measure that is at all attainable by this man, he must gather the forces and elements of his being and ever again protect the unity that is thus won from the cleavage and contradiction that threaten it. For, to quote myself, one cannot do evil with his whole soul, one can do good only with the whole soul.[12] What one must wrest from himself, first, is not yet the good; only when he has first attained his own self does the good thrive through him.

V

The event of illumination corresponds on the plane of the law to the legal confession of guilt, on the plane of faith to the confession of sin. As a social concept, confession of guilt is naturally

---

[12] Martin Buber, *Good and Evil: Two Interpretations;* New York, Scribners, 1953; p. 130.

the most familiar of the three; what takes place here takes place in public in the legal institutions of society.

The confession of sin is spoken by a man when, seeking reconciliation with God, he directly or indirectly steps before the absolute judgment. That may happen in the chorus of the community, as at the Jewish Day of Atonement, or in the whispers of the confessing man into the ear of the confessor, or even in solitude by those who feel themselves as standing before God and their speech as addressing God: the confessing one is always removed from the anonymous publicity of society, but by no means referred to himself. He has one over against him who receives his confession, answers it, "forgives" him—for the Jews, in a significant cooperation with him toward whom the confessing one has become guilty.

The matter is otherwise with the first of the three events in the action of the great conscience, the event of illumination. Here a man ventures to illuminate the depths of a guilt which he has, certainly, recognized as what it is, but not yet in its essence and its meaning for his life. What he is now obliged to do cannot be accomplished in any other place than in the abyss of I-with-me, and it is just this abyss that must be illuminated.

Legal confession of guilt means a dialogue with the representatives of society who rejoin as judges according to the penal law. Religious confession means a dialogue with the absolute divine person who replies in mysterious fashion out of his mystery. As for the illumination of essence, it is in its realest moments not even a monologue, much less a real conversation between an "ego" and a "superego": all speech is exhausted, what takes place here is the mute shudder of self-being. But without this powerful wave of light which illuminates the abyss of mortality, the legal confession of guilt remains without substance in the inner life of the guilty man, no matter how weighty its consequences may be, and the religious confession is only a pathetic prattle that no one hears.

We must not fail to recognize that it has become more difficult for the man of our age than any earlier one to venture self-illumination with awake and unafraid spirit, although he imagines that he knows more about himself than did the man of any earlier time. The inner resistance which shows itself here—a deeper one than all that discloses itself to the genetic investigation of the analyst—has found so valid a representation in two of the characteristic forms of the epic literatures of the nineteenth and twentieth centuries that we cannot do better than to turn to them in order to supplement our understanding of the problem. I mean Nikolai Stavrogin in Dostoevski's novel *The Possessed* and Joseph

K in Kafka's narrative *The Trial.* In our discussion of this subject, the second of these books, as little as it is comparable to the first in artistic power, must still be the more important because in it the present stage of the human problem of guilt has found expression. But in order to see how this later stage is connected with that which preceded it, we must turn our attention first to Dostoevski.

For our formulation of the question it is necessary to proceed from the complete text of the novel, that which contains the chapter of Stavrogin's confession, later expunged by the author on external grounds, and some related material.

Stavrogin was thought of by Dostoevski as the man on the outermost rim of the age who dissolves the meaning of existence through denying it and who manages to destroy himself through the destruction of all over whom he gets power. In the omitted chapter it is told how Stavrogin visits a holy man and brings to him the record of a confession which he declares he wishes to publish. In it he confesses how he raped a little girl. Later he disavows the confession, evidently because he knows from the reaction of the priest as soon as it has been made that it is not able to accomplish what he has expected it to. The content of the confession is true, but the act of making it is fictitious. It has nothing at all to do with Stavrogin's self-illumination, with persevering self-identification, with reconciling renewed relationship with the world. Thus even his "unfeigned need for a public execution" (as Dostoevski states in explanation) is permeated with the fictitious. What Stavrogin desires is "the leap." A fragmentary sketch by Dostoevski informs us unambiguously about this. It says, clearly in this connection, that the priest opposed Stavrogin's intention to publish the confession: "The high priest pointed out that a leap was not necessary, that the man must rather set himself to rights from within—through long work; only then could he complete the leap." "And would it be impossible to do it suddenly?" Stavrogin asks. "Impossible?" rejoins the priest. "From the work of an angel it would become the work of a devil." "Ah," exclaims Stavrogin, "that I already knew myself."

Stavrogin "commits" the confession as he commits his crimes: as an attempt to snatch the genuine existence which he does not possess, but which—nihilist in practice but (in anticipation) existentialist in views—he has recognized as the true good. He is full of "ideas" (Dostoevski even lends him his own!), full of "spirit," but he does not exist. Only after Dostoevski's time, only in our own, will this type of man discover the basic nihilism in existential form after he has learned that he cannot attain to existence by the ways corresponding to his kind of person. Only this is now left to him: to proclaim the spiritful *nihil* as existence and himself as the new man. Stavrogin is not yet so "advanced." All he can do is to kill himself, after all the "demonic" game with ideas, crimes, and confessions—this game that has a goal—has proved itself powerless. The decisive moment—excised in the usual version of the novel as abridged by the author—is precisely the failure of the confession: Stavrogin has wanted the holy man to believe in its existential character and thereby help him, Stavrogin, to existence. But existential confession is possible only as a breaking-through to the great action of the high conscience in self-illumination, persevering self-identification, and a reconciling relationship to the world. This possibility, however, is in Stavrogin's eyes one of two things: either essentially not accorded to him or destroyed by him through his life-game. In Dostoevski's own eyes, however, man is redeemable when he wills redemption *as such* and thereby also his share in it—the great act of the high conscience.

VI

The Possessed was written in 1870, Kafka's *Trial* in 1915. The two books represent two basically different but closely connected situations of human history from which their authors suffered: the one the uncanny negative certainty, "Human values are beginning to shatter," and the other the still more uncanny uncertainty, "Do world-meaning and world-order still have any connection at all with this nonsense and this disorder of the human world?"—an uncertainty that appears to have arisen out of that negative certainty.

Everything in Kafka's book is intended to be uncertain and indefinite, at times to the point of an absurdity, which always remains artistically mastered. This court of justice before which Joseph K is unexpectedly cited because of an unnamed and to him unknown guilt is at once prosaically real and of ghostly indefiniteness, wild, crude, and senselessly disordered through and through. But Joseph K is himself, in all his actions, of hardly less indefiniteness—merely a different kind—as, charged with guilt, he confusedly carries on day after day a life as directionless as before. Directionless, that is, except for the one aim he now pursues, sometimes busily, sometimes incidentally: namely, that of getting free of the court. To this end he occupies himself with indefinite advocates, indefinite women, and other indefinite human instruments in order that they may provide him, in the face of the peculiar ways of this peculiar court, with the protection that he imagines is all he needs. The indefinite guilt with which he is charged occupies him only in so far as he thinks from time to time of composing a written defense in the form of a short description of his life which will explain, in connection with each more important event, on what grounds he then acted thus and not otherwise, and whether he now approves or condemns his manner of acting at that time. Finally there happens what is reported in an unfinished chapter: "From then on K forgot the court."

All this is not to be called chaotic, for in a chaos is hidden a world that shall emerge out of it; here there is no trace of a cosmos that wills to come into being. But one may well call all this taken together—the court, the accused, and the people around him—labyrinthine. The disorder, mounting to absurdity, points toward a secret order, one, however, which nowhere shows itself except by way of a hint, which apparently would first become manifest only if Joseph K did what until the end he does not do— make "the confession" that is demanded of him. But he cannot, as he says, discover the least guilt on account of which one could accuse him. Indeed, he ends later—clearly without quite knowing what he is saying—by uttering the presumptuous words that are not proper to any human mouth: "I am completely guiltless." The thread that leads out of the labyrinth is not to be found in the book; rather this thread exists only when just that happens which did not happen, the "confession of guilt."

But what can be meant here, under the given presuppositions, by making a confession? This question hovers in a strange, altogether intentional paradox. A well-informed young woman says to Joseph K, leaning on his shoulder, "One cannot, in fact, defend oneself against this court; one must make the confession. Make it therefore at the first opportunity. Only then is there any possibility of escaping." And he answers, "You understand much about this court and about the deceit that is necessary here." Since Kafka himself says nothing like this, it can only mean that Joseph, who holds himself, in fact, to be "entirely guiltless," understands that he should make a false confession, and at this moment he does not seem disinclined to do so. Later, however, a painter, who is likewise, as we hear, well-acquainted with the ways of this court, advises him thus: "Since you are guiltless, it is really possible for you to rely on your innocence." Note well: In the same speech the same speaker declares that he has never yet witnessed a single acquittal, but immediately afterwards he says that the decisions of the court were not published, that there exist, however, "legends" of actual acquittals, and that these legends probably contain "a certain truth."

In this atmosphere the action moves forward, and it clearly seems as though the accusation and with it the encouragement to confession are a senseless absurdity, as Joseph K has declared them to be in his speech before the court: "And the meaning of this great organization, gentlemen? It consists in the fact that innocent persons are arrested, and against them a senseless and for the most part, as in my case, inconsequential proceedings are instituted." Some Kafka interpreters take these words to express the essential message of the book. This position is refuted through the further course of the action and through notes in Kafka's diaries relating to it.

I have in mind the chapter, "In the Cathedral," in which it is told how Joseph K comes by accident into a church and is here addressed by name by a clergyman unknown to him, the prison chaplain, who also belongs to the organization of the court but does not act by order of the court. This chapter corresponds exactly to the one excised by Dostoevski from *The Possessed,* in which Stavrogin hands over his confession to the high priest (a chapter which Kafka, moreover, could have known only in an incomplete version, not including the text of the confession). In both a priest is the antagonist, in both it is a matter of a confession of guilt; however, in Dostoevski it is furnished undemanded while in Kafka it is demanded. For it is this demand that the chaplain wishes to convey by the information that the case is going badly, since the court holds the guilt to be proved. "But I am not guilty," answers K, "it's a misunderstanding. And, if it comes to that, how can any man be called guilty? We are all simply men here, one as much as the other." One must listen closely: what is denied here is the ontic character of guilt, the depth of existential guilt beyond all mere violations of taboos. It is just this that Freud wished to deny when he undertook to relativize guilt feeling genetically. And to Joseph K's reply the priest answers, "That is true," which means: Indeed we are all men, and should not overestimate the difference between men. He continues, however, "But that's how all guilty men talk," which means: He who is in question gets off by talking about the others, instead of occupying himself with himself.

Now the priest asks, "What is the next step you propose to take in the matter?" "I'm going to seek more help," answers K. "You cast about too much for outside help," he now hears. And when he still will not understand, the chaplain shrieks at him, "Can't you see two steps in front of you?" He speaks like one who sees a man who still stands there before him as already fallen. What he wants to say with his words, without directly saying it, is that the verdict, "into which the proceedings gradually pass over," now stands at hand, and the verdict itself already means death.

And now, as the last and most extreme effort, the chaplain tells the man, for whose soul and destiny he wrestles in one, that parable of the doorkeeper who stands, as one of countless men, "before the Law," before one of the countless doors leading into the interior of the Law, and of the man who desires entrance here. This man is frightened by the difficulties that await him who dares entrance, according to the information imparted to him by the doorkeeper. He now passes days and years, the entire remainder of his life, sitting sideways before this one out of innumerably many doors, until shortly before his end the keeper discloses to him that this doorway was destined for him alone and now is going to be shut. Joseph K listens to the parable and does not understand it: what then could the men have done to manage to get in? The clergyman does not tell him. Kafka himself, as he records in his diaries, first understood the significance of the story when he read it aloud to his fiancee. On another occasion, he clearly expressed this significance himself in an unforgettable passage in his notebooks: "Confession of guilt, unconditional confession of guilt, door springing open, it appears in the interior of the house of the world whose turbid reflection lay behind walls." The confession is the door springing open. It is the true "breakthrough," by which word Joseph K is falsely accustomed to describe the aspired-for escape from the law.

What does the legal concept of confession of guilt become here? What is so named here is self-illumination, the first and opening event in the action of the great conscience.

Stavrogin makes a confession in words. He describes therein in horrible detail the course of his crime, but both in remembering it and in recording it he remains incapable of self-illumination. He lacks the small light of humility that alone can illuminate the abyss of the guilty self in broad waves. He seeks for some kind of foothold, no matter how meager; then he gives up and kills himself.

Joseph K makes no confession; he refuses to understand that it is necessary for him to do so. In distinction from Stavrogin he is not proud; unlike the latter, he does not distinguish himself from other men. But by that very fact, with his, "We are all simply men here," he escapes the demand to bear into his inner darkness (of which Kafka speaks in his diaries) the cruel and salutary light. He insists that there is no such thing as personal existential guilt. His innermost being knows otherwise—because Kafka, who is closely connected with this Joseph K, knows otherwise—

but he shuns penetrating to this innermost being until it is too late. At this point Franz Kafka and Joseph K seem to have to part company. Kafka had imparted to him something of his own name, he had given him to bear (as he gave to "K" in *The Castle*) his own suffering from a senselessly acting environment; with humorous caricature he had endowed him with his own traits. But now in the decisive hour, according to the logic of the fiction, he lets him say, "How can any man be called guilty?," and lets him lengthily and ingeniously dispute over the story of the doorkeeper, Kafka's most concentrated statement of his life-view, instead of accepting its teaching. As a result, Kafka who understands the depth of existential guilt, must separate himself at this point from Joseph K.

He attains connection with him again, however, through the fact that soon afterwards, when the executors are already leading Joseph K to his death, Kafka lets him concentrate himself in a strong, although still rational, self-recollection. He lets Joseph, who now knows that and how the trial is going to end, say to himself, "I always wanted to snatch at the world with twenty hands, and not for a very laudable motive, either." Joseph K has recognized that he has projected on the disordered human world only his own disorder. His self-recollection is not, of course, the beginning of a self-illumination, but it is a first step toward it, without the man who does it knowing it. And now, before the end, Kafka may again take the foolish man to his heart, although at the very end, before the knife falls on Joseph K, Kafka lets the old foolish notions of some still forgotten objections come into his mind. Perhaps Kafka meant himself by the man whom Joseph K glimpses at the last standing in a window, "a man faint and in-substantial at that distance and at that height": he wants to help his creature and may not.

It might still be asked how the absurd confusion that rules in the court is to be reconciled with the justice of the accusation and the demand. The question places before us a central problem of Kafka's that we find in the background of this novel and of the related novel *The Castle,* where an inaccessible power governs by means of a slovenly bureaucracy. We can extract the answer from an important note in Kafka's diary, from the time of the genesis of *The Trial,* in which he speaks of being occupied with the Biblical figure of the unjust judges. It reads, "I find, therefore, my opinion, or at least the opinion that I have formerly found in me." The Eighty-second Psalm, of which he is clearly speaking here, has as its subject God's judgment over those "sons of God," or angels, to whom He had entrusted the regimen over the human world and who had vilely misused their office and "judged falsely." The content of this late psalm is connected with that of the Oriental myth, elaborated by the Gnostics, of the astral spirits who fatefully determine the destiny of the world, but from whose power that man may become free who dedicates himself to the concealed highest light and enters into rebirth. I have reason to assume that Kafka also knew this myth at that time.[13] In *The Trial* he modified it, in accord with his own contemplation of the world, through letting the just accusation of an inaccessible highest judgment be conveyed by a disorderly and cruel court. Only that man can escape the arm of this court who, out of his own knowledge, fulfills the demand for confession of guilt according to its truth through executing the primal confession, the self-illumination. Only he enters the interior of the Law.

VII

The destiny of both men, that of Stavrogin and that of Joseph K, is determined by their false relationship to their guiltiness.

Stavrogin, of course, plays with the thought of bearing before him like a banner the confession of his most shameful guilt, but he does not bring forth the greater courage to understand in self-illumination his essential being and the origin of his guilt. His feeling, as he says in his last letter, is "too weak and too shallow," his wish "too little strong; it cannot lead me." He declares himself unable to kill himself, for "vexation and shame can never exist in me, and consequently no despair." But immediately thereafter despair overwhelms him and he gives himself up to death.

Joseph K belongs to another, essentially later, more "advanced" generation. Not merely before the world, but also before himself, he refuses to concern himself with an ostensible state of guilt. He refuses to find and illuminate in himself the cause of this indictment which this questionable society casts on him from somewhere — say, from an invisible, unknowable "highest court." Indeed, it now passes as proved, in this his generation, that no real guilt exists; only guilt-feeling and guilt convention. Until the last moment he refuses to enter through the door that still stands open and is only apparently shut; thus the verdict overtakes him.

Both Stavrogin and Joseph K have not taken the crucial hour of man upon themselves, and now have lost it.

It is the crucial hour of man of which we speak. For, to use Pascal's language, the greatness of man is bound up with his misery.

[13] I refer to a question concerning this myth that Kafka put to me at the time of his visit to my house in Berlin in 1911 or 1912.

Man is the being who is capable of becoming guilty and is capable of illuminating his guilt.

I have illustrated through two examples from epic literature the manifold resistance of the human being against self-illumination. But this inner resistance is entirely different from the patient's struggle, well known to the psychoanalyst, against his efforts to convey from the unconscious into the conscious[14] a repressed state of facts of a guilt-like nature. For the guilt which is in question here is not at all repressed into the unconscious. The bearer of existential guilt remains in the realm of conscious existence. This guilt is not one that allows itself to be repressed into the unconscious. It remains in the chamber of memory, out of which it can at any moment penetrate unexpectedly into that of consciousness, without it being possible for any barriers to be erected against this invasion. The memory receives all experiences and actions without the assistance of man. It may, however, retain the ingredients of what is remembered in such a manner that what ascends into the actual remembering does not enter it in its original character. The existential guilt, therefore, does not enter it as such. Only when the human person himself overcomes his inner resistance can he attain to self-illumination.

The "opening door" of self-illumination leads us into no place beyond the law but into the interior of the law. It is the law of man in which we then stand: the law of the identity of the human person as such with himself, the one who recognizes guilt with the one who bears guilt, the one in light with the one in darkness. The hard trial of self-illumination is followed by the still harder, because neverceasing, trial of persevering in this self-identification. But by this is not meant an ever-renewed scourging of the soul with its knowledge of its abyss understood as something inevitably allotted to it. What is meant is an upright and calm perseverance in the clarity of the great light.

If a man were only guilty toward himself, in order to satisfy the demanding summons that meets him at the height of conscience, he would only need to take this one road from the gate of self-illumination, that of persevering. But a man is always guilty toward other beings as well, toward the world, toward the being that exists over against him. From self-illumination he must, in order to do justice to the summons, take not one road but two roads, of which the second is that of reconciliation. By reconciliation is understood here that action from the height of conscience that corresponds on the plane of the law to the customary act of

---

[14] Freud, *A General Introduction to Psychoanalysis;* New York, Liveright, 1935; see Lecture 19.

reparation. In the realm of existential guilt one cannot, of course, "make reparation" in the strict sense—as if the guilt with its consequences could thereby be recalled, as it were. Reconciliation means here, first of all, that I approach the man toward whom I am guilty in the light of my self-illumination—insofar as I can still reach him on earth—acknowledge to his face my existential guilt and help him, insofar as possible, to overcome the consequences of my guilty action. But such a deed can be valid here only as reconciliation if it is done not out of a premeditated resolution, but in the unarbitrary working of the existence I have achieved. And this can happen, naturally, only out of the core of a transformed relationship to the world, a new service to the world with the renewed forces of the renewed man.

This is not the place to speak of the events in the sphere of faith that correspond to the events in the sphere of the high conscience that we have just discussed. For the sincere man of faith, the two spheres are so referred to each other in the practice of his life, and most especially when he has gone through existential guilt, that he cannot entrust himself exclusively to either of them. Both, the human faith not less than the human conscience, can err and err again. And knowing about this their erring, both—conscience not less than faith—must place themselves in the hands of grace. It is not for me to speak in general terms of the inner reality of him who refuses to believe in a transcendent being with whom he can communicate. I have only this to report: that I have met many men in the course of my life who have told me how, acting from the high conscience as men who had become guilty, they experienced themselves as seized by a higher power. These men grew into an existential state to which the name of rebirth is due.

VIII

With all this, I repeat, the psychotherapist in his medical intercourse with his patients has nothing directly to do, not even when he ventures in a particular case to set for himself the goal of an existential healing. The utmost that can be expected of him, as I have said, is only this: that, reaching out beyond his familiar methods, he conduct the patient, whose existential guilt he has recognized, to where an existential help of the self can begin. But to do this, he must know about the reality toward which I have tried to point in this essay.

Herbert Fingarette
Real Guilt and Neurotic Guilt

82　Martin Buber, in his discussion of guilt, expressed a justifiable concern that the psychotherapist and the patient may be seduced into diverting attention from the patient's authentic guilt. In order to elaborate upon this concern of his, Buber makes use of a crucial distinction. On the one hand, he speaks of "authentic," "real," "ontic," and, in its most "intense" form, "existential" guilt. On the other hand, there are "neurotic," "psychological," guilt "feelings": the "anxiety-induced bugbears that are generated in the cavern of the unconscious." Neurotic guilt and real guilt, says Buber, are "fundamentally different."

In one form or another, this radical distinction between "real" guilt and "neurotic" guilt feelings has come to play an important role in the discussions among all those European and American psychotherapists who have been influenced either by existentialist or phenomenological or religious outlooks. It is only accurate to add that many psychotherapists in the United States, before they ever became concerned with these philosophical or religious approaches, had individually come to an appreciation of the "reality" of moral and spiritual issues, the one-sidedness of the purely "psychologizing" approach.

But Buber's radical, ontological distinction, though inspired by an important issue, is not the one that the issue demands. Buber's distinction ultimately defeats its own purpose and obscures the psychological facts as well. As a further consequence, it confuses our understanding of the role of the psychotherapist.

The psychotherapist, according to Buber's formulation, is faced with the dilemma of either evading his duty as a human being or overstepping the bounds of psychotherapy proper. Buber tells us that the "significant actuality" transcends the task and methods of the psychotherapist. "Within his methods," says Buber, "the psychotherapist has to do only with guilt feelings, conscious and unconscious. . . ." "But with a comprehensive service to knowledge and help, he must himself encounter guilt as something of an ontic character. . . ."

This dilemma, with the tension it evokes in practice and the problems in theory, is not associated with the problem of guilt alone. The tension pervades therapy because the ontological distinction in question, once enunciated, suggests analogous distinctions throughout the whole range of therapeutic phenomena. Buber's approach makes fundamental and radical a split between the psychotherapeutic treatment proper, now seen as a technical, "scientific" procedure, and the human encounter. Though the distinction may not be offered in this spirit, this is what it requires if taken seriously. Nor is it helpful to "re-mix" the two in practice by telling the therapist that he, at times, "must" go "beyond professional custom and correct methods." This is a practical but anxiety-evoking compromise which leaves things in theoretical confusion; more unfortunate yet, this unhappy compromise is designed to resolve a problem which has been unnecessarily introduced in the first place.

Let me say at once that I do not argue about the validity of distinguishing between guilt associated with neurotic phenomena and guilt which is not thus associated. It is the merit of Buber and others to have used the psychological-ontological distinction as a device to emphasize that there *is* such a thing as real guilt. Buber properly wishes to stress that guilt is a fundamental and inescapable reality of the *normal* person's existence, that it must not be treated by the therapist as something that ought ideally to be "dissolved" entirely before discharging the patient. Yet here is the rub: Buber's invocation of a metaphysical distinction is from the outset a fatal misstep. It is based on a too ready acceptance of the very psychologism to which it is in spirit opposed. Instead of arguing for the unity of human suffering, whether neurotic or otherwise, Buber, in the manner of Descartes, has divided the human world in two. To the technician he assigns a "merely psychological" realm; his own attention then turns to a spiritual realm.

The proper perspective would focus our attention upon the task of achieving personal integrity, not upon dividing man among two realms. With exceptions which do not concern us here, *all* guilt with which we deal should properly be taken as real guilt, as real as any other guilt, and real in the very same sense of "real." Guilt may be assigned by the patient to the wrong source, but that is a common neurotic error which only makes the guilt *seem* foolish. Our responsibility, whether we be concerned with neurotic or non-neurotic aspects of life, is to face our guilt, to accept it, all of it, and, of course, to do something about it if we will. In psychotherapy, what is at stake is not the dissolving of some kind of pseudo-guilt but two other, quite different things: (1) acceptance of the guilt in conjunction with the identification and acknowledgement of its true source in oneself, and (2) a fresh and honest commitment to living openly with that guilt and the self which engenders it, or a new commitment and a reorganization of the self such that we are no longer guilty.

The distinctive characteristic of the neurotic's guilt is not its unreality but, briefly put, its unacknowledged source in infantile, irrational, immoral commitments which are deeply but surreptitiously at the roots of our being. What is "inauthentic" in "neurotic guilt" is not the guilt but the person, for the neurotic pretends to himself and others that there is no good reason for his being guilty. Often he consciously misassigns his felt guilt to some obviously trivial or inappropriate aspect of his life. Then he and others can focus attention on the inappropriateness and the "irrationality" of his feeling guilty—which in turn suggests the desirability of his "dissolving" that feeling. Meanwhile, as the unacknowledged real basis of the guilt, he harbors within himself, however well disguised, desires and aims in violent conflict with the moral order in which, at bottom, he has his being.

The theses I have now presented dogmatically must be elaborated, and certain obvious objections considered.

Guilt is a moral attribute of persons or selves. If we propose to deal with the "fine structure" of guilt, we must be prepared to have to deal with the "fine structure," the "internal structure" of the person. But our ordinary use of the language of guilt is not readily suited to taking into account the internal complexity of the self. We are fluent in talking of guilt only when we are dealing with a reasonably integrated, mature person, or at least with the person viewed as an unanalyzed unit in the particular situation. In such cases we ascribe guilt or not, as the case may be.

But psychotherapists are professionally concerned with viewing a person's actions on a different level. They see action as the outcome of compromises among conflicting tendencies, to some of which the person blinds himself. These conflicting tendencies are quasi-autonomous dynamic complexes of purpose, affect, behavior, thought—indeed of most of the characteristic features of person-hood. They may be thought of, at least for the moment, as *sub-selves*. The word "complex" is too impersonal. Sullivan's term "self-dynamism" is more suggestive, as is Freud's "fantasy-systems"; but "dynamism" and "system" still emphasize th physical metaphor. Now, my object here is not to introduce a new technical conception. It is merely, by the use of the notion "sub-selves," to bring out more forcefully, and informally, the *person*-like features of these sub-unities. The reader can easily translate "sub-self," if he wishes, into the technical language he prefers.

When Freud wrote that ". . . the id knows no values, no good and evil, no morality,"[1] he pointed to a crucial characteristic of what I have called the sub-selves (though these are not, of course, identical with what Freud means by the id). To be good and evil, there must be choice. But the sub-selves simply press for expression, each in its own way. They are single-minded, stubborn. And since their single-mindedness is of their essence, they do not of themselves have moral attributes — and this reminds us sharply of a respect in which the sub-selves are only person-*like*, not persons. Somehow, the demands of these various sub-selves and of the perceived environmental demands are weighed; a total response is arrived at. In Freudian theory this latter function is assigned to the judging and executive ego. We need not debate such formulations here. The point is that, however one conceptualizes the matter, the various tendencies to action *are* somehow weighed and combined by a person in his overt action. This capacity lies at the core of what the word "person" designates.

The person faces options, then, and not his sub-selves; therefore the person, not a sub-self, can be guilty.

A person is guilty, says Buber, when he "injures an order of the human world. . . ." We may ask: "Under what conditions does this take place? If the sub-selves do not have moral attributes, what shall we say of the neurotic who is "at the mercy" of some of these sub-selves? If the neurotic is the victim of an uncontrollable sub-self, can the neurotic symptom be a moral crime against the "order of the human world"?

This suggests the first of two common objections to the thesis that neurotic guilt is real guilt. I shall take up both these objections in turn and argue as follows: (1) It simply will not do to object that the neurotic guilt is unreal because the person was under "inner compulsion" to act wrongly. (2) Nor will it do to say that he is not really guilty since he only wished, or only fantasied, or only symbolically committed the wrong; it will not do, in short, to say he did not literally do what he unconsciously wished to do, so he is not really guilty. Let us consider the first of these objections.

For the purposes of law or other disciplinary action, we may

---

[1] Sigmund Freud, *New Introductory Lectures on Psychoanalysis* (New York: W. W. Norton & Co., 1933), p. 105.

well allow that a neurotic act was "uncontrollable." In legal matters, for example, we may be legitimately interested in hearing testimony that the person acted under the influence of an "uncontrollable impulse."[2] But in psychotherapy, the lesson the patient must learn is that he cannot divest himself of responsibility by allocating such matters to the class of "bugbears generated in the cavern of the unconscious."

Strictly speaking, the psychoneurotic is in therapy not because his basic values are wrong but because a part of him, a sub-self, is surreptitiously dedicated to aims and modes of conduct which betray his basic values. The neurotic's fundamental moral crisis is one of achieving integrity, not one of changing his basic values — though some change in the latter may well be an indirect consequence of having achieved integrity.

The patient in therapy, therefore, must come to see, to experience, to acknowledge with the full vividness of complete and immediate reality his identity with these hitherto unacknowledged, unconscious sub-selves. He must consciously *realize* the extent to which it is, for example, indeed he who, at least with a part of himself, wants to evade responsibility and to be a child, to be loved as a child, or, for example, that it is he who harbors within him murderous impulses toward his father.

Buber's way of viewing the matter leads naturally to his making the seriously misleading statement that "for the patient it is great relief to be diverted from his authentic guilt feeling to an unambiguous neurotic one." But it should not be a "relief" for the patient to discover his "neurotic" guilt; and in fact it is not. The genuine and insightful acknowledgment of guilt by the neurotic is an insight into a burden he has been carrying, is still carrying, a burden from which he may only now, for the first time, be openly and fully suffering. To achieve relief by saying to oneself that it is "only" an irrational neurotic guilt is a therapeutic evasion as well as a spiritual evasion; it is a defense against true insight.

There is a relief which the patient may legitimately enjoy subsequently; but it has a different source. Suppose the patient accepts the guilt and follows this by achieving insight into the motives which engender the guilt; then, at last, the patient may be able decisively to influence these *motives*. Having rejected or transformed those *motives*, he may feel relieved of his burden of guilt.

Of course we know that good therapeutic technique requires that insight be evoked when that part of the patient which is adult

---

will not be overwhelmed by the experience of guilt. The patient must also be quite aware of other relevant realities, especially that he has in overt deed neither murdered his father nor acted literally as a child. The reasonable adult in the psychoneurotic patient is, after all, the essential therapeutic ally. But it is the first object of insight therapy to enable the patient to accept himself as, in part, unreasonable and childish. I shall come back to these points shortly.

It must be stressed that the person's guilt does not stem merely from the fact that there is a "part" of him, a sub-self, which is irresponsibly infantile. Important as this is, there is another and at least equally important facet to be considered. As we have already noted, sub-selves are not, in themselves, good or evil. It is inevitably the case with the psychoneurotic that, being committed basically to a certain (adult) moral order, he has turned his inward gaze away from the sub-self which is incompatible with that order; but he has done more than avert his gaze: he has then *surreptitiously cooperated.* After all, the sub-self is not a "part" of the person in some mechanical or physical sense of "part." To be a "part" of a *person* is in essence to be in some way accepted as such by the person, to be identified with by the person. The spectrum of neurotic symptomatology is simply the spectrum of those surreptitious alliances between the person and his unacknowledged sub-selves. Where we do not suppose such a surreptitious alliance, we do not speak of neurotic symptoms. Instead, if there is malfunctioning, we speak in non-purposive terms of organic malfunction. Thus the neurotic person is guilty, really guilty, because of this surreptitious alliance with that in himself which aims at injuring "an order of the human world whose foundations he knows and recognizes as those of his own existence. . . ."

The analogy of parent and child may help here—indeed it is more than a mere analogy. Though a parent acknowledges his child's cruel actions and takes steps to prevent them, he may still be held *legally* responsible for the acts of his minor ward. In this case, however, his neighbors do not usually hold the parent to be morally guilty—though we shall have more to say about this shortly. On the other hand, if the parent averts his eyes, and if he surreptitiously arranges opportunities for sadistic acts by the child, then the parent is morally guilty.

Pressing the analogy one step further, we ask: How, if he will, can the parent effectively and humanely deal with the cruelty of his child? If the parent is not to treat the child merely as a target of condemnation or as an inconvenient object, he must to some extent be able to identify himself with the child. If he can tolerate doing this, his stronger and more mature ego may, in alliance with the child's healthy impulses, help find the way to a legitimate resolution of the problem. The parent-child relationship is a symbiotic one in which the weaker, allied with the stronger, moves gradually toward differentiation and genuine independence. The theoretical implications of the parent-child symbiosis hypothesis are consistent with the commonly observed clinical facts. It is a clinical commonplace to find that the parent of an abnormally sadistic child—to continue with this example—has subtly encouraged the child's sadism. The parent evades overt expression of his own sadism through identification with the child. It is this symbiotic aspect of parent-child relations and its roots in identification which completes the parallelism between parent-child and person-sub-self. For, just as we are morally guilty for the sub-selves which we consciously deny, so the parent, through identification, is guilty for the sadistic acts which he has conspired to encourage but which he consciously condemns. In both types of cases, the source of the guilt may not be consciously or correctly known by the person himself, but that source is often easily detectable by the therapist.

The phrase "neurotic guilt" is, then, a handy but misleading metonomy referring to the (genuine) guilt of a neurotic person. It is not unreal because done "under compulsion." The similarity between compulsiveness and compulsion, so illuminating in many contexts, should not blind us to their crucial difference. When I act "under compulsion," it is *really another person* who dominates me. But when I act "compulsively," it is a part of myself, a sub-self with whose demands I surreptitiously identify myself, that dominates. "Neurotic guilt" is the guilt of a person self-blinded, afraid, and secretly untrue to his own adult commitment. "Authentic guilt" is no more authentic as *guilt;* it is the person who acts more authentically toward the guilt by fully acknowledging it and its source.

We turn now to the second objection mentioned earlier: Since the neurotic has merely "fantasied" or only symbolically gratified the demands of the infantile sub-selves, is not his guilt, too, merely a "fantasy," an "illusory" guilt? After all, even if he has indulged, for example, in surreptitious minor aggressions against a father figure, these are far from literal patricide. Disguised and socially accepted forms of dependence on another person are not *literally* the same as acting like a child. Disguised incestuous fantasies are a far cry from literally incestuous acts. The potencies claimed in the neurotic's conscious and unconscious fantasies are precisely the impotencies of his "real" life. Why, if this is all "wishful thinking," is the neurotic *really* guilty?

Here I shall have to state a general thesis first, and then introduce two important qualifications. When stated bluntly, the general thesis still often appears novel and radical. Yet this very thesis is fundamental to twentieth-century dynamic psychiatry and, equally, to the historic moral insights of the major civilizations.[3] The thesis, briefly, is this: moral guilt accrues by virtue of our wishes, not merely our acts. Of course, legal guilt depends primarily upon our acts, though we should note that even here the assessment of motive plays a role. But the question of moral guilt does not wait for acts; it is in profound degree a question of what one harbors in one's heart. This is the gist of Freud's basic concept of "psychic reality." In the psychic economy, the wish is omnipotent. To wish is, psychologically, to have done. Hence a person suffers guilt for his wishes, even his unconscious ones.

This insight, so central to dynamic psychiatry, is not in opposition to the central insights of the great moral teachings. It is ironic that, important as psychotherapists know "matters of the mind" to be, they are still tempted to assume naïvely, as if it were all self-evident, that, morally speaking, "mere" wishes do not count. A wish, morally speaking, seems to them to be "*only* a matter of the mind." This may be because the explicit use of moral language in "scientifically" oriented circles has come to be abandoned to the social critic, the disciplinarian, or the judge — in general, those responsible primarily for controlling or guiding action. The explicit analysis of *personal* morality has tended to be unfashionable and associated with religion, Victorian prissiness, or puritanical rigidity. The sources of this error are no doubt complex, and the psychiatrist's contact with neurotic pseudo-moralizing has not been the most encouraging context in which to take the study of moral language seriously. Whatever the reasons, the fact is that most psychotherapists, in their informal and formal discussions, tacitly assume that only actions and their effects, viewed "literally" and not "symbolically," are what count morally. Since this assumption is made, even though tacitly, we must at least briefly note that, far from being self-evident, it runs counter to central teachings in the great moral traditions.

Jesus taught — and it is central to his teaching — "Ye have heard it was said by them of old time, Thou shalt not commit adultery. . . . But I say unto you that whosoever looketh on a woman to lust after her hath committed adultery with her already in his heart."[4] Jesus did not deny the importance of the law and of works; but

[3] See Herbert Fingarette, "Psychoanalytic Perspectives on Moral Guilt and Responsibility: A Reevaluation," *Philosophy and Phenomenological Research,* XVI (1955), 18–36.
[4] Matthew 5:27–28.

the life with which he was primarily concerned was that of the spirit. This religious-moral insight is congruent with Freud's discovery that it was fantasy, not only actions, which had shaped the character and the fate of his patients.

If we turn to the East, we find that the Bhagavad Gita has taught the Indian peoples that it is to the desires, the motives, and not to the actions, that we must look when we wish to diagnose the spiritual condition of an individual. As for Buddhism, the great Buddhist moral tract, the Dhammapada, begins quite characteristically: "All that we are is the result of what we have thought: it is founded on our thoughts, it is made up of our thoughts." And in the same chapter: "Those who are thoughtless are as if dead already."⁵ Confucius, the great advocate of ritual and tradition, differed from his predecessors precisely in his teaching that it is the inner spirit which is crucial in the carrying out of ritual, that, indeed, in the last analysis, the inward virtues would of themselves be morally definitive if the external world were to prevent one from displaying these virtues in action.⁶

It is, then, not at all self-evident that the wish which is not literally gratified leaves one morally "clean," though perhaps psychically disturbed. On the contrary, the burden of proof lies the other way. Psychotherapists often claim an aversion to introducing moral and philosophical assumptions into their professional doctrine, but the fact is that they do, and the present dubious assumption is a case in point.

Two qualifying comments are necessary with regard to the thesis that, in the moral life, the wish establishes guilt or innocence. The first comment is really not so much a qualification as an explicit statement of what is *not* implied by that thesis. The thesis that one only need wish evil in order to be genuinely guilty is perfectly consistent with the fact that it is worse to commit a real murder than it is to fantasy committing one. To deny this would indeed be to fly in the face of sanity. The question is: In what ways is the one worse than the other?

Part of the answer is obvious and important; but since it is one without any further theoretical interest to us, I shall merely mention it and then go on to the rest of the answer. It is worse to act on an evil wish than it is merely to fantasy the gratification of the wish because the actual suffering inflicted on others is itself an additional evil to cherishing the wish alone. We cannot measure the difference, but the point needs no laboring. This fact is reason enough to entitle us to make vastly different *practical* judgments

---

⁵"Dhammapada," in Lin Yutang, *The Wisdom of China and India* (New York: Modern Library, 1942), pp. 327–328.

⁶See, for one of many examples, Confucius, *Analects*, 7:15.

regarding the actual murderer on the one hand, and, on the other, the neurotic with murderous fantasies (even if these are incorporated in symbolic form in action).

In addition to the social evil of its consequences, however, the overt act increases the evil in another way, a way which is of distinct theoretical interest to us here. The overt commission of the deed by the murderer is the mark of the person's decisive acceptance of the wish. The moral significance of the degree of acceptance becomes clearer when we consider the case of a murderer who was inwardly in great conflict before the decision. Our conviction that there was such conflict tempers our judgment of his guilt, though it in no sense absolves him of it. The neurotic with unconscious murderous wishes is a person who differs from the murderer in this respect: though beset by the demands of a sub-self, he is a person who successfully fights against accepting the demand in its flagrant form. And he does this precisely because overt gratification would rupture the order of the world to which he is basically committed.

Up to this point in my argument, I have emphasized the complicity of the person in his neurosis. But the reverse of the coin is his successful refusal to give in entirely, his refusal to make an open alliance, his temporizing, emasculating, suppressing tactics toward the immoral sub-self. The person who is psychoneurotic in the classical sense of that term is fitted for insight therapy precisely because he is, for the most part, a person committed in deed as well as intent to fighting, however irrationally, the infantile and irresponsible demands of his sub-selves. This fight *is* the neurotic conflict.

We can now see that when the murder is actually committed, the person's burden of guilt is greater than the neurotic's because the acceptance of the murderous wish is more wholehearted; the person has more fully identified himself with the murderous sub-self. And yet, unless he is a psychopath, he may still have to recognize that he has "injured an order of the human world whose foundations he knows and recognizes as those of his own existence." The neurotic, on the other hand, is tempted to murder, but, *on the whole,* he elects decisively not to give in. (And then, as the neurotic symptom shows, he compromises and distorts, and cooperates *to a limited extent,* via the back door, as it were, with the evil he has cast out from the front.) Genuine reluctance to be an accomplice in evil ameliorates guilt just as, for example, *genuine* repentance does—these are facts of the moral life, and also of the psychology of grief and repentance.

Let us return to our essential theme: though we deal with varying degrees of guilt, it is all guilt in the same sense; in the moral, or, if you wish, the existential sense. What is more, the guilt with which we are here concerned is, in practice, guilt in substantial degree. Though the guilt for murderous fantasies may be less in degree than for actual murder, the phrase "less in degree" in these matters does not imply inconsequential. For the neurotic it is not inconsequential. How do we weigh the degree of guilt? The matter, for our purposes, is simple. The neurotic, though maintaining his repressive distortions successfully, may still be so guilty that his life is ruined and his moral fate a tragic one. The special pathos of the neurotic's fate is that the source of the guilt is not understood, its legitimacy often doubly obscured by displacement to venial sins, misdemeanors, nonsense-acts. Not only the amount of suffering and its apparent meaninglessness, but also the degree of irrationality of the defensive maneuvers is a measure of the degree of that guilt. In general, it is clear that the neurotic does not have to act in order to bring his *real* guilt to a burdensome, even a crippling level. He may "do" nothing; yet it may be that, like the Pharisees, his "inward part is full of ravening and wickedness."[7] It is a remarkable error indeed that psychotherapists could deny the genuinely *moral* character of the corruption which is an inward fact just because it has no direct outward expression.

There is, then, no puzzling metaphysical gap between "neurotic guilt" and ontic guilt. The therapist *is* always dealing with what Buber calls the "significant actuality." It is worth repeating that the great value of Buber's ontological distinction is to force us to acknowledge that there *is* a "significant actuality" involved in life and in therapy. But, this lesson once learned, it is time to go further. It is time to see that most of the guilt which is ordinarily considered within the scope of the therapist's "professional custom and correct methods" *is* the significant actuality, not a subjective, half-real, sub-human phenomenon.

We must now take a moment to ask: Is there no possibility of "feeling" guilty when one is not actually guilty? Are there not some forms of pathology in which the "feeling" may arise independently of a sub-self whose demands violate the moral order? This question raises a host of problems, both psychological and philosophical. Fortunately we need not deal with them here because, in order to simplify the analysis, I have restricted the applicability of my theses to adult psychoneurotics. The guilt feelings of the psychoneurotic are ordinarily associated with unconscious sub-selves which strive against the "order of the human world whose foundations he knows and recognizes as

[7]Luke 11:39.

those of his own existence." The generic motive of repression —
as against conscious suppression of impulses — is that the inner
demands are apprehended to be such that to face them openly
would be to threaten one's integrity. The demands the neurotic
represses are infantile in character. Hence they are incompatible
with adult responsibility as well as too primitive in quality to be
acceptable. The sub-self which the person can see how to inte-
grate into his world is one which he will face and accept consciously. But where no solution even seems possible, then repression is instituted. Even where there is no conscious guilt
feeling, it must be assumed that there is some guilt associated
with repression in the neurotic. It is here that Freud and others
have been forced to speak apologetically of "unconscious guilt."
This is because they really mean to refer guilt to the *fact* of radical
inner conflict, but they also still think that guilt is simply a *feeling*
and hence must, by definition, be *felt.* But feeling or no feeling,
the therapist expects that "moral anxiety" will be a significant
element in psychopathology except in cases where he assumes
the patient to be radically immature or defective in a way which
excludes him from the classification "adult psychoneurotic."

The absence in the literature of clear-cut examples illustrating
the supposed radical distinction between neurotic and existential
guilt is good evidence, I hold, that there is no such ontological
distinction to be observed. I myself have read the words but have
looked often and vainly for illustrations which decisively differentiate the two kinds of guilt. I see in the literature exhortations
to make the distinction unaccompanied by usable criteria for
making it. Only the theoretical prejudice that the psychological
is the "merely" psychological has forced people into this radical
verbal dualism in order to preserve the insight, a re-discovery in a
new context, that there is really a moral dimension to life. What
we must now see, in addition, is that *all* insight therapy has the
moral dimension. The only illusion involved in connection with
neurotic guilt is the self-deception of the neurotic as to the occasion of his guilt.

I believe that the analysis I have presented preserves continuity
in psychotherapeutic theory in place of introducing metaphysical
chasms. It is consistent with the moral insights of the great moral
teachers as well as the psychological insights of dynamic psychiatry. It emphasizes the human dignity of the totality of the neurotic's suffering, the reality of his spiritual problem. In addition
to each of these, the view I have presented clarifies the relation
of the psychotherapist to the spiritual adviser or to the wise and
good friend. The psychotherapist is never merely a technician
but is *always* a person in an encounter with another human being

who is bearing genuinely human burdens. The therapist, however, is specially experienced and skilled in connection with one form of human burden. The therapist is concerned, generally, with the failures of the person to achieve or maintain the integrity of the inner community of sub-selves. More specifically, however, he is concerned with these failures insofar as they rely on self-deception, either with regard to the realities of the "external" world or the realities of the "inner" world. The psychotherapist is an expert — insofar as one can be "expert" in human affairs — on the conditions, the motives, and the devices associated with self-deceptive evasion of the world in which one has one's being.

This view of therapy is, I believe, in the same spirit, though not quite the same theoretical framework, as that of Buber's views on the matter.

Friedrich Nietzsche

"Guilt," "Bad Conscience," and the Like

To breed an animal *with the right to make promises*—is not this **95** the paradoxical task that nature has set itself in the case of man? is it not the real problem regarding man?

That this problem has been solved to a large extent must seem all the more remarkable to anyone who appreciates the strength of the opposing force, that of *forgetfulness.* Forgetting is no mere *vis inertiae* as the superficial imagine; it is rather an active and in the strictest sense positive faculty of repression, that is responsible for the fact that what we experience and absorb enters our consciousness as little while we are digesting it (one might call the process "inpsychation") as does the thousandfold process, involved in physical nourishment—so-called "incorporation." To close the doors and windows of consciousness for a time; to remain undisturbed by the noise and struggle of our underworld of utility organs working with and against one another; a little quietness, a little *tabula rasa* of the consciousness, to make room for new things, above all for the nobler functions and functionaries, for regulation, foresight, premeditation (for our organism is an oligarchy)—that is the purpose of active forgetfulness, which is like a doorkeeper, a preserver of psychic order, repose, and etiquette: so that it will be immediately obvious how there could be no happiness, no cheerfulness, no hope, no pride, no *present*, without forgetfulness. The man in whom this apparatus of repression is damaged and ceases to function properly may be compared (and more than merely compared) with a dyspeptic —he cannot "have done" with anything.

Now this animal which needs to be forgetful, in which forget-

From "On the Genealogy of Morals," in *Basic Writings of Nietzsche,* translated by Walter Kaufmann. Copyright © 1966, 1967, 1968 by Random House, Inc. Footnotes have been deleted. Reprinted by permission of the publisher.

ting represents a force, a form of *robust* health, has bred in itself an opposing faculty, a memory, with the aid of which forgetfulness is abrogated in certain cases — namely in those cases where promises are made. This involves no mere passive inability to rid oneself of an impression, no mere indigestion through a once-pledged word with which one cannot "have done," but an active *desire* not to rid oneself, a desire for the continuance of something desired once, a real *memory of the will:* so that between the original "I will," "I shall do this" and the actual discharge of the will, its *act,* a world of strange new things, circumstances, even acts of will may be interposed without breaking this long chain of will. But how many things this presupposes! To ordain the future in advance in this way, man must first have learned to distinguish necessary events from chance ones, to think causally, to see and anticipate distant eventualities as if they belonged to the present, to decide with certainty what is the goal and what the means to it, and in general be able to calculate and compute. Man himself must first of all have become *calculable, regular, necessary,* even in his own image of himself, if he is to be able to stand security for *his own future,* which is what one who promises does!

This precisely is the long story of how *responsibility* originated. The task of breeding an animal with the right to make promises evidently embraces and presupposes as a preparatory task that one first *makes* men to a certain degree necessary, uniform, like among like, regular, and consequently calculable. The tremendous labor of that which I have called "morality of mores" . . . the labor performed by man upon himself during the greater part of the existence of the human race, his entire *prehistoric* labor, finds in this its meaning, its great justification, notwithstanding the severity, tyranny, stupidity, and idiocy involved in it: with the aid of the morality of mores and the social straitjacket, man was actually *made* calculable.

If we place ourselves at the end of this tremendous process, where the tree at last brings forth fruit, where society and the morality of custom at last reveal *what* they have simply been the means to: then we discover that the ripest fruit is the *sovereign individual,* like only to himself, liberated again from morality of custom, autonomous and supramoral (for "autonomous" and "moral" are mutually exclusive), in short, the man who has his own independent, protracted will and the *right to make promises*

—and in him a proud consciousness, quivering in every muscle, of *what* has at length been achieved and become flesh in him, a consciousness of his own power and freedom, a sensation of mankind come to completion. This emancipated individual, with the actual *right* to make promises, this master of a *free* will, this sovereign man—how should he not be aware of his superiority over all those who lack the right to make promises and stand as their own guarantors, of how much trust, how much fear, how much reverence he arouses—he *"deserves"* all three—and of how this mastery over himself also necessarily gives him mastery over circumstances, over nature, and over all more short-willed and unreliable creatures? The "free" man, the possessor of a protracted and unbreakable will, also possesses his *measure of value:* looking out upon others from himself, he honors or he despises; and just as he is bound to honor his peers, the strong and reliable (those with the *right* to make promises)—that is, all those who promise like sovereigns, reluctantly, rarely, slowly, who are chary of trusting, whose trust is a mark of *distinction,* who give their word as something that can be relied on because they know themselves strong enough to maintain it in the face of accidents, even "in the face of fate"—he is bound to reserve a kick for the feeble windbags who promise without the right to do so, and a rod for the liar who breaks his word even at the moment he utters it. The proud awareness of the extraordinary privilege of *responsibility,* the consciousness of this rare freedom, this power over oneself and over fate, has in his case penetrated to the profoundest depths and become instinct, the dominating instinct. What will he call this dominating instinct, supposing he feels the need to give it a name? The answer is beyond doubt: this sovereign man calls it his *conscience.*

3

His conscience?—It is easy to guess that the concept of "conscience" that we here encounter in its highest, almost astonishing, manifestation, has a long history and variety of forms behind it. To possess the right to stand security for oneself and to do so with pride, thus to possess also the *right to affirm oneself*—this, as has been said, is a ripe fruit, but also a *late* fruit: how long must this fruit have hung on the tree, unripe and sour! And for a much longer time nothing whatever was to be seen of any such fruit: no one could have promised its appearance, although everything in the tree was preparing for and growing toward it!

"How can one create a memory for the human animal? How

can one impress something upon this partly obtuse, partly flighty mind, attuned only to the passing moment, in such a way that it will stay there?"

One can well believe that the answers and methods for solving this primeval problem were not precisely gentle; perhaps indeed there was nothing more fearful and uncanny in the whole prehistory of man than his *mnemotechnics.* "If something is to stay in the memory it must be burned in: only that which never ceases to *hurt* stays in the memory" — this is a main clause of the oldest (unhappily also the most enduring) psychology on earth. One might even say that wherever on earth solemnity, seriousness, mystery, and gloomy coloring still distinguish the life of man and a people, something of the terror that formerly attended all promises, pledges, and vows on earth is *still effective:* the past, the longest, deepest and sternest past, breathes upon us and rises up in us whenever we become "serious." Man could never do without blood, torture, and sacrifices when he felt the need to create a memory for himself; the most dreadful sacrifices and pledges (sacrifices of the first-born among them), the most repulsive mutilations (castration, for example), the cruelest rites of all the religious cults (and all religions are at the deepest level systems of cruelties) — all this has its origin in the instinct that realized that pain is the most powerful aid to mnemonics.

In a certain sense, the whole of asceticism belongs here: a few ideas are to be rendered inextinguishable, ever-present, unforgettable, "fixed," with the aim of hypnotising the entire nervous and intellectual system with these "fixed ideas" — and ascetic procedures and modes of life are means of freeing these ideas from the competition of all other ideas, so as to make them "unforgettable." The worse man's memory has been, the more fearful has been the appearance of his customs; the severity of the penal code provides an especially significant measure of the degree of effort needed to overcome forgetfulness and to impose a few primitive demands of social existence as *present realities* upon these slaves of momentary affect and desire.

We Germans certainly do not regard ourselves as a particularly cruel and hardhearted people, still less as a particularly frivolous one, living only for the day; but one has only to look at our former codes of punishments to understand what effort it costs on this earth to breed a "nation of thinkers" (which is to say, *the* nation in Europe in which one still finds today the maximum of trust, seriousness, lack of taste, and matter-of-factness — and with these qualities one has the right to breed every kind of European mandarin). These Germans have employed fearful means to acquire a memory, so as to master their basic mob-instinct and its brutal coarseness. Consider the old German punishments; for example, stoning (the sagas already have millstones drop on the head of the guilty), breaking on the wheel (the most characteristic invention and speciality of the German genius in the realm of punishment!), piercing with stakes, tearing apart or trampling by horses ("quartering"), boiling of the criminal in oil or wine (still employed in the fourteenth and fifteenth centuries), the popular flaying alive ("cutting straps"), cutting flesh from the chest, and also the practice of smearing the wrongdoer with honey and leaving him in the blazing sun for the flies. With the aid of such images and procedures one finally remembers five or six "I will not's," in regard to which one had given one's *promise* so as to participate in the advantages of society—and it was indeed with the aid of this kind of memory that one at last came "to reason"! Ah, reason, seriousness, mastery over the affects, the whole somber thing called reflection, all these prerogatives and showpieces of man: how dearly they have been bought! how much blood and cruelty lie at the bottom of all "good things"!

4

But how did that other "somber thing," the consciousness of guilt, the "bad conscience," come into the world?—And at this point we return to the genealogists of morals. To say it again—or haven't I said it yet?—they are worthless. A brief span of experience that is merely one's own, merely modern; no knowledge or will to knowledge of the past; even less of historical instinct, of that "second sight" needed here above all—and yet they undertake history of morality; it stands to reason that their results stay at a more than respectful distance from the truth. Have these genealogists of morals had even the remotest suspicion that, for example, the major moral concept *Schuld* [guilt] has its origin in the very material concept *Schulden* [debts]? Or that punishment, as requital, evolved quite independently of any presupposition concerning freedom or non-freedom of the will?—to such an extent, indeed, that a *high* degree of humanity had to be attained before the animal "man" began even to make the much more primitive distinctions between "intentional," "negligent," "accidental," "accountable," and their opposites and to take them into account when determining punishments. The idea, now so obvious, apparently so natural, even unavoidable, that had to serve as the explanation of how the sense of justice ever appeared on earth—"the criminal deserves punishment *because* he could have acted differently"—is in fact an extremely late and

subtle form of human judgment and inference: whoever trans-
poses it to the beginning is guilty of a crude misunderstanding of
the psychology of more primitive mankind. Throughout the
greater part of human history punishment was *not* imposed *be-*
cause one held the wrong-doer responsible for his deed, thus
not on the presupposition that only the guilty one should be
punished: rather, as parents still punish their children, from
anger at some harm or injury, vented on the one who caused
it—but this anger is held in check and modified by the idea that
every injury has its *equivalent* and can actually be paid back,
even if only through the *pain* of the culprit. And whence did this
primeval, deeply rooted, perhaps by now ineradicable idea draw
its power—this idea of an equivalence between injury and pain?
I have already divulged it: in the contractual relationship between
creditor and *debtor,* which is as old as the idea of "legal subjects"
and in turn points back to the fundamental forms of buying,
selling, barter, trade, and traffic.

5

When we contemplate these contractual relationships, to be
sure, we feel considerable suspicion and repugnance toward
those men of the past who created or permitted them. This was
to be expected from what we have previously noted. It was here
that *promises* were made; it was here that a memory had to be
made for those who promised; it is here, one suspects, that we
shall find a great deal of severity, cruelty, and pain. To inspire
trust in his promise to repay, to provide a guarantee of the seriousness and sanctity of his promise, to impress repayment as a
duty, an obligation upon his own conscience, the debtor made a
contract with the creditor and pledged that if he should fail to
repay he would substitute something else that he "possessed,"
something he had control over; for example, his body, his wife,
his freedom, or even his life (or, given certain religious presuppositions, even his bliss after death, the salvation of his soul,
ultimately his peace in the grave: thus it was in Egypt, where the
debtor's corpse found no peace from the creditor even in the
grave—and among the Egyptians such peace meant a great
deal). Above all, however, the creditor could inflict every kind of
indignity and torture upon the body of the debtor; for example,
cut from it as much as seemed commensurate with the size of
the debt—and everywhere and from early times one had exact
evaluations, *legal* evaluations, of the individual limbs and parts
of the body from this point of view, some of them going into horrible and minute detail. I consider it as an advance, as evidence

of a freer, more generous, *more Roman* conception of law when the Twelve Tables of Rome decreed it a matter of indifference how much or how little the creditor cut off in such cases: *"si plus minusve secuerunt, ne fraude esto."*[1]

Let us be clear as to the logic of this form of compensation: it is strange enough. An equivalence is provided by the creditor's receiving, in place of a literal compensation for an injury (thus in place of money, land, possessions of any kind), a recompense in the form of a kind of *pleasure*—the pleasure of being allowed to vent his power freely upon one who is powerless, the voluptuous pleasure *"de faire le mal pour le plaisir de le faire,"*[2] the enjoyment of violation. This enjoyment will be the greater the lower the creditor stands in the social order, and can easily appear to him as a most delicious morsel, indeed as a foretaste of higher rank. In "punishing" the debtor, the creditor participates in a *right of the masters:* at last he, too, may experience for once the exalted sensation of being allowed to despise and mistreat someone as "beneath him"—or at least, if the actual power and administration of punishment has already passed to the "authorities," to *see* him despised and mistreated. The compensation, then, consists in a warrant for and title to cruelty.—

6

It was in *this* sphere then, the sphere of legal obligations, that the moral conceptual world of "guilt," "conscience," "duty," "sacredness of duty" had its origin: its beginnings were, like the beginnings of everything great on earth, soaked in blood thoroughly and for a long time. And might one not add that, fundamentally, this world has never since lost a certain odor of blood and torture? (Not even in good old Kant: the categorical imperative smells of cruelty.) It was here, too, that that uncanny intertwining of the ideas "guilt and suffering" was first effected—and by now they may well be inseparable. To ask it again: to what extent can suffering balance debts or guilt? To the extent that to *make* suffer was in the highest degree pleasurable, to the extent that the injured party exchanged for the loss he had sustained, including the displeasure caused by the loss, an extraordinary counterbalancing pleasure: that of *making* suffer—a genuine *festival,* something which, as aforesaid, was prized the more highly the more violently it contrasted with the rank and social standing of the creditor. This is offered only as a conjecture; for

---

[1] If they have secured more or less, let that be no crime.
[2] Of doing evil for the pleasure of doing it.

the depths of such subterranean things are difficult to fathom, besides being painful; and whoever clumsily interposes the concept of "revenge" does not enhance his insight into the matter but further veils and darkens it (—for revenge merely leads us back to the same problem: "how can making suffer constitute a compensation?").

It seems to me that the delicacy and even more the tartuffery of tame domestic animals (which is to say modern men, which is to say us) resists a really vivid comprehension of the degree to which *cruelty* constituted the great festival pleasure of more primitive men and was indeed an ingredient of almost every one of their pleasures; and how naïvely, how innocently their thirst for cruelty manifested itself, how, as a matter of principle, they posited "disinterested malice" (or, in Spinoza's words, *sympathia malevolens*) as a *normal* quality of man—and thus as something to which the conscience cordially *says Yes!* A more profound eye might perceive enough of this oldest and most fundamental festival pleasure of man even in our time; in *Beyond Good and Evil*, section 229 (and earlier in *The Dawn*, sections 18, 77, 113) I pointed cautiously to the ever-increasing spiritualization and "deification" of cruelty which permeates the entire history of higher culture (and in a significant sense actually constitutes it). In any event, it is not long since princely weddings and public festivals of the more magnificent kind were unthinkable without executions, torturings, or perhaps an auto-da-fé, and no noble household was without creatures upon whom one could heedlessly vent one's malice and cruel jokes. (Consider, for instance, Don Quixote at the court of the Duchess. Today we read *Don Quixote* with a bitter taste in our mouths, almost with a feeling of torment, and would thus seem very strange and incomprehensible to its author and his contemporaries: they read it with the clearest conscience in the world as the most cheerful of books, they laughed themselves almost to death over it). To see others suffer does one good, to make others suffer even more: this is a hard saying but an ancient, mighty, human, all-too-human principle to which even the apes might subscribe; for it has been said that in devising bizarre cruelties they anticipate man and are, as it were, his "prelude." Without cruelty there is no festival: thus the longest and most ancient part of human history teaches —and in punishment there is so much that is *festive!*—

7

With this idea, by the way, I am by no means concerned to furnish our pessimists with more grist for their discordant and creaking mills of life-satiety. On the contrary, let me declare expressly that in the days when mankind was not yet ashamed of its cruelty, life on earth was more cheerful than it is now that pessimists exist. The darkening of the sky above mankind has deepened in step with the increase in man's feeling of shame *at man*. The weary pessimistic glance, mistrust of the riddle of life, the icy No of disgust with life—these do not characterize the most *evil* epochs of the human race: rather do they first step into the light of day as the swamp weeds they are when the swamp to which they belong comes into being—I mean the morbid softening and moralization through which the animal "man" finally learns to be ashamed of all his instincts. On his way to becoming an "angel" (to employ no uglier word) man has evolved that queasy stomach and coated tongue through which not only the joy and innocence of the animal but life itself has become repugnant to him—so that he sometimes holds his nose in his own presence and, with Pope Innocent the Third, disapprovingly catalogues his own repellent aspects ("impure begetting, disgusting means of nutrition in his mother's womb, baseness of the matter out of which man evolves, hideous stink, secretion of saliva, urine, and filth").

Today, when suffering is always brought forward as the principal argument *against* existence, as the worst question mark, one does well to recall the ages in which the opposite opinion prevailed because men were unwilling to refrain from *making* suffer and saw in it an enchantment of the first order, a genuine seduction *to* life. Perhaps in those days—the delicate may be comforted by this thought—pain did not hurt as much as it does now; at least that is the conclusion a doctor may arrive at who has treated Negroes (taken as representatives of prehistoric man—) for severe internal inflammations that would drive even the best constituted European to distraction—in the case of Negroes they do *not* do so. (The curve of human susceptibility to pain seems in fact to take an extraordinary and almost sudden drop as soon as one has passed the upper ten thousand or ten million of the top stratum of culture; and for my own part, I have no doubt that the combined suffering of all the animals ever subjected to the knife for scientific ends is utterly negligible compared with *one* painful night of a single hysterical bluestocking.) Perhaps the possibility may even be allowed that this joy in cruelty does not really have to have died out: if pain hurts more today, it simply requires a certain sublimation and subtilization, that is to say it has to appear translated into the imaginative and psychical and adorned with such innocent names that even the tenderest and most hypocritical conscience is not suspicious of them ("tragic pity" is one such name; *"les nostalgies de la croix"*[3] is another).

What really arouses indignation against suffering is not suffering as such but the senselessness of suffering: but neither for the Christian, who has interpreted a whole mysterious machinery of salvation into suffering, nor for the naïve man of more ancient times, who understood all suffering in relation to the spectator of it or the causer of it, was there any such thing as *senseless* suffering. So as to abolish hidden, undetected, unwitnessed suffering from the world and honestly to deny it, one was in the past virtually compelled to invent gods and genii of all the heights and depths, in short something that roams even in secret, hidden places, sees even in the dark, and will not easily let an interesting painful spectacle pass unnoticed. For it was with the aid of such inventions that life then knew how to work the trick which it has always known how to work, that of justifying itself, of justifying its "evil." Nowadays it might require other auxiliary inventions (for example, life as a riddle, life as an epistemological problem). "Every evil the sight of which edifies a god is justified": thus spoke the primitive logic of feeling—and was it, indeed, only primitive? The gods conceived of as the friends of *cruel* spectacles—oh how profoundly this ancient idea still permeates our European humanity! Merely consult Calvin and Luther. It is certain, at any rate, that the *Greeks* still knew of no tastier spice to offer their gods to season their happiness than the pleasures of cruelty. With what eyes do you think Homer made his gods look down upon the destinies of men? What was at bottom the ultimate meaning of Trojan Wars and other such tragic terrors? There can be no doubt whatever: they were intended as *festival plays* for the gods; and, insofar as the poet is in these matters of a more "godlike" disposition than other men, no doubt also as festival plays for the poets.

It was in the same way that the moral philosophers of Greece later imagined the eyes of God looking down upon the moral struggle, upon the heroism and self-torture of the virtuous: the "Herakles of duty" was on a stage and knew himself to be; virtue without a witness was something unthinkable for this nation of actors. Surely, that philosophers' invention, so bold and so fateful, which was then first devised for Europe, the invention of "free will," of the absolute spontaneity of man in good and in evil, was devised above all to furnish a right to the idea that the interest of the gods in man, in human virtue, *could never be exhausted.* There must never be any lack of real novelty, of really unprecedented tensions, complications, and catastrophies on

[3] The nostalgia of the cross.

the stage of the earth: the course of a completely deterministic world would have been predictable for the gods and they would have quickly grown weary of it — reason enough for those *friends of the gods,* the philosophers, not to inflict such a deterministic world on their gods! The entire mankind of antiquity is full of tender regard for "the spectator," as an essentially public, essentially visible world which cannot imagine happiness apart from spectacles and festivals. — And, as aforesaid, even in great *punishment* there is so much that is festive!

8

To return to our investigation: the feeling of guilt, of personal obligation, had its origin, as we saw, in the oldest and most primitive personal relationship, that between buyer and seller, creditor and debtor: it was here that one person first encountered another person, that one person first *measured himself* against another. No grade of civilization, however low, has yet been discovered in which something of this relationship has not been noticeable. Setting prices, determining values, contriving equivalences, exchanging — these preoccupied the earliest thinking of man to so great an extent that in a certain sense they constitute thinking *as such:* here it was that the oldest kind of astuteness developed; here likewise, we may suppose, did human pride, the feeling of superiority in relation to other animals, have its first beginnings. Perhaps our word "man" (*manas*) still expresses something of precisely *this* feeling of self-satisfaction: man designated himself as the creature that measures values, evaluates and measures, as the "valuating animal as such."

Buying and selling, together with their psychological appurtenances, are older even than the beginnings of any kind of social forms of organization and alliances: it was rather out of the most rudimentary form of personal legal rights that the budding sense of exchange, contract, guilt, right, obligation, settlement, first *transferred* itself to the coarsest and most elementary social complexes (in their relations with other similar complexes), together with the custom of comparing, measuring, and calculating power against power. The eye was now focused on this perspective; and with that blunt consistency characteristic of the thinking of primitive mankind which is hard to set in motion but then proceeds inexorably in the same direction, one forthwith arrived at the great generalization, "everything has its price; *all* things can be paid for" — the oldest and naïvest moral canon of *justice,* the beginning of all "good-naturedness," all "fairness," all "good will," all "objectivity" on earth. Justice on this elementary level is the good will among parties of approximately equal power to come to terms with one another, to reach an "understanding" by means of a settlement—and to *compel* parties of lesser power to reach a settlement among themselves.—

9

Still retaining the criteria of prehistory (this prehistory is in any case present in all ages or may always reappear): the community, too, stands to its members in that same vital basic relation, that of the creditor to his debtors. One lives in a community, one enjoys the advantages of a communality (oh what advantages! we sometimes underrate them today), one dwells protected, cared for, in peace and trustfulness, without fear of certain injuries and hostile acts to which the man *outside,* the "man without peace," is exposed—a German will understand the original connotations of *Elend*[4]—since one has bound and pledged oneself to the community precisely with a view to injuries and hostile acts. What will happen *if this pledge is broken?* The community, the disappointed creditor, will get what repayment it can, one may depend on that. The direct harm caused by the culprit is here a minor matter; quite apart from this, the lawbreaker is above all a "breaker," a breaker of his contract and his word *with the whole* in respect to all the benefits and comforts of communal life of which he has hitherto had a share. The lawbreaker is a debtor who has not merely failed to make good the advantages and advance payments bestowed upon him but has actually attacked his creditor: therefore he is not only deprived henceforth of all these advantages and benefits, as is fair—he is also reminded *what these benefits are really worth.* The wrath of the disappointed creditor, the community, throws him back again into the savage and outlaw state against which he has hitherto been protected: it thrusts him away—and now every kind of hostility may be vented upon him. "Punishment" at this level of civilization is simply a copy, a *mimus,* of the normal attitude toward a hated, disarmed, prostrated enemy, who has lost not only every right and protection, but all hope of quarter as well; it is thus the rights of war and the victory celebration of the *vae victis!*[5] in all their mercilessness and cruelty—which explains why it is that war itself (including the warlike sacrificial cult) has provided all the *forms* that punishment has assumed throughout history.

[4] Misery. Originally, exile.
[5] Woe to the losers!

As its power increases, a community ceases to take the individual's transgressions so seriously, because they can no longer be considered as dangerous and destructive to the whole as they were formerly: the malefactor is no longer "set beyond the pale of peace" and thrust out; universal anger may not be vented upon him as unrestrainedly as before — on the contrary, the whole from now on carefully defends the malefactor against this anger, especially that of those he has directly harmed, and takes him under its protection. A compromise with the anger of those directly injured by the criminal; an effort to localize the affair and to prevent it from causing any further, let alone a general, disturbance; attempts to discover equivalents and to settle the whole matter (*compositio*); above all, the increasingly definite will to treat every crime as in some sense *dischargeable,* and thus at least to a certain extent to *isolate* the criminal and his deed from one another — these traits become more and more clearly visible as the penal law evolves. As the power and self-confidence of a community increase, the penal law always becomes more moderate; every weakening or imperiling of the former brings with it a restoration of the harsher forms of the latter. The "creditor" always becomes more humane to the extent that he has grown richer; finally, how much injury he can endure without suffering from it becomes the actual *measure* of his wealth. It is not unthinkable that a society might attain such a *consciousness of power* that it could allow itself the noblest luxury possible to it — letting those who harm it go *unpunished.* "What are my parasites to me?" it might say. "May they live and prosper: I am strong enough for that!"

The justice which began with, "everything is dischargeable, everything must be discharged," ends by winking and letting those incapable of discharging their debt go free: it ends, as does every good thing on earth, by *overcoming itself.* This self-overcoming of justice: one knows the beautiful name it has given itself — *mercy;* it goes without saying that mercy remains the privilege of the most powerful man, or better, his — beyond the law.

11

Here a word in repudiation of attempts that have lately been made to seek the origin of justice in quite a different sphere — namely in that of *ressentiment.* To the psychologists first of all, presuming they would like to study *ressentiment* close up for once, I would say: this plant blooms best today among anarchists and anti-Semites—where it has always bloomed, in hidden places, like the violet, though with a different odor. And as like must always produce like, it causes us no surprise to see a repetition in such circles of attempts often made before—see above, section 14—to sanctify *revenge* under the name of *justice*—as if justice were at bottom merely a further development of the feeling of being aggrieved—and to rehabilitate not only revenge but all *reactive* affects in general. To the latter as such I would be the last to raise any objection: in respect to the entire biological problem (in relation to which the value of these affects has hitherto been underrated) it even seems to me to constitute a *service*. All I draw attention to is the circumstance that it is the spirit of *ressentiment* itself out of which this new nuance of scientific fairness (for the benefit of hatred, envy, jealousy, mistrust, rancor, and revenge) proceeds. For this "scientific fairness" immediately ceases and gives way to accents of deadly enmity and prejudice once it is a question of dealing with another group of affects, affects that, it seems to me, are of even greater biological value than those reactive affects and consequently deserve even more to be *scientifically* evaluated and esteemed: namely, the truly *active* effects, such as lust for power, avarice, and the like. (E. Dühring: *The Value of Life; A Course in Philosophy;* and, fundamentally, *passim.*)

So much against this tendency in general: as for Dühring's specific proposition that the home of justice is to be sought in the sphere of the reactive feelings, one is obliged for truth's sake to counter it with a blunt antithesis: the *last* sphere to be conquered by the spirit of justice is the sphere of the reactive feelings! When it really happens that the just man remains just even toward those who have harmed him (and not merely cold, temperate, remote, indifferent: being just is always a *positive* attitude), when the exalted, clear objectivity, as penetrating as it is mild, of the eye of justice and *judging* is not dimmed even under the assault of personal injury, derision, and calumny, this is a piece of perfection and supreme mastery on earth—something it would be prudent not to expect or to *believe* in too readily. On the average, a small dose of aggression, malice, or insinuation certainly suffices to drive the blood into the eyes—and fairness out of the eyes—of even the most upright people. The active, aggressive, arrogant man is still a hundred steps closer to justice than the reactive man; for he has absolutely no need to take a false and prejudiced view of the object before him in the way the reactive man does and is bound to do. For that reason the aggressive man, as the stronger, nobler, more courageous, has in fact also had at all times a *freer* eye, a *better* conscience on his side: conversely, one can see who has the invention of the "bad conscience" on his conscience—the man of *ressentiment!*

Finally, one only has to look at history: in which sphere has the entire administration of law hitherto been at home—also the need for law? In the sphere of reactive men, perhaps? By no means: rather in that of the active, strong, spontaneous, aggressive. From a historical point of view, law represents on earth—let it be said to the dismay of the above-named agitator (who himself once confessed: "the doctrine of revenge is the red thread of justice that runs through all my work and efforts")—the struggle *against* the reactive feelings, the war conducted against them on the part of the active and aggressive powers who employed some of their strength to impose measure and bounds upon the excesses of the reactive pathos and to compel it to come to terms. Wherever justice is practiced and maintained one sees a stronger power seeking a means of putting an end to the senseless raging of *ressentiment* among the weaker powers that stand under it (whether they be groups or individuals)—partly by taking the object of *ressentiment* out of the hands of revenge, partly by substituting for revenge the struggle against the enemies of peace and order, partly by devising and in some cases imposing settlements, partly by elevating certain equivalents for injuries into norms to which from then on *ressentiment* is once and for all directed. The most decisive act, however, that the supreme power performs and accomplishes against the predominance of grudges and rancor—it always takes this action as soon as it is in any way strong enough to do so—is the institution of *law,* the imperative declaration of what in general counts as permitted, as just, in its eyes, and what counts as forbidden, as unjust: once it has instituted the law, it treats violence and capricious acts on the part of individuals or entire groups as offenses against the law, as rebellion against the supreme power itself, and thus leads the feelings of its subjects away from the direct injury caused by such offenses; and in the long run it thus attains the reverse of that which is desired by all revenge that is fastened exclusively to the viewpoint of the person injured: from now on the eye is trained to an ever more *impersonal* evaluation of the deed, and this applies even to the eye of the injured person himself (although last of all, as remarked above).

"Just" and "unjust" exist, accordingly, only after the institution of the law (and *not*, as Dühring would have it, after the perpetration of the injury). To speak of just or unjust *in itself* is quite senseless; *in itself,* of course, no injury, assault, exploitation, destruction can be "unjust," since life operates *essentially,* that is in its basic functions, through injury, assault, exploitation, destruction and simply cannot be thought of at all without this character. One must indeed grant something even more unpalatable: that, from the highest biological standpoint, legal conditions can never be other than *exceptional conditions,* since they constitute a partial restriction of the will of life, which is bent upon power, and are subordinate to its total goal as a single means: namely, as a means of creating *greater* units of power. A legal order thought of as sovereign and universal, not as a means in the struggle between power-complexes but as a means of *preventing* all struggle in general — perhaps after the communistic cliché of Dühring, that every will must consider every other will its equal — would be a principle *hostile to life,* an agent of the dissolution and destruction of man, an attempt to assassinate the future of man, a sign of weariness, a secret path to nothingness. —

12

Yet a word on the origin and the purpose of punishment — two problems that are separate, or ought to be separate: unfortunately, they are usually confounded. How have previous genealogists of morals set about solving these problems? Naïvely, as has always been their way: they seek out some "purpose" in punishment, for example, revenge or deterrence, then guilelessly place this purpose at the beginning as *causa fiendi*[6] of punishment, and — have done. The "purpose of law," however, is absolutely the last thing to employ in the history of the origin of law: on the contrary, there is for historiography of any kind no more important proposition than the one it took such effort to establish but which really *ought to be* established now: the cause of the origin of a thing and its eventual utility, its actual employment and place in a system of purposes, lie worlds apart; whatever exists, having somehow come into being, is again and again reinterpreted to new ends, taken over, transformed, and redirected by some power superior to it; all events in the organic world are a subduing, a *becoming master,* and all subduing and becoming master involves a fresh interpretation, an adaptation through which any previous "meaning" and "purpose" are necessarily obscured or even obliterated. However well one has understood the *utility* of any physiological organ (or of a legal institution, a social custom, a political usage, a form in art or in a religious cult), this means nothing regarding its origin: however uncomfortable and dis-

[6]The cause of the origin.

agreeable this may sound to older ears—for one had always believed that to understand the demonstrable purpose, the utility of a thing, a form, or an institution, was also to understand the reason why it originated—the eye being made for seeing, the hand being made for grasping.

Thus one also imagined that punishment was devised for punishing. But purposes and utilities are only *signs* that a will to power has become master of something less powerful and imposed upon it the character of a function; and the entire history of a "thing," an organ, a custom can in this way be a continuous sign-chain of ever new interpretations and adaptations whose causes do not even have to be related to one another but, on the contrary, in some cases succeed and alternate with one another in a purely chance fashion. The "evolution" of a thing, a custom, an organ is thus by no means its *progressus* toward a goal, even less a logical *progressus* by the shortest route and with the smallest expenditure of force—but a succession of more or less profound, more or less mutually independent processes of subduing, plus the resistances they encounter, the attempts at transformation for the purpose of defense and reaction, and the results of successful counteractions. The form is fluid, but the "meaning" is even more so.

The case is the same even within each individual organism: with every real growth in the whole, the "meaning" of the individual organs also changes; in certain circumstances their partial destruction, a reduction in their numbers (for example, through the disappearance of intermediary members) can be a sign of increasing strength and perfection. It is not too much to say that even a partial *diminution of utility,* an atrophying and degeneration, a loss of meaning and purposiveness—in short, death—is among the conditions of an actual *progressus,* which always appears in the shape of a will and way to *greater power* and is always carried through at the expense of numerous smaller powers. The magnitude of an "advance" can even be measured by the mass of things that had to be sacrificed to it; mankind in the mass sacrificed to the prosperity of a single *stronger* species of man—that *would* be an advance.

I emphasize this major point of historical method all the more because it is in fundamental opposition to the now prevalent instinct and taste which would rather be reconciled even to the absolute fortuitousness, even the mechanistic senselessness of all events than to the theory that in all events a *will to power* is operating. The democratic idiosyncracy which opposes everything that dominates and wants to dominate, the modern *misarchism* (to coin an ugly word for an ugly thing) has permeated the realm of the spirit and disguised itself in the most spiritual forms to such a degree that today it has forced its way, has acquired the *right* to force its way into the strictest, apparently most objective sciences; indeed, it seems to me to have already taken charge of all physiology and theory of life — to the detriment of life, as goes without saying, since it has robbed it of a fundamental concept, that of *activity.* Under the influence of the above-mentioned idiosyncracy, one places instead "adaptation" in the foreground, that is to say, an activity of the second rank, a mere reactivity; indeed, life itself has been defined as a more and more efficient inner adaptation to external conditions (Herbert Spencer). Thus the essence of life, its *will to power,* is ignored; one overlooks the essential priority of the spontaneous, aggressive, expansive, form-giving forces that give new interpretations and directions, although "adaptation" follows only after this; the dominant role of the highest functionaries within the organism itself in which the will to life appears active and form-giving is denied. One should recall what Huxley reproached Spencer with — his "administrative nihilism": but it is a question of rather *more* than mere "administration."

13

To return to our subject, namely *punishment,* one must distinguish two aspects: on the one hand, that in it which is relatively *enduring,* the custom, the act, the "drama," a certain strict sequence of procedures; on the other, that in it which is *fluid,* the meaning, the purpose, the expectation associated with the performance of such procedures. In accordance with the previously developed major point of historical method, it is assumed without further ado that the procedure itself will be something older, earlier than its employment in punishment, that the latter is *projected* and interpreted *into* the procedure (which has long existed but been employed in another sense), in short, that the case is *not* as has hitherto been assumed by our naïve genealogists of law and morals, who have one and all thought of the procedure as *invented* for the purpose of punishing, just as one formerly thought of the hand as invented for the purpose of grasping.

As for the other element in punishment, the fluid element, its "meaning," in a very late condition of culture (for example, in modern Europe) the concept "punishment" possesses in fact not *one* meaning but a whole synthesis of "meanings": the previous history of punishment in general, the history of its employment for the most various purposes, finally crystallizes into a kind of unity that is hard to disentangle, hard to analyze and, as must be emphasized especially, totally *indefinable.* (Today it is impossible to say for certain *why* people are really punished: all concepts in which an entire process is semiotically concentrated elude definition; only that which has no history is definable.) At an earlier stage, on the contrary, this synthesis of "meanings" can still be disentangled, as well as changed; one can still perceive how in each individual case the elements of the synthesis undergo a shift in value and rearrange themselves accordingly, so that now this, now that element comes to the fore and dominates at the expense of the others; and under certain circumstances one element (the purpose of deterrence perhaps) appears to overcome all the remaining elements.

To give at least an idea of how uncertain, how supplemental, how accidental "the meaning" of punishment is, and how one and the same procedure can be employed, interpreted, adapted to ends that differ fundamentally, I set down here the pattern that has emerged from consideration of relatively few chance instances I have noted. Punishment as a means of rendering harmless, of preventing further harm. Punishment as recompense to the injured party for the harm done, rendered in any form (even in that of a compensating affect). Punishment as the isolation of a disturbance of equilibrium, so as to guard against any further spread of the disturbance. Punishment as a means of inspiring fear of those who determine and execute the punishment. Punishment as a kind of repayment for the advantages the criminal has enjoyed hitherto (for example, when he is employed as a slave in the mines). Punishment as the expulsion of a degenerate element (in some cases, of an entire branch, as in Chinese law: thus as a means of preserving the purity of a race or maintaining a social type). Punishment as a festival, namely as the rape and mockery of a finally defeated enemy. Punishment as the making of a memory, whether for him who suffers the punishment—so-called "improvement"—or for those who witness its execution. Punishment as payment of a fee stipulated by the power that protects the wrongdoer from the excesses of revenge. Punishment as a compromise with revenge in its natural state when the latter is still maintained and claimed as a privilege by powerful clans. Punishment as a declaration of war and a war measure against an enemy of peace, of the law, of order, of the authorities, whom, as a danger to the community, as one who has broken the contract that defines the conditions under which it exists, as a rebel, a traitor, and breaker of the peace, one opposes with the means of war. —

This list is certainly not complete; it is clear that punishment is overdetermined by utilities of all kinds. All the more reason, then, for deducting from it a *supposed* utility that, to be sure, counts in the popular consciousness as the most essential one—belief in punishment, which for several reasons is tottering today, always finds its strongest support in this. Punishment is supposed to possess the value of awakening the *feeling of guilt* in the guilty person; one seeks in it the actual *instrumentum* of that psychical reaction called "bad conscience," "sting of conscience." Thus one misunderstands psychology and the reality of things even as they apply today: how much more as they applied during the greater part of man's history, his prehistory!

It is precisely among criminals and convicts that the sting of conscience is extremely rare; prisons and penitentiaries are *not* the kind of hotbed in which this species of gnawing worm is likely to flourish: all conscientious observers are agreed on that, in many cases unwillingly enough and contrary to their own inclinations. Generally speaking, punishment makes men hard and cold; it concentrates; it sharpens the feeling of alienation; it strengthens the power of resistance. If it happens that punishment destroys the vital energy and brings about a miserable prostration and self-abasement, such a result is certainly even less pleasant than the usual effects of punishment—characterized by dry and gloomy seriousness.

If we consider those millennia *before* the history of man, we may unhesitatingly assert that it was precisely through punishment that the development of the feeling of guilt was most powerfully *hindered*—at least in the victims upon whom the punitive force was vented. For we must not underrate the extent to which the sight of the judicial and executive procedures prevents the criminal from considering his deed, the type of his action *as such,* reprehensible: for he sees exactly the same kind of actions practiced in the service of justice and approved of and practiced with a good conscience: spying deception, bribery, setting traps, the whole cunning and underhand art of police and prosecution, plus robbery, violence, defamation, imprisonment, torture, murder, practiced as a matter of principle and without even emotion to excuse them, which are pronounced characteristics of the various forms of punishment—all of them therefore actions which his judges in no way condemn and repudiate *as such,* but only when they are applied and directed to certain particular ends.

The "bad conscience," this most uncanny and most interesting plant of all our earthly vegetation, did *not* grow on this soil; indeed, during the greater part of the past the judges and punishers themselves were *not at all* conscious of dealing with a "guilty person." But with an instigator of harm, with an irresponsible piece of fate. And the person upon whom punishment subsequently descended, again like a piece of fate, suffered no "inward pain" other than that induced by the sudden appearance of something unforeseen, a dreadful natural event, a plunging, crushing rock that one cannot fight.

15

This fact once came insidiously into the mind of Spinoza (to the vexation of his interpreters, Kuno Fischer, for example, who make a real *effort* to misunderstand him on this point), when one afternoon, teased by who knows what recollection, he mused on the question of what really remained to him of the famous *morsus conscientiae*[7]—he who had banished good and evil to the realm of human imagination and had wrathfully defended the honor of his "free" God against those blasphemers who asserted that God effected all things *sub ratione boni*[8] ("but that would mean making God subject to fate and would surely be the greatest of all absurdities"). The world, for Spinoza, had returned to that state of innocence in which it had lain before the invention of the bad conscience: what then had become of the *morsus conscientiae?*

"The opposite of *gaudium*,"[9] he finally said to himself—"a sadness accompanied by the recollection of a past event that flouted all of our expectations." *Eth.III, propos. XVIII, schol. I. II.* Mischiefmakers overtaken by punishments have for thousands of years felt in respect of their "transgressions" *just as Spinoza did:* "here something has unexpectedly gone wrong," *not:* "I ought not to have done that." They submitted to punishment as one submits to an illness or to a misfortune or to death, with that stout-hearted fatalism without rebellion through which the Russians, for example, still have an advantage over us Westerners in dealing with life.

If there existed any criticism of the deed in those days, it was prudence that criticized the deed: the actual *effect* of punishment must beyond question be sought above all in a heightening of prudence, in an extending of the memory, in a will henceforth to go to work more cautiously, mistrustfully, secretly, in the insight

[7] Sting of conscience.
[8] For a good reason.
[9] Joy.

that one is definitely too weak for many things, in a kind of improvement in self-criticism. That which can in general be attained through punishment, in men and in animals, is an increase of fear, a heightening of prudence, mastery of the desires: thus punishment *tames* men, but it does not make them "better" — one might with more justice assert the opposite. ("Injury makes one prudent," says the proverb: insofar as it makes one prudent it also makes one bad. Fortunately, it frequently makes people stupid.)

16

At this point I can no longer avoid giving a first, provisional statement of my own hypothesis concerning the origin of the "bad conscience": it may sound rather strange and needs to be pondered, lived with, and slept on for a long time. I regard the bad conscience as the serious illness that man was bound to contract under the stress of the most fundamental change he ever experienced — that change which occurred when he found himself finally enclosed within the walls of society and of peace. The situation that faced sea animals when they were compelled to become land animals or perish was the same as that which faced these semi-animals, well adapted to the wilderness, to war, to prowling, to adventure: suddenly all their instincts were disvalued and "suspended." From now on they had to walk on their feet and "bear themselves" whereas hitherto they had been borne by the water: a dreadful heaviness lay upon them. They felt unable to cope with the simplest undertakings; in this new world they no longer possessed their former guides, their regulating, unconscious and infallible drives: they were reduced to thinking, inferring, reckoning, co-ordinating cause and effect, these unfortunate creatures; they were reduced to their "consciousness," their weakest and most fallible organ! I believe there has never been such a feeling of misery on earth, such a leaden discomfort — and at the same time the old instincts had not suddenly ceased to make their usual demands! Only it was hardly or rarely possible to humor them: as a rule they had to seek new and, as it were, subterranean gratifications.

All instincts that do not discharge themselves outwardly *turn inward* — this is what I call the *internalization* of man: thus it was that man first developed what was later called his "soul." The entire inner world, originally as thin as if it were stretched between two membranes, expanded and extended itself, acquired depth, breadth, and height, in the same measure as outward discharge was *inhibited*. Those fearful bulwarks with which the political organization protected itself against the old instincts of freedom—punishments belong among these bulwarks—brought about that all those instincts of wild, free, prowling man turned backward *against man himself.* Hostility, cruelty, joy in persecuting, in attacking, in change, in destruction—all this turned against the possessors of such instincts: *that* is the origin of the "bad conscience."

The man who, from lack of external enemies and resistances and forcibly confined to the oppressive narrowness and punctiliousness of custom, impatiently lacerated, persecuted, gnawed at, assaulted, and maltreated himself; this animal that rubbed itself raw against the bars of its cage as one tried to "tame" it; this deprived creature, racked with homesickness for the wild, who had to turn himself into an adventure, a torture chamber, an uncertain and dangerous wilderness—this fool, this yearning and desperate prisoner became the inventor of the "bad conscience." But thus began the gravest and uncanniest illness, from which humanity has not yet recovered, man's suffering *of man, of himself*—the result of a forcible sundering from his animal past, as it were a leap and plunge into new surroundings and conditions of existence, a declaration of war against the old instincts upon which his strength, joy, and terribleness had rested hitherto.

Let us add at once that, on the other hand, the existence on earth of an animal soul turned against itself, taking sides against itself, was something so new, profound, unheard of, enigmatic, contradictory, *and pregnant with a future* that the aspect of the earth was essentially altered. Indeed, divine spectators were needed to do justice to spectacle that thus began and the end of which is not yet in sight—a spectacle too subtle, too marvelous, too paradoxical to be played senselessly unobserved on some ludicrous planet! From now on, man is *included* among the most unexpected and exciting lucky throws in the dice game of Heraclitus' "great child," be he called Zeus or chance; he gives rise to an interest, a tension, a hope, almost a certainty, as if with him something were announcing and preparing itself, as if man were not a goal but only a way, an episode, a bridge, a great promise.—

17

Among the presuppositions of this hypothesis concerning the origin of the bad conscience is, first, that the change referred to was not a gradual or voluntary one and did not represent an organic adaptation to new conditions but a break, a leap, a compulsion, an ineluctable disaster which precluded all struggle and even all *ressentiment.* Secondly, however, that the welding of a hitherto unchecked and shapeless populace into a firm form was not only instituted by an act of violence but also carried to its conclusion by nothing but acts of violence—that the oldest "state" thus appeared as a fearful tyranny, as an oppressive and remorseless machine, and went on working until this raw material of people and semi-animals was at last not only thoroughly kneaded and pliant but also *formed.*

I employed the word "state": it is obvious what is meant—some pack of blond beasts of prey, a conqueror and master race which, organized for war and with the ability to organize, unhesitatingly lays its terrible claws upon a populace perhaps tremendously superior in numbers but still formless and nomad. That is after all how the "state" began on earth: I think that sentimentalism which would have it begin with a "contract" has been disposed of. He who can command, he who is by nature "master," he who is violent in act and bearing—what has he to do with contracts! One does not reckon with such natures; they come like fate, without reason, consideration, or pretext; they appear as lightning appears, too terrible, too sudden, too convincing, too "different" even to be hated. Their work is an instinctive creation and imposition of forms; they are the most involuntary, unconscious artists there are—wherever they appear something new soon arises, a ruling structure that *lives,* in which parts and functions are delimited and coordinated, in which nothing whatever finds a place that has not first been assigned a "meaning" in relation to the whole. They do not know what guilt, responsibility, or consideration are, these born organizers; they exemplify that terrible artists' egoism that has the look of bronze and knows itself justified to all eternity in its "work," like a mother in her child. It is not in *them* that the "bad conscience" developed, that goes without saying—but it would not have developed *without them,* this ugly growth, it would be lacking if a tremendous quantity of freedom had not been expelled from the world, or at least from the visible world, and made as it were *latent* under their hammer blows and artists' violence. This *instinct for freedom* forcibly made latent— we have seen it already—this instinct for freedom pushed back and repressed, incarcerated within and finally able to discharge and vent itself only on itself: that, and that alone, is what the *bad conscience* is in its beginnings.

18

One should guard against thinking lightly of this phenomenon merely on account of its initial painfulness and ugliness. For fundamentally it is the same active force that is at work on a grander scale in those artists of violence and organizers who build states, and that here, internally, on a smaller and pettier scale, directed backward, in the "labyrinth of the breast," to use Goethe's expression, creates for itself a bad conscience and builds negative ideals—namely, the *instinct for freedom* (in my language: the will to power); only here the material upon which the form-giving and ravishing nature of this force vents itself is man himself, his whole ancient animal self—and *not,* as in that greater and more obvious phenomenon, some *other* man, *other* men. This secret self-ravishment, this artists' cruelty, this delight in imposing a form upon oneself as a hard, recalcitrant, suffering material and in burning a will, a critique, a contradiction, a contempt, a No into it, this uncanny, dreadfully joyous labor of a soul voluntarily at odds with itself that makes itself suffer out of joy in making suffer—eventually this entire *active* "bad conscience" —you will have guessed it—as the womb of all ideal and imaginative phenomena, also brought to light an abundance of strange new beauty and affirmation, and perhaps beauty itself.—After all, what would be "beautiful" if the contradiction had not first become conscious of itself, if the ugly had not first said to itself: "I am ugly"?

This hint will at least make less enigmatic the enigma of how contradictory concepts such as *selflessness, self-denial, self-sacrifice* can suggest an ideal, a kind of beauty; and one thing we know henceforth—I have no doubt of it—and that is the nature of the *delight* that the selfless man, the self-denier, the self-sacrificer feels from the first: this delight is tied to cruelty.

So much for the present about the origin of the moral value of the "unegoistic," about the soil from which this value grew: only the bad conscience, only the will to self-maltreatment provided the conditions for the *value* of the unegoistic.—

19

The bad conscience is an illness, there is no doubt about that, but an illness as pregnancy is an illness. Let us seek out the conditions under which this illness has reached its most terrible and most sublime height; we shall see what it really was that thus entered the world. But for that one needs endurance—and first of all we must go back again to an earlier point of view.

The civil-law relationship between the debtor and his creditor, discussed above, has been interpreted in an, historically speaking, exceedingly remarkable and dubious manner into a relationship in which to us modern men it seems perhaps least to belong: namely into the relationship between the present generation and its ancestors.

Within the original tribal community—we are speaking of primeval times—the living generation always recognized a juridical duty toward earlier generations, and especially toward the earliest; which founded the tribe (and by no means a merely sentimental obligation: there are actually reasons for denying the existence of the latter for the greater part of human history). The conviction reigns that it is only through the sacrifices and accomplishments of the ancestors that the tribe *exists*—and that one has to *pay them back* with sacrifices and accomplishments: one thus recognizes a *debt* that constantly grows greater, since these forebears never cease, in their continued existence as powerful spirits, to accord the tribe new advantages and new strength. In vain, perhaps? But there is no "in vain" for these rude and "poor-souled" ages. What can one give them in return? Sacrifices (initially as food in the coarsest sense), feasts, music, honors; above all, obedience—for all customs, as works of the ancestors, are also their statutes and commands: can one ever give them enough? This suspicion remains and increases; from time to time it leads to a wholesale sacrifice, something tremendous in the way of repayment to the "creditor" (the notorious sacrifice of the first-born, for example; in any case blood, human blood).

The *fear* of the ancestor and his power, the consciousness of indebtedness to him, increases, according to this kind of logic, in exactly the same measure as the power of the tribe itself increases, as the tribe itself grows ever more victorious, independent, honored, and feared. By no means the other way round! Every step toward the decline of a tribe, every misfortune, every sign of degeneration, of coming disintegration always *diminishes* fear of the spirit of its founder and produces a meaner impression of his cunning, foresight, and present power. If one imagines this rude kind of logic carried to its end, then the ancestors of the *most powerful* tribes are bound eventually to grow to monstrous dimensions through the imagination of growing fear and to recede into the darkness of the divinely uncanny and unimaginable: in the end the ancestor must necessarily be transfigured into a *god*. Perhaps this is even the origin of gods, an origin therefore out of *fear!* . . . And whoever should feel obliged to add, "but out of piety also!" would hardly be right for the greater part of the existence of man, his prehistory. To be sure, he would be quite right for the *intermediate* age, in which the noble tribes developed—who indeed paid back their originators, their ancestors (heroes, gods) with interest all the qualities that had become palpable in themselves, the *noble* qualities. We shall take another look later at the ennoblement of the gods (which should not be confused with their becoming "holy"); let us first of all follow to its end the course of this whole development of the consciousness of guilt.

20

History shows that the consciousness of being in debt to the deity did not by any means come to an end together with the organization of communities on the basis of blood relationship. Even as mankind inherited the concepts "good and bad" from the tribal nobility (along with its basic psychological propensity to set up orders of rank), it also inherited, along with the tribal and family divinities, the burden of still unpaid debts and of the desire to be relieved of them. (The transition is provided by those numerous slave and dependent populations who, whether through compulsion or through servility and mimicry, adapted themselves to their masters' cult of the gods: this inheritance then overflows from them in all directions.) The guilty feeling of indebtedness to the divinity continued to grow for several millennia — always in the same measure as the concept of God and the feeling for divinity increased on earth and was carried to the heights. (The entire history of ethnic struggle, victory, reconciliation, fusion, everything that precedes the definitive ordering of rank of the different national elements in every great racial synthesis, is reflected in the confused genealogies of their gods, in the sagas of the gods' struggles, victories, and reconciliations; the advance toward universal empires is always also an advance toward universal divinities; despotism with its triumph over the independent nobility always prepares the way for some kind of monotheism.)

The advent of the Christian God, as the maximum god attained so far, was therefore accompanied by the maximum feeling of guilty indebtedness on earth. Presuming we have gradually entered upon the *reverse* course, there is no small probability that with the irresistible decline of faith in the Christian God there is now also a considerable decline in mankind's feeling of guilt; indeed, the prospect cannot be dismissed that the complete and definitive victory of atheism might free mankind of this whole feeling of guilty indebtedness toward its origin, its *causa prima.* Atheism and a kind of *second innocence* belong together. —

21

So much for a first brief preliminary on the connection of the concepts "guilt" and "duty" with religious presuppositions: I have up to now deliberately ignored the moralization of these concepts (their pushing back into the conscience; more precisely, the involvement of the *bad* conscience with the concept of god); and at the end of the last section I even spoke as if this moralization had not taken place at all, and as if these concepts were now necessarily doomed since their presupposition, the faith in our "creditor," in God, had disappeared. The reality is, to a fearful degree, otherwise.

The moralization of the concepts guilt and duty, their being pushed back into the *bad* conscience, actually involves an attempt to *reverse* the direction of the development described above, or at least to bring it to a halt: the *aim* now is to preclude pessimistically, once and for all, the prospect of a final discharge; the *aim* now is to make the glance recoil disconsolately from an iron impossibility; the *aim* now is to turn back the concepts "guilt" and "duty" — back against whom? There can be no doubt: against the "debtor" first of all, in whom from now on the bad conscience is firmly rooted, eating into him and spreading within him like a polyp, until at last the irredeemable debt gives rise to the conception of irredeemable penance, the idea that it cannot be discharged ("*eternal* punishment"). Finally, however, they are turned back against the "creditor," too: whether we think of the *causa prima* of man, the beginning of the human race, its primal ancestor who is from now on burdened with a curse ("Adam," "original sin," "unfreedom of the will"), or of nature from whose womb mankind arose and into whom the principle of evil is projected from now on ("the diabolizing of nature"), or of existence in general, which is now considered *worthless as such* (nihilistic withdrawal from it, a desire for nothingness or a desire for its antithesis, for a different mode of being, Buddhism and the like) — suddenly we stand before the paradoxical and horrifying expedient that afforded temporary relief for tormented humanity, that stroke of genius on the part of Christianity: God himself sacrifices himself for the guilt of mankind, God himself makes payment to himself, God as the only being who can redeem man from what has become unredeemable for man himself — the creditor sacrifices himself for his debtor, out of *love* (can one credit that?), out of love for his debtor! —

22

You will have guessed *what* has really happened here, *beneath* all this: that will to self-tormenting, that repressed cruelty of the animal-man made inward and scared back into himself, the creature imprisoned in the "state" so as to be tamed, who invented

13

the bad conscience in order to hurt himself after the *more natural*
vent for this desire to hurt had been blocked—this man of the
bad conscience has seized upon the presupposition of religion
so as to drive his self-torture to its most gruesome pitch of severity and rigor. Guilt before *God:* this thought becomes an in-
strument of torture to him. He apprehends in "God" the ultimate
antithesis of his own ineluctable animal instincts; he reinterprets
these animal instincts themselves as a form of guilt before God
(as hostility, rebellion, insurrection against the "Lord," the
"father," the primal ancestor and origin of the world); he stretches
himself upon the contradiction "God" and "Devil"; he ejects
from himself all his denial of himself, of his nature, naturalness,
and actuality, in the form of an affirmation, as something existent,
corporeal, real, as God, as the holiness of God, as God the Judge,
as God the Hangman, as the beyond, as eternity, as torment without end, as hell, as the immeasurability of punishment and guilt.

In this psychical cruelty there resides a madness of the will
which is absolutely unexampled: the *will* of man to find himself
guilty and reprehensible to a degree that can never be atoned for;
his *will* to think himself punished without any possibility of the
punishment becoming equal to the guilt; his *will* to infect and
poison the fundamental ground of things with the problem of
punishment and guilt so as to cut off once and for all his own
exit from this labyrinth of "fixed ideas"; his *will* to erect an ideal—
that of the "holy God"—and in the face of it to feel the palpable
certainty of his own absolute unworthiness. Oh this insane,
pathetic beast—man! What ideas he has, what unnaturalness,
what paroxysms of nonsense, what *bestiality of thought* erupts
as soon as he is prevented just a little from being a *beast in deed!*

All this is interesting, to excess, but also of a gloomy, black,
unnerving sadness, so that one must forcibly forbid oneself to
gaze too long into these abysses. Here is *sickness,* beyond any
doubt, the most terrible sickness that has ever raged in man; and
whoever can still bear to hear (but today one no longer has ears
for this!) how in this night of torment and absurdity there has
resounded the cry of *love,* the cry of the most nostalgic rapture,
of redemption through *love,* will turn away, seized by invincible
horror.—There is so much in man that is hideous!—Too long, the
earth has been a madhouse!—

23

This should dispose once and for all of the question of how the
"holy God" originated.

That the conception of gods *in itself* need not lead to the degradation of the imagination that we had to consider briefly, that there are *nobler* uses for the invention of gods than for the self-crucifixion and self-violation of man in which Europe over the past millennia achieved its distinctive mastery — that is fortunately revealed even by a mere glance at the *Greek gods,* those reflections of noble and autocratic men, in whom *the animal* in man felt deified and did *not* lacerate itself, did *not* rage against itself! For the longest time these Greeks used their gods precisely so as to ward off the "bad conscience," so as to be able to rejoice in their freedom of soul — the very opposite of the use to which Christianity put its God. They went *very far* in this direction, these splendid and lion-hearted children; and no less an authority than the Homeric Zeus himself occasionally gives them to understand that they are making things too easy for themselves. "Strange!" he says once — the case is that of Aegisthus, a *very* bad case —

Strange how these mortals so loudly complain of the gods!
We alone produce evil, they say; yet themselves
Make themselves wretched through folly, even counter to fate.[10]

Yet one can see and hear how even this Olympian spectator and judge is far from holding a grudge against them or thinking ill of them on that account: "how *foolish* they are!" he thinks when he observes the misdeeds of mortals — and "foolishness," "folly," a little "disturbance in the head," this much even the Greeks of the strongest, bravest age conceded of themselves as the reason for much that was bad and calamitous — foolishness, *not* sin! do you grasp that?

Even this disturbance in the head, however, presented a problem: "how is it possible? how could it actually have happened to heads such as *we* have, we men of aristocratic descent, of the best society, happy, well-constituted, noble, and virtuous?" — thus noble Greeks asked themselves for centuries in the face of every incomprehensible atrocity or wantonness with which one of their kind had polluted himself. "He must have been deluded by a *god,*" they concluded finally, shaking their heads. . . . This expedient is *typical* of the Greeks. . . . In this way the gods served in those days to justify man to a certain extent in his wickedness, they served as the originators of evil — in those days they took upon themselves, not the punishment but, what is *nobler,* the guilt.

[10] *Odyssey,* I, line 32ff.

I end up with three question marks; that seems plain. "What are you really doing, erecting an ideal or knocking one down?" I may perhaps be asked.

But have you ever asked yourselves sufficiently how much the erection of *every* ideal on earth has cost? How much reality has had to be misunderstood and slandered, how many lies have had to be sanctified, how many consciences disturbed, how much "God" sacrificed every time? If a temple is to be erected *a temple must be destroyed:* that is the law — let anyone who can show me a case in which it is not fulfilled!

We modern men are the heirs of the conscience-vivisection and self-torture of millennia: this is what we have practiced longest, it is our distinctive art perhaps, and in any case our subtlety in which we have acquired a refined taste. Man has all too long had an "evil eye" for his natural inclinations, so that they have finally become inseparable from his "bad conscience." An attempt at the reverse would *in itself* be possible — but who is strong enough for it? — that is, to wed the bad conscience to all the *unnatural* inclinations, all those aspirations to the beyond, to that which runs counter to sense, instinct, nature, animal, in short all ideals hitherto, which are one and all hostile to life and ideals that slander the world. To whom should one turn today with *such* hopes and demands?

One would have precisely the *good* men against one; and, of course, the comfortable, the reconciled, the vain, the sentimental, the weary.

What gives greater offense, what separates one more fundamentally, than to reveal something of the severity and respect with which one treats oneself? And on the other hand — how accommodating, how friendly all the world is toward us as soon as we act as all the world does and "let ourselves go" like all the world!

The attainment of this goal would require a *different* kind of spirit from that likely to appear in this present age: spirits strengthened by war and victory, for whom conquest, adventure, danger, and even pain have become needs; it would require habituation to the keen air of the heights, to winter journeys, to ice and mountains in every sense; it would require even a kind of sublime wickedness, an ultimate, supremely self-confident mischievousness in knowledge that goes with great health; it would require, in brief and alas, precisely this *great health!*

Is this even possible today? — But some day, in a stronger age than this decaying, self-doubting present, he must yet come to us, the *redeeming* man of great love and contempt, the creative spirit whose compelling strength will not let him rest in any aloofness or any beyond, whose isolation is misunderstood by the people as if it were flight *from* reality — while it is only his absorption, immersion, penetration *into* reality, so that, when he one day emerges again into the light, he may bring home the *redemption* of this reality: its redemption from the curse that the hitherto reigning ideal has laid upon it. This man of the future, who will redeem us not only from the hitherto reigning ideal but also from that which was bound to grow out of it, the great nausea, the will to nothingness, nihilism; this bell-stroke of noon and of the great decision that liberates the will again and restores its goal to the earth and his hope to man; this Antichrist and antinihilist; this victor over God and nothingness — *he must come one day.* —

25

But what am I saying? Enough! Enough! At this point it behooves me only to be silent; or I shall usurp that to which only one younger, "heavier with future," and stronger than I has a right — that to which only *Zarathustra* has a right, *Zarathustra the godless.* —

John Rawls

The Sense of Justice

In *Emile* Rousseau asserts that the sense of justice is no mere   **127**
moral conception formed by the understanding alone, but a true
sentiment of the heart enlightened by reason, the natural outcome of our primitive affections. In the first part of this paper I
set out a psychological construction to illustrate the way in which
Rousseau's thesis might be true. In the second part I use several
of the ideas elaborated in formulating this construction to consider two questions which arise in the systematic analysis of the
concept of justice.

These two questions are: first, to whom is the obligation of
justice owed? — that is, in regard to whom must one regulate
one's conduct as the principles of justice require? — and second,
what accounts for men's doing what justice requires? Very briefly,
the answers to these questions are as follows: to the first, the
duty of justice is owed to those who are capable of a sense of
justice; and to the second, if men did not do what justice requires,
not only would they not regard themselves as bound by the principles of justice, but they would be incapable of feeling resentment and indignation, and they would be without ties of friendship and mutual trust. They would lack certain essential elements
of humanity.

Throughout, I think of a sense of justice as something which
persons have. One refers to it when one says, for example, that
cruel and unusual punishments offend one's sense of justice. It
may be aroused or assuaged, and it is connected not only with
such moral feelings as resentment and indignation but also, as I
shall argue, with such natural attitudes as mutual trust and affection. The psychological construction is designed to show how
the sense of justice may be viewed as the result of a certain

John Rawls, "The Sense of Justice," *The Philosophical Review*, LXXII (1963),
281–305; reprinted with the permission of the author and *The Philosophical Review*.

natural development; it will be useful in understanding why the capacity for a sense of justice is the fundamental aspect of moral personality in the theory of justice.

II

Before setting out the psychological construction I should like to consider the background of the two questions. The main problem in giving a systematic analysis of the concept of justice is to derive and to arrange the principles associated with the concept. These principles are those which account for the considered judgments of competent persons concerning the justice of political and social institutions. Institutions are understood as those publicly recognized systems of rules which are generally acted upon and which, by defining offices and positions, rights and duties, give political and social activity its form and structure. Now the family of principles associated with the concept of justice can be characterized as those principles which rational persons would acknowledge when the constraints of morality are imposed upon them in circumstances which give rise to questions of justice. These circumstances are those in which persons make conflicting demands on their common institutions and in which they regard themselves as representing or possessing legitimate interests the claims of which they are prepared to press on one another. Questions of justice and fairness arise when free persons, who have no authority over one another, are participating in their common institutions and among themselves settling or acknowledging the rules which define them and which determine the resulting shares in their benefits and burdens. An institution is just or fair, then, when it satisfies the principles which those who participate in it could propose to one another for mutual acceptance from an original position of equal liberty. To derive the familiar principles of justice is to show how they would be mutually acknowledged; and to arrange these principles is to determine their respective priorities, given the nature of the cases to which they apply.

When the concept of justice is applied to the basic structure of the political and social system, the principles associated with the concept are the following: (i) each person participating in it or affected by it has an equal right to the most extensive liberty compatible with a like liberty for all; and (ii) inequalities (as defined and permitted by the pattern of distribution of rights and duties) are arbitrary unless it is reasonable to expect that they will work out for everyone's advantage, and provided that the positions and offices to which they attach, or from which they may be gained, are open to all. (I state these principles here and sketch their derivation as they are used in the formulation of the psychological construction. The idea underlying this derivation I shall call the conception of justice as fairness.)

The derivation of these principles is indicated by the following analytic construction. Imagine a number of rational and mutually self-interested persons situated in an initial position of equal liberty. Assume that they are to propose and acknowledge before one another general principles applicable to their common institutions as standards by which their complaints against these institutions are to be judged. They do not begin by registering complaints; instead they try to agree to criteria by which a complaint is to be counted as legitimate. Their procedure for this is that each person is allowed to propose the principles upon which he wishes his own complaints to be tried, this privilege being subject to three conditions. It is understood (i) that if the principles one proposes are accepted, the complaints of others will be similarly tried; (ii) that no one's complaints will be heard until everyone is roughly of one mind as to how complaints are to be judged; and (iii) that the principles proposed and acknowledged on any one occasion are binding, failing special circumstances, on all future occasions. The main idea of the procedure is that everyone should be required to make in advance a firm commitment, which others also may reasonably be expected to make, and that no one be given the opportunity to tailor the canons of a legitimate complaint to fit his own special condition and then to discard them when they no longer suit his purpose. The principles accepted will express the standards in accordance with which each person is willing to have his interests limited on the supposition that the interests of others will be limited in the same way. The restrictions which would so arise may be thought of as those which a person would keep in mind if he were designing a social system in which his enemy were to assign him his place. The two principles of justice previously mentioned are those which would be acknowledged given the conditions of this analytic construction; they constitute the principles of justice in this fundamental case.

Now one can distinguish three instances in which the concept of equality applies. The first is to institutions as part of their definition. The notion of an institution involves the concept of equality in that the notion of an activity in accordance with rules implies that similar cases, as defined by these rules, are to be treated similarly. Next, the concept of equality applies to the structure of an institution, or of a social system. What equality requires, in the case of the fundamental constitution of society, is included in the two principles of justice. In general, an institution satisfies the demands of equality if it is in accordance with the principles which would be acknowledged by rational and mutually self-interested persons from an original position of equal liberty. Finally, the concept of equality applies to the original position itself, giving rise to the first question: namely, what qualifies a person as holding an original position so that in one's dealings with him one is required to conduct oneself in accordance with principles that could be acknowledged by everyone from an initial position of equality? The answer to this question, I shall argue below, is that it is necessary and sufficient that he be capable, to a certain minimum degree, of a sense of justice.

The second question—namely, what accounts for men's doing what justice requires—arises in the following manner. If the argument of the analytic construction is correct, the concept of justice has associated with it a certain family of principles. The concept of morality, when imposed upon rational and self-interested persons, gives rise to certain definite constraints. A person who has a morality not only accepts general and universal principles as limiting the pursuit of his own interests as well as those of others, but these principles must state certain specific restrictions. Among rational persons a morality without certain familiar principles of justice is impossible. The argument of the analytic construction does not show, however, that rational persons as participants in a scheme of co-operation will do what justice requires in particular cases. The aim of the analytic construction is to derive the principles of justice which apply to institutions. How persons will act in the particular circumstances when, as the rules specify, it is their turn to do their part is a different question altogether. Those engaged in an institution will indeed normally do their part if they feel bound to act on the principles which they would acknowledge under the conditions of the analytic construction. But their feeling bound in this way is not itself accounted for by this construction, and it cannot be accounted for as long as the parties are described solely by the concept of rationality.

In the psychological construction to follow, the stages of a development are described by which the sense of justice might arise from our primitive natural attitudes. This construction may be regarded as purely hypothetical. I do not claim that it represents what actually takes place. Nevertheless, I have tried to make it reasonably plausible and to include in it only those psychological principles which are compatible with our conception of ourselves as moral beings. I shall use several of the ideas elaborated in stating this construction to answer the two questions.

The psychological construction by which the sense of justice might develop consists of three parts representing the development of three forms of guilt feelings in this order: authority guilt, association guilt, and principle guilt. There are other forms of guilt feelings, and in other connections it would be essential to discuss them; but for the moment, these other forms may be left aside. The central place given to the feeling of guilt is a matter of convenience and simply a way of arranging what is said about the moral feelings.

To characterize authority guilt, let us suppose an institutional situation in which certain persons are subject to the general precepts or to the particular injunctions of others. The specific case to be taken is the relation of parents and their children. Assume that those subject—the children—love, trust, and have faith in those in authority, the parents. Let us suppose also that those subject are not in a position to question the general precepts or particular injunctions which they are expected to obey, either because they do not have sufficient knowledge and understanding or because they lack the concept of justification, both being the case with children. Suppose, further, to avoid needless complications, that the precepts and injunctions given are reasonable, so that the attitudes of love, trust, and faith are not misplaced. Given these conditions, which involve the natural attitudes of love, trust, and faith within a certain institutional background, it follows that those subject will manifest what I shall call authority guilt when they violate the precepts set to them. Their action will be recognized and experienced as a breach of the relation of love and trust with the authoritative person. An absence of guilt feelings would betray an absence of love and trust. Guilt feelings are shown (among other ways) in the inclination to confess and to ask forgiveness in order to restore the previous relation; they are part of what defines a relation as one of love and trust.

These remarks require further elaboration. Assume that this psychological law holds: the child, moved by certain instincts and regulated only (if at all) by rational self-love, comes to love, and to recognize the love of, the parent if the parent manifestly loves the child. The parents' love of the child involves an evident intention to care for the child, to do for him as his rational self-love inclines; it involves taking joy in his presence, the support of his sense of competence, and manifest pleasure at his success. One may suppose that in time the love of the parent will foster in the child an equal love for the parent, and that while the capacity for love is innate it requires special circumstances for its development. The parents' love for the child, then, may explain a child's love for his parents; his love for them does not have — indeed, cannot have — a rational explanation in terms of his antecedent instincts and desires. He does not love them in order to insure, say, his security, although he could seem to love them for this reason. That his love of them does not have a rational explanation follows from the concept of love: to love another is to care for him for his own sake as his rational self-love would incline. The child's love of his parents has an explanation — namely, that they first loved him — but not a rational explanation by reference to his original self-love.

If, then, one accepts this psychological principle and assumes that the child's love is an ordered structure of dispositions, of a sentiment, how will it show itself? Here it is necessary to keep in mind the peculiar feature of the authority situation: namely, that the child does not have his own standards of criticism. He is not in a position rationally to reject parental injunctions, so that, if he loves and trusts them, he will accept their precepts. He will also strive to live up to them as worthy objects of esteem, and he will accept their way of judging him. He will impose on himself the standards they embody, and he will judge himself as they would when he violates their precepts. The child will do these things, given his peculiar position in the authority situation, if he does, as we assume, love and trust his parents. At the same time, the child is tempted to transgress the parental precepts. He may wish to rebel against their authority which, in so far as the parents succeed in giving him self-esteem, is a humiliating reminder of his dependence. His own desires may exceed the limits of what is permitted, so that the precepts are experienced as unbearable constraints. The child will have feelings of hatred for the parents, but if he loves them, then once he has given in to temptation and violated their injunctions, he will in part take up their attitude toward himself. He will be disposed to reveal his fault by confession and to seek reconciliation. One who is ashamed redeems himself by successful achievement, but one subject to authority guilt wants to be forgiven and to have the previous relation restored. In these various inclinations and their expression are shown the feelings of guilt. Their absence would manifest an absence of love and trust.

IV

The second part of the psychological construction describes the generation of association guilt. The setting of this form of guilt involves the participation in a joint activity of those who regard themselves as associates. These joint activities may take various forms from social institutions proper to games. I assume it is known to all the participants that the rules defining the scheme of co-operation do in fact satisfy the two principles of justice and I also suppose that the derivation of these principles, as given in the analytic construction, is understood. This knowledge may be more or less intuitive, but I assume that these facts are nevertheless known.

Now let us suppose that, given a system of joint activity meeting these conditions—perhaps some scheme of economic co-operation—the participants are bound by ties of friendship and mutual trust, and rely on one another to do their part. I suppose that these feelings have been generated in any given person by his participating in the activity itself. I assume as a second psychological law that if a person's capacity for fellow-feeling has been realized in accordance with the first law, then, where another, engaged with him in a joint activity known to satisfy the two principles, with evident intention lives up to his duty of fair play, friendly feelings toward him develop as well as feelings of trust and mutual confidence. (One may suppose the participants introduced into the scheme one by one over a period of time, and in this way acquiring these feelings as the others fulfill their duty of fair play.) So if participants in a joint enterprise regularly act with evident intention in accordance with their duty of fair play, they will tend to acquire ties of friendship and mutual trust.

Now given these feelings and relations against the background of a scheme of co-operation known to satisfy the stated conditions, if a person fails to do his part he will experience feelings of association guilt. These feelings will show themselves in various ways: in the inclination to make good the loss to others (reparation) and to admit what one has done and to apologize; in the inclination to ask for reinstatement and to acknowledge and to accept reproofs and penalties; and in a diminished ability to be angry with others should they likewise fail to do their part. The absence of such inclinations would betray the absence of ties of friendship and relations of mutual trust. It would manifest a capacity to associate with others in disregard of those principles which one knows would be mutually acknowledged. It would show that one had no qualms about the losses inflicted on others (or gains taken from them) as a consequence of one's own acts, and that one was not troubled by the breaches of mutual confidence by which others are deceived. If there are ties of friendship and mutual trust, there exist these various inhibitions and reactions to failing to do one's part. If these inhibitions and reactions are lacking, one has at best only a show of fellow-feeling and mutual trust.

It may be observed that the effect of the second psychological law and the attitudes generated by it play an important part in maintaining schemes of co-operation known to satisfy the two principles of justice (stated in Section II). For such schemes are liable to at least two types of instability. Instability of the first kind is present when, if any one person knows that the others will do their part, it will be worth his while not to do his: the consequences of one person's not doing his part if others do theirs may go unnoticed, or may have no ostensible effect, so that an alternative use of one's time and effort is a personal gain. Such a system of co-operation is unstable: each is tempted to depart from it if he thinks others will keep it going. Since each is aware of another's temptation, mutual trust is in danger of breaking down. Instability of the second kind is present when it is the case that if any one person knows or reasonably supposes that others will not do their part, it will be worth his while to be the first, or among the first, not to do his, or even dangerous for him not to be. These two kinds of instability are related in that if the first kind obtains, then one may think that others will not do their part, and this may bring about instability of the second kind. Where both kinds are present the scheme of co-operation is fragile and participants are moved to withdraw, or even to be afraid not to. (Disarmament schemes are subject to instability of both kinds.) Hobbes seems to have been the first to place the problem of such unstable situations at the center of the question of political obligation. One way of interpreting the Hobbesian sovereign is as an agency added to unstable systems of co-operation in such a way that it is no longer to anyone's advantage not to do his part given that others will do theirs. By keeping watch and enforcing sanctions, the sovereign acts to inhibit violations and to restore the system when violations occur; and the belief in the sovereign's efficacy removes instability of both kinds.

Now relations of friendship and mutual trust have a similar effect. Once a system of co-operation satisfying the stated conditions is set up and a period of uncertainty survived, the passage of time renders it more stable, given an evident intention on the part of all to do their part. The generation of feelings of friendship and mutual trust tends to reinforce the scheme of co-operation. A greater temptation is required and, should violations occur, the feelings of guilt, shown in wishing to make reparation and the like, will tend to restore the broken relations. Thus not only may such a system of co-operation be stable in the sense that when each man thinks the others will do their part there is no tendency for him not to do his; it may be inherently stable in the sense that the persistence of the scheme generates, in accordance with the second psychological law, inclinations which further support it. The effect, then, of relations of friendship and mutual trust is analogous to the role of the sovereign; only in this case it is the consequence of a certain psychological principle of human nature in such systems, and of the implications of the generated attitudes.

V

The third part of the psychological construction concerns principle guilt. In both the previous forms of guilt I have supposed it to be connected with an actual natural attitude toward certain particular persons: with authority guilt these persons are parents, and in association guilt they are fellow-associates. Very often, however, we feel guilty for doing something when those injured or put at a disadvantage are not persons with whom we are tied by any form of particular fellow-feeling. To account for feelings of guilt of this kind—principle guilt—I assume a third psychological law as follows: given that the attitudes of love and trust, friendly feelings and mutual respect, have been generated in accordance with the two previous psychological laws, then, if a person (and his associates) are the beneficiaries of a successful and enduring institution or scheme of co-operation known to satisfy the two principles of justice, he will acquire a sense of justice. This will show itself in at least two ways: first, in an acceptance of those particular institutions which are just (as defined by the two principles) and from which he and his associates have benefited. This acceptance of particular institutions shows itself in feeling guilty for infractions which harm other persons even though these persons are not the objects of any particular fellow-feelings. It may be that they have not yet had sufficient opportunity to show an evident intention of doing their part, and so are not yet the object of such feelings by the second law. Or it may be that the institution is too large to allow occasion for such particular ties to be established. The sense of justice will manifest itself second in a willingness to work for (or at least not to oppose) the setting up of just institutions, or for the reform of existing ones where justice requires it. Guilt feelings associated with the sense of justice are characterized as principle guilt feelings since in their explanation reference is made to principles, in this case to principles of justice. These principle guilt feelings spring from breaches of institutions accepted as satisfying the principles of justice, or from resistance to reforms which those principles are seen to require.

Principle guilt is, then, connected with the acceptance of the principles of justice. It represents a step beyond the understanding of their derivation which is all that is presupposed by association guilt. One might say that principle guilt is guilt proper. It is, as the two previous forms of guilt were not, a complete moral feeling. For this reason authority and association guilt should be spoken of with the prefixed adjective. They are not, as defined, complete moral feelings although they include many of the characteristic aspects of moral feelings. Once the full development to principle guilt has taken place, however, and the principles of justice which specify the conditions of association guilt are accepted, then the infractions which gave rise to association guilt will be guilt proper; for now the reference to the accepted principle is given in a person's explanation of his feeling. Furthermore, where the ties of natural attitudes are present in the form of friendship and mutual trust, the feelings of guilt will be greater than where they are absent. The transmuted association guilt will reinforce principle guilt. If one assumes that an appropriate guilt feeling—that is, one based on true beliefs concerning what one has done—implies a fault, and that a greater feeling of guilt implies a greater fault, one can infer that conduct giving rise to association guilt feelings is wrong. Thus all the violations of the natural attitudes generated by association—in particular friendship, affection, and mutual trust—are wrong.

The sense of justice helps to maintain schemes of co-operation just as the natural attitudes of friendship and trust do. The acceptance of the principles of justice implies, failing a special explanation, an avoidance of their violation and a recognition that advantages gained in conflict with them are without value; and should such violations nevertheless occur, in cases of temptation, feelings of guilt will tend to restore joint activity. To grasp this fact, one has only to consider the variety of inclinations and inhibitions in which these feelings are expressed. A system in which each person has, and is known by everyone to have, a sense of justice is inherently stable. Other things being equal, the forces making for its stability increase as time passes. (It may nevertheless break down at a later time if outside elements make for increasingly greater temptations.) This inherent stability is a direct consequence of the reciprocal relation between the second and third psychological laws. The psychological construction as a whole is consistent and self-reinforcing: it is intrinsically stable. To explain this properly one would have to bring the institutions constituting the setting for authority guilt under the regulation of the principles of justice, but there is no insuperable difficulty in this.

VI

It is evident that the foregoing psychological construction relies heavily on the concept of a moral feeling. It will prove useful to make a brief digression and to discuss the main features of this concept. These features may be given by considering the chief questions which must be asked in examining the concepts of the various moral feelings.

There are, first, such questions as: (a) what are the various linguistic expressions which are used to give voice to the having of a particular moral feeling, and the significant variations, if any, between the expressions for different feelings? (b) what are the characteristic behavioral manifestations of a particular moral feeling, and what are the ways in which a person characteristically betrays how he feels? (c) what are the characteristic sensations and kinesthetic feelings, if any, which go with a given moral feeling? When a person is angry, for example, he may feel hot; he may tremble and feel a tightening in his stomach; he may be unable to talk without his voice shaking; or he may be unable to suppress certain gestures. But if there are such characteristic sensations and behavioral manifestations for at least some moral feelings, these will not be, in any case, guilt, or shame, or whatever the feeling is. Such characteristic sensations and manifestations are neither necessary nor sufficient in particular instances for someone to feel guilty or ashamed. This is not to deny that some characteristic sensations and behavioral manifestations of disturbance may be necessary if one is overwhelmed by feelings of guilt, or if one is intensely ashamed. To feel guilty or ashamed it is often sufficient, however, that a person sincerely say that he feels guilty or ashamed, provided that he has the concept of guilt or of shame and that he is prepared to give an appropriate explanation of why he feels as he does.

This fact introduces perhaps the main question in examining the moral feelings, namely: (d) what is the definitive type of explanation required for having a given moral feeling, and how do these explanations differ from one feeling to another? Thus, when someone says that he feels guilty, what sort of explanation do we expect and within what limits? Certainly not any account is acceptable. Even such a phenomenon as neurotic guilt feelings, which is recognized as a deviation from the definitive case, is accepted as a kind of guilt feeling only because of the special kind of explanation accepted for these departures from the norm, and because it is supposed that a fuller psychological investigation will reveal the similarity with other guilt feelings. In general, it is a necessary condition and a defining feature of moral feelings that the person's explanation invokes a moral concept and its associated principle(s) and thereby makes a reference to an acknowledged right or a wrong. For example, a person feels guilty because he knows that he has taken more than his share and treated others unfairly, or a person feels ashamed because he has been cowardly and not spoken out. What distinguishes the different moral feelings are the principles and faults which their explanations typically invoke. The same act may give rise to both guilt and shame, say, if the person regards the action, as it is often possible to do, as each feeling requires. One who cheats may feel both guilty and ashamed: guilty because he has violated a trust and unfairly advanced himself, ashamed because by resorting to such means he admits his lack of ability and has given in to weakness. It may be remarked here that for a person to have a moral feeling it is not necessary that everything asserted in his explanation be true. A person may be in error, for example, in thinking that he has taken more than his share. He may not be guilty. But his explanation is in order since it is of the right sort and the beliefs it expresses are sincere.

Next, there is a group of questions concerning the bearing of the moral feelings on action. Thus, (e) what are the characteristic intentions, endeavors, and inclinations of a person having the feeling; what are the sorts of things he feels like doing, or feels unable to do? An angry person characteristically tries to strike back or to block the purposes of the person at whom he is angry. One who is plagued by authority guilt is disposed to reveal his fault and to attempt to set matters right by confession and reconciliation, whereas one who suffers from association guilt is inclined to admit what he has done and to ask for reinstatement, to acknowledge and to accept reproofs and penalties, and also he finds himself less able to be angry with others when they behave wrongly. Again, one can ask: (f) what feelings and responses does a person having the feeling expect on the part of other persons, and how does he anticipate that they will act toward him, as this is shown, say, in various characteristic distortions in his interpretation of others' conduct toward him? Also, (g) what are the characteristic temptations to actions giving rise to the given feeling and how characteristically is the feeling resolved or gotten rid of? Some such connections with action are also, in addition to an appropriate explanation, a necessary condition for having a moral feeling. (The last two questions have played little part in the construction which sets out the forms of guilt feeling, but they would be important, for example, in distinguishing feelings of guilt from feelings of shame.)

Finally, a question which I have emphasized is: (h) what, if any, is the natural basis of a moral feeling? There are two distinct kinds of questions involved here. One is: if a person, given his circumstances, fails to have a certain moral feeling, is there a natural attitude which would thereby be shown to be absent? The other is: if a person, given his circumstances, has a moral feeling, is there a natural attitude which would thereby be shown to be present? In presenting the psychological construction I have been concerned solely with the first kind of question. This construction provides a background for the second kind also, but I have left it entirely aside. Thus I have held that, in the context of the authority situation, the existence of love and trust for those in authority implies feelings of guilt for violating authoritative injunctions, and that the absence of such guilt feelings implies the absence of the natural attitudes of love and trust. Similarly, in the context of associative arrangements, the natural attitudes of friendship, affection, and mutual trust imply feelings of guilt for recognized violations of duties of fair play, and the absence of such guilt feelings implies an absence of the natural attitudes of friendship, affection, and mutual trust. These propositions are not, then, to be confused with their converses, which raise different problems altogether.

The thought here is that, by definition, a natural attitude and a moral feeling are both orderings of certain characteristic dispositions, and that the dispositions connected with the natural attitudes and those connected with the moral feelings are related, in such a way that the absence of certain moral feelings implies the absence of certain natural attitudes; or, alternatively, that the presence of certain natural attitudes implies a liability to certain moral feelings. These propositions are necessary truths: they hold in virtue of the relations between the concepts of the moral feelings and the natural attitudes. How this is so may be grasped from an example. If A loves B, then, failing a special explanation, A is afraid for B when B is threatened and tries to ward off the danger; and when C attacks B, A is angry with C and strives to prevent his attack from succeeding. Unless there are special circumstances, A is joyful when together with B, and when B suffers injury or dies, A is stricken with grief; and so on. Love is a sentiment—that is, among other things, a set of dispositions to experience and to manifest these primary emotions in a certain way. Now the necessary truths of the form mentioned above simply assert that the disposition to feel guilty in certain circumstances is just as much a defining feature of the natural attitude of love as the disposition to be joyful in the other's presence or to be sorrowful at his hurt.

For the argument to follow, the essential points about the moral feelings are these: (a) these feelings are not to be identified with characteristic sensations and behavioral manifestations, even if those exist, but must be understood as essentially including certain types of explanation and certain connections with conduct and natural attitudes; (b) these feelings presuppose the acceptance of certain moral principles which are invoked in their explanation, and in part what distinguish different feelings are the different principles occurring in these explanations; and (c) these feelings have necessary connections with certain natural attitudes such as love, affection, and mutual trust, and were a liability to these feelings completely absent there would be an absence also of these natural attitudes.

VII

Consider now the second question: namely, what accounts for men's acting on their duty of justice in particular cases? When they have a sense of justice, an answer is that they accept the principles of justice and regard themselves bound to act in accordance with schemes of co-operation which satisfy these principles when it comes their turn. This explanation is perfectly satisfactory. Moreover, it is often a sufficient reason for one's doing one's part that the principles of justice require it; or, more generally, that doing so is in accordance with principles which would be acknowledged in an original position of equal liberty. I should like, however, to view the second question in another way. I want to consider what follows from the assumption that certain persons would never act in accordance with their duty of justice except as reasons of self-interest and expediency dictate.

From what was said about association guilt it would follow that between any two such persons participating in a scheme of co-operation there are no ties of friendship and mutual trust. If such ties existed they would accept reasons other than those of expediency and self-interest for their acting fairly. This consequence is relatively obvious. But it also follows that, barring self-deception, these persons are incapable of feeling resentment and indignation toward another's actions as being unjust. If one of them cheats and deceives another, and this is found out, none of them has a ground for complaint. The injured cannot feel resentment; the others cannot feel indignation. They do not accept the principles of justice, and they experience no inhibitions from principle guilt feelings for breaches of their duty of fair play. Resentment and indignation are moral feelings. Resentment is our reaction to the injuries and harms which the wrongs of others inflict upon us, and indignation is our reaction to the injuries which the wrongs of others inflict on others. Both resentment and indignation require, then, an explanation which invokes a moral concept, say the concept of justice, and its associated principles and so makes a reference to a right or a wrong. In order to experience resentment and indignation one must accept the principles which specify these rights and wrongs. By hypothesis the members of this scheme neither accept these principles nor experience any inhibition from principle guilt feelings. Now to deny that these persons are capable of resentment and indignation is not to say that they might not be angry or annoyed with one another. A person without a sense of justice may be enraged at someone who fails to act fairly. But anger and annoyance are distinct from resentment and indignation; they are not, as resentment and indignation are, moral feelings. No doubt there are many behavioral similarities between these feelings: the emotional display in expression and gesture may sometimes be indistinguishable. Still, the explanation of the feeling will normally enable us to tell them apart.

One may say, then, that a person who lacks a sense of justice and who would never act as justice requires except as self-interest and expediency prompt, not only is without ties of friendship, affection, and mutual trust, but is incapable of experiencing resentment and indignation. Thus a person who lacks a sense of justice is also without certain natural attitudes and certain moral feelings of a particularly elementary kind. Put another way, one who lacks a sense of justice lacks certain fundamental attitudes and capacities included under the notion of humanity. Now the moral feelings are admittedly unpleasant, in some extended sense of unpleasant; but there is no way for us to avoid a liability to them without disfiguring ourselves. This liability is the price of love and trust, of friendship and affection, and of a devotion to institutions and traditions from which we have benefited and which serve the general interests of mankind. Moreover, as long as men are possessed of interests and aspirations of their own, as long as they are prepared in the pursuit of their own ends and ideals to press their claims on one another—that is, so long as the conditions giving rise to questions of justice obtain among them—it is inevitable that, given temptation and passion, this liability will be realized. (Since being moved by ends and ideals of excellence implies a liability to humiliation and shame, and an absence of a liability to humiliation and shame implies a lack of such ends and ideals, one can say of shame and humiliation also that they are a part of the notion of humanity.) Now the fact that one who lacks a sense of justice, and thereby a liability to guilt, lacks thereby certain fundamental attitudes and capacities included under the notion of humanity is not to be taken as a reason for acting as justice dictates. But this fact is an important truth. By understanding what it would be like not to have a sense of justice—that it would be to lack part of our humanity, too—we are led to understand our having this sense.

VIII

Consider now the first question: namely, to whom is the obligation of justice owed, that is, in regard to beings of what kind must we regulate our conduct by the principles of justice? Put another way, what qualifies a being as entitled to hold an initial position of equal liberty, so that in our dealings with him we are required to conduct ourselves in accordance with principles which could be acknowledged in such a position? The answer to this question is that it is necessary and sufficient that the being is capable of a sense of justice. This answer requires some explanation.

First I shall try to show that the capacity for a sense of justice is sufficient. The capacity for a sense of justice includes these capacities: to understand, at least in an intuitive way, the meaning and content of the principles of justice and their application to particular institutions; to understand, at least in an intuitive way, the derivation of these principles as indicated in the analytic construction; and to have the capacities of feeling, attitude, and conduct, mentioned in the three laws of the psychological construction. None of these capacities imposes conditions which are at all stringent, and I assume that they are satisfied to the required degree by the vast majority of mankind. Now the thought behind taking the capacity for a sense of justice as sufficient is that the principles of justice are characterized as those principles which persons could propose to one another for mutual acceptance in an original position of equal liberty. In this position it is assumed that there is an absence of information; in particular, it is assumed that the parties do not know their social position, nor do they know their peculiar talents and abilities—that is, their native assets. Briefly, they do not know how they have fared in the natural lottery. Nevertheless, in the original position, knowing the possibility (or allowing for it) of different native endowments, it is rational for them to acknowledge the two principles of justice. These principles require that any special benefits for those more fortunate in the natural lottery must be gained in ways which at the same time improve the condition of the less fortunate. The parties in the original positions are assumed to be moral persons abstracted from certain kinds of knowledge of themselves and their situation. Yet they have the capacity to understand and to give the undertaking which the analytic construction describes, and then to act on it: that is, they have the capacity expressed by the sense of justice. To say that the sense of justice is sufficient is to say, then, that the duty of justice is owed to those who could participate in the contractual situation of the original position and act on it. And, indeed, this is sufficient, for in the conception of justice of the analytic construction the consequences of the natural lottery are irrelevant in the original position. The unknown distribution of talents and abilities may, however, be exploited in accordance with principles which everyone in the original position would acknowledge.

Moreover, the capacity for a sense of justice need be possessed only to the extent required for participation in the original position. Certainly some persons have a greater capacity for a sense of justice than others. These persons may properly be placed in positions where the judicial virtues are especially fitting, but their superior capacity should be regarded as any other advantage in the natural lottery, the benefits from it being subject to the principles of justice. A special capacity for a sense of justice may qualify a man for certain offices, then, but assuming that a certain minimum is satisfied, these peculiar gifts are not a proper ground for establishing different grades of citizenship. The minimum is sufficient to share in the position of equal citizenship in a constitutional democracy.

To show that a capacity for a sense of justice is necessary is perhaps more difficult. One has a reluctance, moreover, to admit that this capacity is necessary, for one is averse to granting that any human being might not be owed the duty of justice. Yet if one holds that a capacity for a sense of justice is necessary and that a human being may lack this capacity, one allows for this possibility. But perhaps this reluctance is merely the aversion to admitting that any human being is incapable of a sense of justice. In any case, it seems almost certain that at least the vast majority of mankind have a capacity for a sense of justice and that, for all practical purposes, one may safely assume that all men originally possess it. It is plausible to suppose that any being capable of language is capable of the intellectual performances required to have a sense of justice; and, given these intellectual powers, the capacity for the natural attitudes of love and affection, faith and mutual trust, appears to be universal. There seems to be no doubt then that the minimum requisites for the development of a sense of justice are possessed by men as part of their original natural capacity, and it is this original capacity which is said to be necessary. It is another question entirely whether the duty of justice is owed to persons who, although they possessed the capacity originally, have lost it through no fault of their own: through illness or accident, or from experiencing such a deprivation of affection in childhood that their capacity for the natural attitudes has not developed properly.

The following considerations may show that a capacity for a sense of justice is necessary. First, it does not follow from a person's not being owed the duty of justice that he may be treated in any way that one pleases. We do not normally think of ourselves as owing the duty of justice to animals, but it is certainly wrong to be cruel to them. Their capacity for feeling pleasure and pain, for some form of happiness, is enough to establish this. To deny that this capacity is sufficient is not, then, to license everything. Other faults will still be possible, since the principles of humanity and liberality are more extensive in their application. On the other hand, something must account for animals not being owed the duty of justice, and a plausible explanation is their lack of the capacity for a sense of justice and the other capacities which this sense presupposes.

Again, one might say that the duty of justice is owed only to those who can complain of not being justly treated. Since, as previously argued, a person lacking a sense of justice cannot himself complain nor feel resentment if others do not act in regard to him as the principles of justice require, the duty of justice, it might be held, is not owed to him. This suggestion follows from the idea that if a person has a right to something, it must be that he can claim it and protest its not being given him. This idea is not incompatible with there being persons who claim rights for others in certain types of situations. For example, one thinks of guardians for children and of trustees for others' rights in special cases. In the instance of children, one supposes that the capacity for a sense of justice is there and only awaits development. Guardians must secure this development and they must decide for their wards in view of what a person is presumed to want and to claim once he reaches the age of reason. The case at hand, however, supposes that there never was nor will there ever be the capacity. If it is said that others might nevertheless complain, one could say that the duty, if there is one, is owed to them. In any case, the analytic construction excludes this possibility *qua* the initial position, so that accepting this basis of the necessity of a sense of justice would accord with that construction.

Finally, one may follow Kant in holding that a good will or, in the present case, a sense of justice is a necessary condition of the worthiness to be happy. One may hold that the sense of justice is a necessary part of the dignity of the person, and that it is this dignity which puts a value upon the person distinct from and logically prior to his capacity for enjoyment and his ability to contribute to the enjoyment of others through the development of his talents. It is because of this dignity that the conception of justice as fairness is correct in viewing each person as an individual sovereign, as it were, none of whose interests are to be sacrificed for the sake of a greater net balance of happiness but rather only in accordance with principles which all could acknowledge in an initial position of equal liberty. In the absence of a sense of justice on everyone's part, there would be, it might be said, no objection to the utilitarianism principle. In the absence of this capacity, the liability to pleasure and pain, to joy and sorrow, might be taken as alone relevant, and the greatest happiness principle would be entirely natural. Certainly in the absence of the capacity for a sense of justice no one could complain if the utilitarian principle were applied, and so the possession of a sense of justice is necessary for the conception of justice as fairness to hold. But lack of a sense of justice would undermine our capacity to identify ourselves with and to care about a society of such persons, if such a society could exist. We would not be moved by its injustices, since what they cannot resent and be indignant about among themselves we cannot resent and be indignant about for them. This is not to say that we might not be moved by the cruelties of such a society, but from the standpoint of justice, it would not be a society which aroused our moral feelings.

The capacity for a sense of justice is, then, necessary and sufficient for the duty of justice to be owed to a person — that is, for a person to be regarded as holding an initial position of equal liberty. This means that one's conduct in relation to him must be regulated by the principles of justice or, more generally, by the principles which rational and self-interested persons could acknowledge before one another in such a position. This conclusion may be contrasted with two other possible views. It is distinct from classical utilitarianism which holds that a capacity for pleasure and pain, for joy and sorrow, is sufficient for being a full subject of rights. The conclusion is also distinct from an aristocratic ethic which takes as necessary certain attributes and capacities such as strength, beauty, and superior intelligence, and which would impose the requirement of initial equality only within the same rank and allow original inequalities between superior and lower ranks. Such an aristocratic doctrine can only be maintained, I think, if one assumes a specific obligation on the parties in the original position: namely, the obligation to develop human persons of a certain style and aesthetic grace, or the obligation to the pursuit of knowledge and the cultivation of the arts, or both. I cannot discuss here the propriety of this assumption, or whether if it were accepted it would justify the inequalities commonly associated with aristocracy. It suffices to say that in the analytic construction no such obligation is assumed. The sole constraints imposed are those expressed in the formal elements of the concept of morality, and the only circumstances assumed are those exhibiting the conflicts of claims which give rise to questions of justice. The natural consequence of this construction is that the capacity for the sense of justice is the fundamental aspect of moral personality in the theory of justice.

Gerhart Piers and
Milton B. Singer
Shame

A. Structure of Shame

We realize then that most previous authors consider shame a **147** comparatively insignificant emotion or anxiety, more or less a result of conflicts over sexual strivings, usually in the particular form of exhibitionism. Only Erikson and Alexander ascribe to shame an importance equal to "guilt" in human pathology.

In the following I shall attempt to describe the differences between the two even sharper, both phenomenologically and dynamically.

To start with, I suggest, by way of definition, a structural description of shame which will then be discussed in more detail in the following chapters.

The following seem to me properties of Shame which clearly differentiate it from Guilt:

(1) Shame arises out of a tension between the Ego and the Ego-Ideal, not between Ego and Super-Ego as in guilt.

(2) Whereas guilt is generated whenever a boundary (set by the Super-Ego) is touched or transgressed, shame occurs when a goal (presented by the Ego-Ideal) is not being reached. It thus indicates a real "shortcoming." Guilt anxiety accompanies transgression; shame, failure.

(3) The unconscious, irrational threat implied in shame anxiety is abandonment and not mutilation (castration) as in guilt.

(4) The Law of Talion does not obtain in the development of shame, as it generally does in guilt.

Several of the terms used here require further elaboration. An attempt will then be made to validate the entire thesis through observations of both normal and clinical phenomena.

Reprinted from *Shame and Guilt, A Psychoanalytic and Cultural Study* by Gerhart Piers, M.D., and Milton B. Singer, Ph.D. By permission of W. W. North & Company, Inc. Copyright 1953 by Charles C Thomas. Copyright © 1971 by W. W. Norton & Company, Inc. Footnotes have been deleted. The author of parts A and B is Dr. Piers, and Professor Singer is the author of part C.

B. Ego-Ideal and Super-Ego

I have suggested that Shame represents a tension between Ego and Ego-Ideal, rather than between Ego and Super-Ego. It seems immaterial whether one wishes to regard the Ego-Ideal merely as one particular aspect of the Super-Ego, or as a psychological formation entirely separate and independent from the latter. In *The Ego and the Id,* (1923) Freud uses both terms interchangeably throughout. As is well known, he clearly describes them there as a "precipitate in the Ego from that sexual phase of development which was dominated by the Oedipus complex." However, in a different passage he adds that the Super-Ego is also a result of the prolonged helplessness and dependency of the human animal. He points out the two-facedness of the Super-Ego which not only exhorts the Ego to become like father, but also forbids to attempt certain things which are father's prerogative. Freud feels that this state of affairs has derived from the formidable task to repress the Oedipus complex. To achieve this — in deference to the Super-Ego — the Ego borrows strength from the Father as Ideal.

It should be possible to arrive at a greater clarity about the function of the Ego-Ideal as distinguished from the Super-Ego, since these two aspects of "superstructure" in the Ego have different — at times opposing — integrative tasks, and their respective generic sources, too, can be differentiated.

Firstly, the Ego-Ideal appears to contain *a core of narcissistic omnipotence.* The amount of it is, of course, subject to tremendous individual variation. Needless to say that a "too-much" makes for a great variety of pathological conditions with overinflated, grandiose or perfectionistic Ideals that put the Ego under unbearable tensions. But to maintain a minimum of primitive omnipotence seems to be necessary to establish such healthy, integrative functions as self-confidence, hope and trust in others. Possibly it also requires a minimum of magic belief in one's invulnerability or immortality to make for physical courage and to help counteract realistic fear of injury and death.

Secondly, the Ego-Ideal represents the sum of the *positive identifications* with the parental images. Both the loving, the reassuring parent, the parent who explicitly and implicitly gives the permission to become like him, and the narcissistically expecting parent and the parent who imposes his own unobtained ideals on the child, may be represented here.

Thirdly, the Ego-Ideal contains layers of *later identifications,* more superficial, to be sure, and more subject to change than the earlier ones, but of the greatest social importance. The "social role" that an individual assumes in any given social situation, is largely determined by the structure of these developmentally later parts of his Ego-Ideal. There is a continuous psychological interchange between the individual Ego-Ideal and its projections in the form of collective Ideals. It is important to recognize that the images that go into the formation of this part of the Ego-Ideal do not have to be parental ones at all. The sibling group and the peer group are much more significant.

Fourthly, the Ego-Ideal is in continuous dynamic interfunction with the unconscious and conscious *awareness of the Ego's potentialities.* This part of the Ego-Ideal must contain the *goals* of what has been variously termed "instinct of mastery," "mastery principle," etc. A better term for what I have in mind might be "maturation drive." It would signify a psychic representation of all the growth, maturation and individuation processes in the human being, beginning with the most primitive organizational functions made possible by the progressive myelinization of the nervous system in infancy up to those highly complex functions that strive for what is somewhat romantically referred to as self-realization. As far as I can see, nobody has better envisioned the far-reaching meaning of the "maturation drive" (without naming it such) nor described it more beautifully than the phenomenologist, *Erwin Straus,* in an essay *Die aufrechte Haltung.* The successful exertion of this "maturation drive" in accordance with the Ego-Ideal is accompanied by a sense of pleasure which *Karl Buehler* has termed "Funktionslust" — the pleasure experienced in and through one's own well-functioning. This "lust" is of course essentially a "narcissistic," not a libidinous one, although sexual pleasure ideally combines both.

It will be clearer now why I prefer to use the more inclusive term "shame" rather than "inferiority feelings." The latter term implies comparison with external figures, hence does not quite express this completely internalized tension between Ego and Ego-Ideal. The two terms stand in somewhat similar relationship to each other as "guilt feelings" and "fear of punishment." Also, "inferiority feeling" does not well describe that particular inner tension which stems from failure to reach one's own potentialities.

It will be equally clear now that we mean by "shame" something quite different from "sexual shame." It is related to what *Hegel* must have had in mind when he wrote: "Shame does not mean to be ashamed of loving, say on account of exposing or surrendering the body . . . but to be ashamed that love is not complete, that . . . there still be something inimical in oneself which keeps love from reaching completion and perfection."

Shame then occurs whenever goals and images presented by the Ego-Ideal are not reached. If shame can reach such a degree that it appears as conscious anxiety it must imply a severe unconscious threat to the Ego. This threat, however, is not the fear of the wrath of the parental images, or in other words, fear of annihilation or mutilation proferred as punishment by the Super-Ego under the Talion principle. Behind the feeling of shame stands not the fear of hatred, but the fear of *contempt* which, on an even deeper level of the unconscious, spells fear of *abandonment,* the death by emotional starvation. The parent who uses as educational tools the frequent exposure of the child's immaturity ("Look how foolish, dumb, clumsy you are!") will be the one to lay the foundation of such fear of contempt. We suspect, however, that the deeper rooted shame anxiety is based on the fear of the parent who walks away "in disgust," and that this anxiety in turn draws its terror from the earlier established and probably ubiquital separation anxiety.

Withdrawal of love can be a threat only from positive images. It is as if the loved parental images, or the projected power and life sustaining sources of one's own omnipotence threaten to abandon the weakling who fails to reach them. Accordingly, on a higher, social and more conscious level of individual development, it is again not fear of active punishment by superiors which is implied in shame anxiety, but social expulsion, like ostracism. *Fenichel* was, therefore, right when he, although still assuming that shame was the specific reaction to scoptophilia, suspected that it was not just a fear of the "evil eye," i.e., a peculiar form of castration anxiety. Indeed, it is not the malevolently destructive eye, but the all-seeing, all-knowing eye which is feared in the condition of shame, God's eye which reveals all shortcomings of mankind. . . .

C. Internal vs. External Sanctions

The prevailing criterion for distinguishing shame and guilt cultures has been the distinction between external and internal sanctions. If a culture depends primarily on external sanctions, it is considered to be a shame culture; whereas if it depends on internal sanctions it is a guilt culture. This does not necessarily imply that shame is the only form of external sanction, or guilt the only form of internal sanction, but the assumption is made that shame and guilt are the principal representatives of external and internal sanctions respectively.

An early and influential development of this approach will be found in Margaret Mead's *Cooperation and Competition among Primitive Peoples*. This is a series of individual studies of 13 primitive cultures, a landmark in the comparative method of testing generalizations about human nature by cross-cultural comparison of similar material. While the major interest of the study is in cooperation and competition, a good deal of attention is also devoted to the formation of character by cultural agencies, and it is in this context that the systematic survey of internal and external sanctions occurs.

Mead defines *sanctions* as "mechanisms by which conformity is obtained, by which desired behavior is induced and undesired behavior prevented." If the individual child "so internalizes the standards that he obeys them in the absence of force exerted from the outside," then he is obeying *internal sanctions.* And "once these are established within the character of the individual they operate automatically." As examples of the operation of internal sanctions, Mead cites obeying a taboo for fear of death or disease, or abstaining from illicit sex activities for fear of punishment by the ghosts.

If, on the other hand, the growing individual has not so internalized his culture's standards, but responds only to "forces which must be set in motion by others"—such as ridicule, abuse, execution of a royal decree—then he is responding to *external sanctions.*

The major internal sanctions found among the 13 primitive cultures are guilt, anxiety over loss of love, anxiety over loss of health, fear of loss of strength, fear of being shamed, fear of loss of status, anxiety over failure to achieve, pride, fear of offending against the system, and the sense of one's own position, which must be kept inviolate.

The major external sanctions are withdrawal of health and affection by members of the group, sorcery and accusation of sorcery, threat of starvation, threat of death, punishment of person, destruction of offender's property, expulsion, threat of force, public shaming, divesting of reputation, ritual scolding and ridicule, a well enforced judicial system, and the public invocation of some of the internal sanctions of guilt and pride.

These lists of internal and external sanctions are not, however, a sufficient clue to the classification of the 13 cultures as shame or guilt cultures. Only two of the 13—the Manus and the Arapesh—are classified as guilt cultures, with character structures roughly similar to the Western European. The use of shame as a principal external sanction is said to be characteristic of all the North American Indian cultures. The remaining cultures using combinations of internal and external sanctions—and occasionally the power of central authority—are not explicitly classified as either shame or guilt cultures.

In Mead's tabulated lists of sanctions, shame appears as an internal sanction in the form of "fear of being shamed," as well as an external sanction in the form of shaming, ridicule, etc. Why then is not shame considered to be as much of an internal sanction as guilt? To this question Mead gives two answers: (1) shame may become an internal sanction when it is strongly developed; and (2) shame requires an audience who know about the misdeed, whereas guilt operates in the psyche without an audience. "In societies in which the individual is controlled by fear of being shamed, he is safe if no one knows of his misdeeds; he can dismiss his misbehavior from his mind . . . but the individual who feels guilt must repent and *atone* for his *sin*." "Guilt is a response to a past threat . . . which seems to be internalized in the character, and reenactment of analogous situations throughout life invokes the earlier fears and makes it necessary to establish the internal balance of the personality."

This obviously complicates the difference between internal and external sanctions as a criterion for distinguishing shame and guilt cultures, since it adds to that criterion three others: the strength of development of the shame sanctions, the presence or absence of an audience, and the age at which the sanction is internalized. But these qualifications will not suffice to distinguish shame from guilt sanctions. In the tabulated sanctions for the different cultures, shame as an internal sanction appears whenever shaming as an external sanction is listed. So in about seven of these cultures, shame is strongly enough developed to have become an internal sanction. Where it has become an internal sanction, cannot fear of being shamed operate as a sanction even in the absence of an audience? Can it be so easily dismissed from the mind if no audience is physically present? In a recent paper Mead notes that shame has sometimes been "internalized to such an extent that an Indian alone in the middle of a lake could be so shamed by his paddle breaking that he would commit suicide." Does this not suggest that feelings of shame may be aroused in the absence of an audience?

Perhaps shame does not require that an audience be present physically, but only in phantasy; perhaps the Indian canoeist thought of what people would say when he got back. This is, of course, a common experience: in prospective and retrospective phantasies we anticipate or remember humiliating experiences and feel ashamed. George Bernard Shaw tells in his autobiography of having felt so humiliated by an incident in his childhood that he was not able to master his shame over it and tell anyone about it until he was an old man. But this is not confined to shame, for in feelings of remorse and in apprehensions of discovery and punishment we also experience a kind of guilt which requires a reference to an audience. Even Kant's categorical imperative contains a reference to the audience of all rational men. It is not the presence of an audience (actual or imaginary) which is decisive for distinguishing shame from guilt. Both shame and guilt may be experienced in the actual presence of an audience or when the audience is present only as an internalized "other" (H. S. Sullivan's "eidetic other," G. H. Mead's "me" and "generalized other"). Robinson Crusoe was as much dominated by inner shame as he was by guilt.

That there are forms of guilt dependent on an audience and in this respect resembling the fear of being shamed may be granted, but it may be argued that this does not yet take account of genuine guilt feelings—the unconscious sense of guilt—which is experienced in solitude and contains no conscious or realistic reference to an audience, punishment, or misdeeds. Is this not perhaps the decisive point of difference from shame? The unconscious sense of guilt which produces a restless anxiety pressing for punishment of the individual without any realistic basis has, I suppose, been often enough observed by psychoanalysts to be taken for a fact. Their theory, too, that this sense of guilt derives from hostile feelings acquired in childhood towards punitive parents seems plausible enough. In this meaning, guilt is an internalized response to a past threat—as Margaret Mead calls it. But I do not think that guilt differs from shame even in this respect, for as Piers so well points out, there is also an unconscious form of shame. This form of inner shame may also be without any conscious reference to an audience, and need involve only the anxiety of failing to live up to one's ideals. It, too, may be regarded as an internalized response to a past threat, but what has been internalized are the ideals of the loving parents and the past threat unconsciously reactivated is abandonment by those loving parents and loss of their love.

The practical conclusion of this discussion is that we cannot distinguish shame and guilt in terms of external and internal sanctions respectively, for there are "inner" forms of shame paralleling almost exactly the forms of guilt. Nor can we save the internal-external criterion by saying that shame requires an audience and guilt does not, or that guilt involves a reenactment of a childhood response and shame does not, for these additional criteria will only serve to differentiate among the forms of shame and among the forms of guilt but not to distinguish shame from guilt. Excessive reliance on the internal-external criterion for distinguishing shame from guilt, and the failure to develop more adequate criteria, has in the past been responsible for a number of confusions in the attempts to use shame and guilt sanctions as a basis for classifying cultures. Some of the most common of these are the identification of inner shame with guilt; the failure to see that "internal" sanctions like fear of loss of status and position, and anxiety over failure to achieve, and over loss of love and pride, are very closely related to shame sanctions (recognizing this might change the classification of Manus and Arapesh from guilt to shame cultures); the confusion of conscious and unconscious guilt; and the practically universal assumption that the presence of "shaming," ridicule, and other forms of insult imply a shame culture, despite the fact that such "external" sanctions might generate guilt and are not in any case necessary for arousing shame. These confusions have combined to encourage the emphasis on the external side of shame and on the internal side of guilt, an emphasis congenial to the notion that most cultures of the world use shame as an external sanction and have yet not advanced to the internal moral sanctions characteristic of our own culture. There is little question that the classification of cultures into shame and guilt cultures would have to be substantially changed once we abandoned the internal-external sanction criterion. We might lose a neat classification but we should gain much greater understanding of the role of shame and guilt in different cultures.

Erik H. Erikson

Autonomy *v.*
Shame and Doubt

In describing the growth and the crises of the human person as a series of alternative basic attitudes such as trust *v.* mistrust, we take recourse to the term a 'sense of', although, like a 'sense of health', or a 'sense of being unwell', such 'senses' pervade surface and depth, consciousness and the unconscious. They are, then, at the same time, ways of *experiencing* accessible to introspection; ways of *behaving,* observable by others; and unconscious *inner states* determinable by test and analysis. It is important to keep these three dimensions in mind, as we proceed.

Muscular maturation sets the stage for experimentation with two simultaneous sets of social modalities: holding on and letting go. As is the case with all of these modalities, their basic conflicts can lead in the end to either hostile or benign expectations and attitudes. Thus, to hold can become a destructive and cruel retaining or restraining, and it can become a pattern of care: to have and to hold. To let go, too, can turn into an inimical letting loose of destructive forces, or it can become a relaxed 'to let pass' and 'to let be'.

Outer control at this stage, therefore, must be firmly reassuring. The infant must come to feel that the basic faith in existence which is the lasting treasure saved from the rages of the oral stage, will not be jeopardized by this about-face of his, this sudden violent wish to have a choice, to appropriate demandingly, and to eliminate stubbornly. Firmness must protect him against the potential anarchy of his as yet untrained sense of discrimination, his inability to hold on and to let go with discretion. As his environment encourages him to 'stand on his own feet', it must protect him against meaningless and arbitrary experiences of shame and of early doubt.

The latter danger is the one best known to us. For if denied the gradual and well-guided experience of the autonomy of free choice (or if, indeed, weakened by an initial loss of trust) the child will turn against himself all his urge to discriminate and to manipulate. He will overmanipulate himself, he will develop a precocious conscience. Instead of taking possession of things in order to test them by purposeful repetition, he will become obsessed by his own repetitiveness. By such obsessiveness, of course, he then learns to repossess the environment and to gain power by stubborn and minute control, where he could not find large-scale mutual regulation. Such hollow victory is the infantile model for a compulsion neurosis. It is also the infantile source of later attempts in adult life to govern by the letter, rather than by the spirit.

Shame is an emotion insufficiently studied, because in our civilization it is so early and easily absorbed by guilt. Shame supposes that one is completely exposed and conscious of being looked at: in one word, self-conscious. One is visible and not ready to be visible; which is why we dream of shame as a situation in which we are stared at in a condition of incomplete dress, in night attire, 'with one's pants down'. Shame is early expressed in an impulse to bury one's face, or to sink, right then and there, into the ground. But this, I think, is essentially rage turned against the self. He who is ashamed would like to force the world not to look at him, not to notice his exposure. He would like to destroy the eyes of the world. Instead he must wish for his own invisibility. This potentiality is abundantly used in the educational method of 'shaming' used so exclusively by some primitive peoples. Visual shame precedes auditory guilt, which is a sense of badness to be had all by oneself when nobody watches and when everything is quiet—except the voice of the superego. Such shaming exploits an increasing sense of being small, which can develop only as the child stands up and as his awareness permits him to note the relative measures of size and power.

Too much shaming does not lead to genuine propriety but to a secret determination to try to get away with things, unseen—if, indeed, it does not result in defiant shamelessness. There is an impressive American ballad in which a murderer to be hanged on the gallows before the eyes of the community, instead of feeling duly chastened, begins to berate the onlookers, ending every salvo of defiance with the words, 'God damn your eyes.' Many a small child, shamed beyond endurance, may be in a chronic mood (although not in possession of either the courage or the words) to express defiance in similar terms. What I mean by this sinister reference is that there is a limit to a child's and an adult's endurance in the face of demands to consider himself, his body, and his wishes as evil and dirty, and to his belief in the infallibility of those who pass such judgement. He may be apt to turn things around, and to consider as evil only the fact that they exist: his chance will come when they are gone, or when he will go from them.

Doubt is the brother of shame. Where shame is dependent on the consciousness of being upright and exposed, doubt, so clinical observation leads me to believe, has much to do with a consciousness of having a front and a back—and especially a 'behind'. For this reverse area of the body, with its aggressive and libidinal focus in the sphincters and in the buttocks, cannot be seen by the child, and yet it can be dominated by the will of others. The 'behind' is the small being's dark continent, an area of the body which can be magically dominated and effectively invaded by those who would attack one's power of autonomy and who would designate as evil those products of the bowels which were felt to be all right when they were being passed. This basic sense of doubt in whatever one has left behind forms a substratum for later and more verbal forms of compulsive doubting; this finds its adult expression in paranoiac fears concerning hidden persecutors and secret persecutions threatening from behind (and from within the behind).

This stage, therefore, becomes decisive for the ratio of love and hate, cooperation and wilfulness, freedom of self-expression and its suppression. From a sense of self-control without loss of self-esteem comes a lasting sense of good will and pride; from a sense of loss of self-control and of foreign overcontrol comes a lasting propensity for doubt and shame.

If, to some reader, the 'negative' potentialities of our stages seem overstated throughout, we must remind him that this is not only the result of a preoccupation with clinical data. Adults, and seemingly mature and unneurotic ones, display a sensitivity concerning a possible shameful 'loss of face' and fear of being attacked 'from behind' which is not only highly irrational and in contrast to the knowledge available to them, but can be of fateful import if related sentiments influence, for example, interracial and international policies.

We have related basic trust to the institution of religion. The lasting need of the individual to have his will reaffirmed and delineated within an adult order of things which at the same time reaffirms and delineates the will of others has an institutional safeguard in the *principle of law and order.* In daily life as well as in the high courts of law—domestic and international—this principle apportions to each his privileges and his limitations, his obligations and his rights. A sense of rightful dignity and lawful independence on the part of adults around him gives to the child of good will the confident expectation that the kind of autonomy fostered in childhood will not lead to undue doubt or shame in later life. Thus the sense of autonomy fostered in the child and modified as life progresses, serves (and is served by) the preservation in economic and political life of a sense of justice.

Helen Merrell Lynd
The Nature
of Shame

In this chapter I shall attempt to enter further into the nature of **159**
the feeling of shame. I am not trying to build up any logical, or
perhaps even consistent, definition of shame. Rather, I shall
approach the feeling of shame from different directions and in
different ways, and present situations that have been described
by various writers as giving rise to a sense of shame. This assumes that there are some common characteristics of the feelings of shame that may occur in a variety of circumstances, and
possibly some common characteristics among these diverse
circumstances.

The different aspects or characteristics of shame, mentioned
separately for purposes of examination, are so intermeshed with
each other that each can be fully perceived and understood only
within the context of the whole experience.

Exposure, Particularly Unexpected Exposure

Experiences of shame appear to embody the root meaning of
the word—to uncover, to expose, to wound. They are experiences
of exposure, exposure of peculiarly sensitive, intimate, vulnerable
aspects of the self. The exposure may be to others but, whether
others are or are not involved, it is always, as will be shown more
fully below, exposure to one's own eyes.

The particular aspects of the self especially vulnerable to exposure differ in different cultures.[1] Adam and Eve felt shame in

From *On Shame and the Search for Identity,* © 1958, by Helen Merrell Lynd.
Reprinted by permission of Harcourt Brace Jovanovich, Inc. The editor has re-
numbered footnotes.

[1] The terms culture and society are sometimes used by anthropologists and other
social scientists as virtually synonymous, and writers who do differentiate them have
no common usage. I use the two terms . . . [here] in ways that do not require fine
distinctions between them. In general, I use society for the organized institutions
of a social group that constitute its functioning and provide for its survival as a
group; culture for the shared, learned traditions of a group that are passed on from
one generation to the next. But in some places it seems appropriate to use culture
in the wider anthropological sense that includes both the functioning society and
its traditions.

becoming aware of their own nakedness. Throughout our Western civilization shame is related to the uncovering of nakedness. The terms *Scham* and *Schamgefühl* in German carry the implication of uncovered nudity, and *Scham* is part of the compound words referring particularly to the genitals.

In other societies shame may be more related to exposure while eating, to exposure of certain kinds of contact with kinfolk or with certain kinfolk, to exposure in initiation ceremonies or other stylized rituals surrounded with special sanctions, and to a whole range of patterns of social intercourse and social custom that it does not occur to us to cover up. This would suggest that there is a recognizable feeling of shame that arises in different societies, although the particular aspects of the self related to that feeling and the situations that give rise to it differ widely from one society to another.

Even within our own Western society there are wide individual differences as to what it is most shameful to have uncovered. For Philip in *Of Human Bondage*[2] it was his clubfoot, still more his feeling about allowing it to be exposed. For Virginia Woolf it was her writing and her ability, as a writer, to stand aside and observe the misery of others: "Is the time ever coming when I can endure to read my own writing in print without blushing — shivering and wishing to take cover?"[3] For Rousseau it was his lie accusing the maid of having stolen Mademoiselle Pontal's ribbon, which he himself had stolen.[4] For Kitty in *Anna Karenina* it was the open exposure of her love for Vronsky which was unreturned;[5] for Anna herself it was the secret recognition within herself of her love for Vronsky.[6] Dmitri Karamazov, on trial for murdering his father, suffered his greatest misery at having to take off his socks.

They were very dirty . . . and now everyone could see it. And what was worse he disliked his feet. All his life he had thought both his big toes hideous. He particularly loathed the coarse, flat, crooked nail on the right one, and now they would all see it. Feeling intolerably ashamed . . .[7]

[2] W. Somerset Maugham, *Of Human Bondage*, Modern Library, p. 47.

[3] Quoted in Aileen Pippett, *The Moth and the Star*, Little, Brown, 1955, pp. 108, 323–4.

[4] Rousseau, *Confessions*, Modern Library, pp. 88–9.

[5] Tolstoy, *Anna Karenina*, Modern Library, p. 95. (All page references to *Anna Karenina* are to the Modern Library edition, but in some cases Nathan Haskell Dole's and Louise and Aylmer Maude's translations are used when they seem more revealing than Constance Garnett's translation.)

[6] *Ibid.*, p. 119.

[7] Dostoyevsky, *The Brothers Karamazov*, Modern Library, p. 587.

Not wholly dissimilar was the experience of Mr. Pinkerton, the gray little amateur detective. All his life ashamed of penury, he preferred to be hanged for murder rather than to produce his alibi which would have involved the admission of mousy economy — that he had gone to a sixpenny rather than a shilling washroom. Freud pointed out that in some people shame may be excited less by feelings associated specifically with sex than by certain other feelings one is loath to admit to oneself.[8]

Closer examination of some of these experiences raises further questions about the nature of shame. For Rousseau, as for Dmitri Karamazov and for Mr. Pinkerton, exposure or fear of exposure to other persons certainly added to the sense of shame. But I think that this public exposure of even a very private part of one's physical or mental character could not in itself have brought about shame unless one had already felt within oneself, not only dislike, but shame for these traits. It is also true that if one discovered that one was not alone in having these traits shame would in one sense be alleviated by being shared; but if one still felt these characteristics as mean and ugly no matter how many people had them, shame would in another sense be extended.

Philip's exposure of his clubfoot also raises the question of the relation of exposure to others and to oneself. After the school bully had twisted his arm until Philip put his foot out of bed to let the boys see his clubfoot

Philip . . . had got his teeth in the pillow so that his sobbing should be inaudible. He was not crying for the pain they had caused him, nor for the humiliation he had suffered when they looked at his foot, but with rage at himself because, unable to stand the torture, he had put out his foot of his own accord.[9]

Exposure to others was less painful to Philip than the exposure to himself of his own weakness. This incident also raises the questions, discussed later, of the extent to which an experience of shame is the result of a voluntary action which one brings on oneself or something which comes on one from without, and of the importance of the element of the unexpected in shame. Both deliberate and involuntary action may be involved. Maugham does not say whether the yielding to pain came suddenly for Philip. But it is more than possible that the final giving in and showing of his foot was unexpected, and that each time it occurred it had an element of surprise as if it had happened wholly against his will.

[8] "A Child Is Being Beaten" (1919), *Collected Papers*, Vol. II, p. 172.
[9] *Of Human Bondage*, p. 47.

Anna Karenina lays bare wide varieties of shame experienced by very different kinds of people. In all of them, though other persons are sometimes present and involved, it is the exposure of oneself to oneself that is crucial. No one but Anna knew of her feelings as she recalled her encounters with Vronsky.

[*On the train returning from Moscow she*] *reviewed all her memories of her visit . . . they were all pleasant and good. She remembered the ball, she remembered Vronsky . . . she recalled all her relations with him; there was nothing to be ashamed of. But at the same time in these reminiscences the sense of shame kept growing stronger and stronger . . . that inward voice, whenever she thought of Vronsky, seemed to say: "Warmly, very warmly, passionately."*[10]

No one but Anna knew of the unmerited sharp reproof she gave to her dressmaker, nor of the shame it brought to her because she knew it resulted from her thoughts of Vronsky.[11] The shame that Anna and Vronsky felt after their first intercourse was shame that each felt differently and that was unshared.

. . . There was something horrible and revolting [*to each of them*] *in the memory of what had been bought at this fearful price of shame. The shame in the presence of their physical nakedness crushed her and took hold of him.*[12]

It was Anna alone who knew of her shame and alarm "at the new spiritual condition in which she found herself. She felt as though everything were beginning to be double in her soul."[13]

Levin felt not only the shame of rejection by Kitty, these "wounds that never healed," but also the shame known only to himself that followed a "fall" from chastity.[14] (This last is similar to the shame Philip felt in showing his clubfoot, a deliberate act which was, nevertheless, each time unexpected.) Kitty, recalling painfully to herself a year later the loving glance she had cast at Vronsky at the ball, said that she had acted "worse than badly,—shamefully."[15]

Dostoevski, who knew so many hidden aspects of shame, rec-

[10] *Anna Karenina*, p. 119.
[11] *Ibid.*, p. 131.
[12] *Ibid.*, p. 176.
[13] *Ibid.*, p. 342.
[14] *Ibid.*, p. 179.
[15] *Ibid.*, p. 263.

ognized that the deepest shame is exposure to oneself even though no one else may pay any attention to or even know of it.

Even in forty years I would remember with loathing and humiliation those filthiest, most ludicrous, and most awful moments in my life. No one could have gone out of his way to degrade himself more shamelessly.[16]

The Scarlet Letter, an unfolding of shame, does not fail to note that the deepest shame is not shame in the eyes of others but weakness in one's own eyes. Public exposure may even be a protection against this more painful inner shame. Dimmesdale said, "Happy are you, Hester, that wear the scarlet letter openly upon your bosom! Mine burns in secret!"[17] This raises the question of when public knowledge re-enforces and when it is an easing of shame known to oneself.

However much schools of psychoanalysis may differ in their explanations of fear of exposure, shame, humiliation, there can be no doubt of the extent to which shame operates in the analytic hour, nor of the intensification of shame if there is a lack of understanding, or any sign of contempt, on the part of the analyst. But, here again, shame is the outcome not only of exposing oneself to another person but of the exposure to oneself of parts of the self that one has not recognized and whose existence one is reluctant to admit.

There is a particularly deep shame in deceiving other persons into believing something about oneself that is not true. No one else knows of it; one has lied to oneself. This comes about in part because one doesn't know how to fit shame into the network of other emotions with which it is interwoven. It is closely associated with anger and bitterness, emotions that according to our code should be repressed, and may be turned against the self. Not knowing what should be done with shame one's first impulse is to conceal it, and this may produce further shame.

The exposure to oneself is at the heart of shame. In reviewing Stendhal's *Diaries,* Auden expressed surprise that Stendhal found it hard to admit certain things to himself and asked, "How can admitting anything to oneself be daring?"[18] In raising this remarkable question Auden reflects the extent to which many

[16] *Notes from the Underground* in *The Short Novels of Dostoevsky,* Dial Press, 1945, p. 184.

[17] Nathaniel Hawthorne, *The Scarlet Letter,* Houghton Mifflin, Riverside Press, p. 85. See also the reference to "the child of its father's guilt and its mother's shame." (*Ibid.,* p. 141.)

[18] W. H. Auden in the *New Yorker,* Dec. 18, 1954, pp. 142–3.

people at present have become insensitive to the experience of shame and to the deep ambiguities in human nature in which it is rooted.

More than other emotions, shame involves a quality of the unexpected; if in any way we feel it coming we are powerless to avert it. This is in part because of the difficulty we have in admitting to ourselves either shame or the circumstances that give rise to shame. Whatever part voluntary action may have in the experience of shame is swallowed up in the sense of something that overwhelms us from without and "takes us" unawares. We are taken by surprise, caught off guard, or off base, caught unawares, made a fool of. It is as if we were suddenly invaded from the rear where we cannot see, are unprotected, and can be overpowered.[19]

Kafka's *The Trial* is a study of the shame and bewilderment that may come from being taken by surprise, unprepared. "One is so unprepared," says K. He felt "the shame of being delivered into the hands of these people by his sudden weakness." " 'I don't know this law,' said K"; ". . . this unexpected question confused the man, which was the more deeply embarrassing as he was obviously a man of the world"; "One day—quite unexpectedly—some Judge will take up the documents . . . and order an immediate arrest."[20]

As in the case of Philip's suddenly giving in and showing his clubfoot, the phenomenon of unexpected yielding to physical and mental torture has been observed in the extreme conditions of concentration camps when persons felt the shame of being helpless and defeated, of being betrayed by their own bodies and minds.[21] ". . . victims of the Nazi inquisition have [said] that the moment of surrender occurred suddenly and against their will. For days they had faced the fury of their interrogators, and then suddenly they fell apart. 'All right, all right, you can have anything you want.' "[22]

---

[19] Cf. Paul Schilder on the importance of the image of one's own body, *Image and Appearance of the Human Body*, Kegan Paul, Trench, Trubner, 1935; Erikson, *Childhood and Society*, p. 224; and Kurt Goldstein's discussion of anxiety as something that "gets at us from the back . . . coming from no particular place," in "The Effect of Brain Damage On The Personality," *Psychiatry*, Vol. 15, No. 3, Aug. 1952, p. 256.

Cf. also James Rae, "On Shame," *Journal of Mental Science*, Vol. 62, No. 259, Oct. 1916, pp. 756–7: ". . . physical signs and accompaniments of shame . . . [show] a confusion of thought. . . . To exhibit the extreme of grief the Greek artist painted a curtain to conceal the face as if from shame at revealing emotion."

[20] Franz Kafka, *The Trial*, Knopf, 1937, pp. 27, 84, 10, 79, 199.

[21] See, for example, Agnes Keith, *Three Came Home*, Michael Joseph, 1948.

[22] Joost A. M. Meerloo, *The Rape of the Mind: The Psychology of Thought Control, Menticide, and Brainwashing*, World Publishing Co., 1956, p. 75. Cf. also *ibid.*, p. 91, and William Sargant, *Battle for the Mind: A Physiology of Conversion and Brain-washing*, Heinemann, 1957.

Blushing manifests the exposure, the unexpectedness, the involuntary nature of shame. One's feeling is involuntarily exposed openly in one's face; one is uncovered. With blushing comes the impulse to "cover one's face," "bury one's face," "sink into the ground." "When the heart's past hope the face is past shame," says a Scottish proverb.

This association of shame with involuntary exposure of the face appears in both the Old and the New Testaments.

They looked unto him, and were lightened: and their faces were not ashamed.[23]

[I] said, O my God, I am ashamed and blush to lift up my face to thee . . .[24]

Were they ashamed when they had committed abomination? Nay, they were not at all ashamed, neither could they blush . . .[25]

Shakespeare associates changes of color in the face with the uncovering of shame.

> *No, Plantagenet,*
> *'Tis not for fear but anger that thy cheeks*
> *Blush for pure shame to counterfeit our roses,*
> *And yet thy tongue will not confess thy error.*[26]
>
> *Thou changed and self-cover'd thing, for shame!*
> *Bemonster not thy feature!*[27]

Different as are the varieties of shame experienced by the different persons in *Anna Karenina*, all are accompanied by blushing.

"My words must make a deep impression on you, since you remember them so well," said Levin, and, suddenly conscious that he had said just the same thing before, he grew red in the face.[28]

"Oh, [my husband] doesn't even know," [Anna] said, and suddenly a hot flush came over her face; her cheeks, her brow, her neck crimsoned, and tears of shame came into her eyes.[29]

[23] Psalms 34:5.
[24] Ezra 9:6.
[25] Jeremiah 6:15.
[26] *Henry VI*, Part I, II, iv, 64–7.
[27] *King Lear*, IV, ii, 62–3.
[28] *Anna Karenina*, p. 62.
[29] *Ibid.*, p. 224.

On seeing [Anna, her husband] would have risen, but changed his mind, then his face flushed hotly—for the first time since Anna had known him he blushed, and he got up quickly and went to meet her, looking not at her eyes, but above them at her forehead and hair.[30]

The feeling of unexpectedness marks one of the central contrasts between shame and guilt. This unexpectedness is more than suddenness in time; it is also an astonishment at seeing different parts of ourselves, conscious and unconscious, acknowledged and unacknowledged, suddenly coming together, and coming together with aspects of the world we have not recognized.[31] Patterns of events (inner and outer) of which we are not conscious come unexpectedly into relation with those of which we are aware. In situations in which we feel guilty, choice, foresight, awareness in regard to a specific act are at least possible. Being taken unpleasantly by surprise, the impossibility of ordered behavior, the sudden sense of exposure, of being unable to deal with what is happening, characterize shame. It is as if a self of which we were not aware makes us unable to grasp the situation and to control what we do. In shame, says Erikson, one is conscious of being—when one is unprepared—exposed, looked at, all around.[32]

Incongruity or Inappropriateness

Being taken unawares is shameful when what is suddenly exposed is incongruous with, or glaringly inappropriate to, the situation, or to our previous image of ourselves in it.[33] There is nothing *wrong* with what we have done; no sin has been committed. But discrepancy appears between us and the social situation, between what we feel from within and what appears to us, and perhaps to others, seen from without. We have acted on the assumption of being one kind of person living in one kind of surroundings, and unexpectedly, violently, we discover that these assumptions are false. We had thought that we were able

---

[30] *Ibid.*, p. 377.

[31] See Max Scheler, *La Pudeur*, throughout.

[32] *Childhood and Society*, p. 223, and "On the Sense of Inner Identity," in Robert P. Knight and Cyrus R. Friedman, eds., *Psychoanalytic Psychiatry and Psychology: Clinical and Theoretical Papers*, Austen Riggs Center, Vol. I, International Universities Press, 1954, p. 355.

[33] Not all being taken unawares is shameful, and not all incongruity is shameful. Delight may come upon us unexpectedly and may be enhanced by elements of incongruity. Unexpectedness and incongruity are, nevertheless, essential elements in shame.

to see around certain situations and, instead, discover in a moment that it is we who are exposed; alien people in an alien situation can see around us.

Bernard Shaw believed that men are never at home in society, that they remain in a false position until "they have realized their possibilities. . . . They are tormented by a continual shortcoming in themselves; yet they irritate others by a continual overweening. . . . This finding of one's place may be made very puzzling by the fact that there is no place in ordinary society for extraordinary individuals."[34] Extraordinary individuals might include, in a sense wider than Shaw's, deviant, or innovating, or revolutionary, as well as markedly creative and independent individuals.

The attempt to understand experiences of being suddenly out of key with one's environment, and the recognition that such experiences may occur more often and more acutely for exceptional, or, as Shaw says, for extraordinary, individuals raises a question, suggested earlier, that should be borne in mind throughout this discussion: Does the feeling of shame imply an acceptance of the validity[35] of the values or standards of the society in relation to which one feels ashamed? Or, may there be personal or widely human values (if not standards) not wholly derived from the culture, in terms of which one judges not only oneself but one's society as well?

My tentative hypothesis is that the second comes closer to the truth, that aspects of the phenomenon of shame can be understood only with reference to transcultural values, and that this awareness of values beyond one's own society is one of the distinctions between shame and guilt.

This statement needs immediate qualification, and it is not easy to state this view exactly, still less to substantiate it. If a person were wholly independent of the demands and conventions of his society, he might not feel shame, but the feeling of shame for the values of one's society, and the transcending of personal shame, would seem to depend upon having some perspective, some standards of significance, against which one can call into question the codes of one's immediate culture. The

[34] George Bernard Shaw, *Selected Prose,* Dodd, Mead, 1952, p. 35. The finding of a place in society that is accepted by others is related to the Chinese concept of being "in face." Erving Goffman has discussed this concept in relation to feelings of inferiority and shame. "When a person senses that he is in face he typically responds with feelings of confidence and assurance. . . . [If he feels in wrong face or out of face he is] likely to feel ashamed and inferior . . . [he] had relied upon the encounter to support an image of self to which he had become emotionally attached and which he now finds threatened." ("On Face-Work," *Psychiatry,* Vol. 18, No. 3, Aug. 1955, p. 214.)

[35] Acceptance of legitimacy of standards should be distinguished from acceptance of their validity. One may recognize that certain things are required by law without believing that the laws are valid.

occasion for the comparison and the feeling of the need for it may arise out of a situation of shame in which there was initially no separate awareness of the values of one's culture as something to be questioned against the perspective of wider values. Some latent readiness to recognize this wider perspective must, however, have been present. Huckleberry Finn's conscience persistently nagged him because he did not report the Negro Jim, a runaway slave. According to the only moral code he had been taught, Jim was Miss Watson's property, and he ought to paddle ashore and tell someone that Jim was almost free. His guilt was compounded when he heard Jim talk of buying or stealing his children, who were the property of another owner. Huckleberry Finn had no doubt that he was doing wrong, but, because of some wider feeling of human decency that he could not name, he could not bring himself to do what his society called right.[36] The distinctions that some psychologists and philosophers have made between social codes and sources of shame beyond the moral codes of any society cannot be ignored, and these distinctions invite further exploration.[37] Complete cultural relativism need not be regarded as either as simple or as final as it was held to be by many people when it first provided a valuable corrective to ideas of absolute or authoritarian moral values. Never losing sight of the extent to which standards and values are the result of a particular upbringing in a particular society, we can now begin the exploration of common human desires, decencies, and values—and of the variety and richness of human values—that may be appealed to beyond those that are shaped by particular societies or particular cultural traditions.

The possibility of transcultural values is a highly complex question, which will be approached in different ways in what follows. It involves selective identification with different aspects of one's culture, and the individual combining of these selected aspects into new forms as well as identifications with wider values beyond those of one's immediate culture.[38] It also involves the distinction between feeling shame for things that one believes one should feel ashamed of and feeling shame that one is ashamed of feeling because one does not actually accept the standards on which it is based. Some of these things will be examined more fully later. I bring in this digression at this point

[36] Mark Twain, *Huckleberry Finn*, Harper, 1923, pp. 126–32.

[37] See, for example, Kurt Riezler, "Comment on the Social Psychology of Shame"; Arnold Isenberg, "Natural Pride and Natural Shame"; Max Scheler, *La Pudeur*.

[38] Cf. Franz Alexander's statement that feelings of inferiority and inadequacy, unlike feelings of guilt, are not connected with any sense of justice. ("Remarks about the Relation of Inferiority Feelings to Guilt Feelings," p. 44.)

in order that the aspects of shame described, in particular the feeling of inappropriateness and incongruity, may be seen as not necessarily wholly dependent on acceptance of the standards of the immediate society.

Finding oneself in a position of incongruity, not being accepted as the person one thought one was, not feeling at home in a world one thought one knew, can occur repeatedly throughout life. Sudden awareness of discrepancy may be brought about by changes in the social situation, for example, in a society of great mobility where an individual may unexpectedly find himself in an unfamiliar position, with the things he had taken for granted no longer there; or it may come about through changes in the person which put him out of key with a stable situation; or through changes outside the range of the more visible social structure.[39]

The loss of the identity one thought one had is in many ways more painful and disconcerting than the tortuous process of discovering identity that Shaw describes. This feeling of loss of identity can come about through changes in relations to one's family or friends or through changes in a professional or social situation to which one was committed. It is one of the painful characteristics of old age. The very identifications of oneself with one's body, one's mind, and the responses of other persons to the person one has been are no longer there and cannot be relied upon. Awareness of these changes in identity as they occur may be a special anguish.

> How can it really be
> That I was that young Tess
> And that before long I shall be
> The 'old princess,' the old wife of the Field Marshal?
> Look! There goes the old Duchess Theresia.
> How can it happen?
> Why should God do it
> While I am I and remain I?
> And if He does it
> Why does He permit me
> To look at all this with so clear a mind?[40]

The disconcertion arising from this juxtaposition of different perspectives explains the Biblical association of shame with

---

[39] Cf. Anselm Strauss, *An Essay on Identity* (mimeographed), University of Chicago, 1957, p. 128.

[40] From *Der Rosenkavalier.*

confusion and confounding.[41] One is confounded by the inappropriate, and at a loss as to the means of restoring congruity.

Lear felt shame over the uncontrollable tears which were inappropriate for a king and for a man:

> *Life and death! I am asham'd*
> *That thou hast power to shake my manhood thus;*
> *That these hot tears, which break from me perforce,*
> *Should make thee worth them. . . .*[42]

Rejected by his daughters so that he felt himself

> *. . . [a] slave,*
> *A poor, infirm, weak, and despis'd old man*[43]

he struggled to regain his sense of congruence by proclaiming himself "every inch a king!"[44]

Dostoevski sensed with peculiar sensitivity congruence and incongruence and the lasting impact of the exposure involved in "unseemly" or inappropriate behavior.

> *. . . fifteen years later I should still in my imagination see Liza, always with the pitiful, distorted, inappropriate smile which was on her face at that minute.*[45]

Virginia Woolf liked to think of herself as indifferent to public opinion, striving in her writing only to find the best artistic medium for her perceptions. The discovery that the appraisals of reviewers could wound her violated in disconcerting fashion her image of herself.

> *. . . opened the* Spectator *and read W. L. on me again. . . . Well L. says I should be contemptible to mind. Yes: but I do mind for 10 minutes: I mind being in the light again. . . . I must take a pull on myself. . . . I think I shall be free from the infection by Monday.*[46]

---

[41] It is this disconcertion that is the basis of the aspect of shame called embarrassment. Webster defines embarrass as: to hinder from liberty of thought or movement, to impede, perplex, or disconcert. Embarrassment is often an initial feeling in shame before shame is either covered up or explored as a means of further understanding of oneself and of the situation that gave rise to it.

[42] *King Lear*, I, iv, 318–21.

[43] *Ibid.*, III, ii, 19–20.

[44] *Ibid.*, IV, vi, 109.

[45] *Notes from the Underground*, p. 207.

[46] *A Writer's Diary*, p. 223.

Tolstoy makes clear both the shame of discrepancy arising from the sudden loss of all known landmarks in oneself and in the world, and the way in which one seizes upon familiar details of daily life in an effort to regain a sense of one's own identity and rootedness in the social situation.

Of Anna Karenina, surprised in the shameful awareness of her feeling for Vronsky as she journeyed from Moscow to Petersburg, he says:

. . . something seemed to choke her, and all objects and sounds in the wavering semi-darkness surprised her by their exaggerated proportions. She kept having moments of doubt as to whether the train were going backwards or forwards, or were standing still altogether; was it Annuska there, sitting next her, or was it a stranger?

"What is that on the hook?—my fur shuba or an animal? And what am I doing here? Am I myself, or some one else?"[47]

When Anna reached home she immersed herself in the familiar to dispel shame.

The hour before dinner . . . she employed sitting with her son . . . in arranging her things, and in reading and answering the letters and notes heaped up on her writing-table.

The sensation of causeless shame, and the agitation from which she had suffered so strangely during her journey, now completely disappeared. Under the conditions of her ordinary every-day life, she felt calm, and free from reproach, and she was filled with wonder as she recalled her condition of the night before.[48]

Different as Levin was from Anna, his experience of the shame of incongruity and of the surmounting of shame paralleled hers.

On the journey he . . . was overcome by the chaos of conflicting opinions, self-dissatisfaction, and a sense of shame. But when he got out at his station, and perceived his one-eyed coachman, Ignat, with his Kaftan collar turned up; . . . when Ignat, as he was tucking in the robes, told him all the news of the village . . . then it seemed to him that the chaos resolved itself a little, and his shame and dissatisfaction passed away. . . .

[47] *Anna Karenina*, p. 120.
[48] *Ibid.*, p. 129.

He felt himself again, and no longer wished to be a different person.[49]

It is peculiarly characteristic of these situations of suddenly experienced incongruity or discrepancy that evoke shame that they are often occasioned by what seems a "ridiculously" slight incident. An ostensibly trivial incident has precipitated intense emotion. What has occurred is harmless in itself and has no evil pragmatic outcome. It is the very triviality of the cause — an awkward gesture, a gaucherie in dress or table manners, "an untimely joke" always "a source of bitter regret,"[50] a gift or a witticism that falls flat, an expressed naïveté in taste, a mispronounced word, ignorance of some unimportant detail that everyone else surprisingly knows — that helps to give shame its unbearable character. "Some of those eccentricities are less often pardoned than vices," says Balzac of Père Goriot.[51] "Men blush for their crimes much less than for their weaknesses or vanity."[52] "Goldsmith was reserved because his foibles are of the kind men conceal; his ludicrous mishaps in dress, his preoccupation with his ugliness and awkwardness, his poverty, his fear of ridicule."[53]

Tolstoy makes the fact that shame is an open wound occasioned by a slight incident one of the distinctions between shame and guilt. He says of Levin:

There had been in his past, as in every man's, actions recognized by him as bad, for which his conscience ought to have tormented him; but the memory of these evil actions was far from causing him so much suffering as these trivial but humiliating reminiscences. These wounds never healed.[54]

Part of Dostoevski's power lies in his revelation of the way in which an outwardly trivial incident can become invested with profound human emotion and be transformed into an event of tremendous import. It was this slight occasion for much feeling that bewildered Velchaninov.

. . . he felt as though someone had caught him in something shameful. He was bewildered and surprised.

[49] *Ibid.*, p. 109.

[50] Joseph Conrad, *Chance*, Doubleday, Doran, 1914, p. 223.

[51] Honoré de Balzac, *Père Goriot*, Modern Library, p. 18.

[52] Jean de la Bruyère, *Les "Caractères" de Théophraste*, Librairie Larousse, 1949, Vol. II.

[53] V. S. Pritchett, review of Virginia Woolf, *The Captain's Death Bed and Other Essays*, New Statesman and Nation, May 13, 1950.

[54] *Anna Karenina*, pp. 178–9.

"Then there must be reasons for my being so angry . . . apropos of nothing . . . at a mere reminiscence."[55]

It is in part because of his realization of the informing power for the individual of the seemingly insignificant that Dostoevski's novels, whatever his intentions, can never be primarily political or religious tracts, nor any of his characters simply an embodiment of an idea. Stavrogin's attention could always remain held by "a trifle." Mary Lebyatkin could blush and become "terribly ashamed" over a "slight accident" as she did not over her position as the unacknowledged wife of Stavrogin—or rather the fall could suddenly bring her bodily awkwardness and her whole position into painful awareness; Mrs. Stavrogin's calling the Sistine Madonna the Dresden Madonna could bring into focus the whole of her relation to Mrs. Lembke.[56] It is for this reason, too, that no matter how sordid the details that Dostoevski introduces they never remain only sordid, and that it is difficult for him to remain wholly alien from any of his characters. He *is* the four brothers Karamazov; he is Mr. Verkhovensky as well as Shatov and Kirilov; General Yepanchin as well as Myshkin.[57]

Faulkner's *Light in August* is a study in shame. Here, too, it is the small details that probe the depths of pain. More than in his uncertainty about his Negro blood, more than in the indignity of McEachern's cruelty or his wife's self-distrustful kindness, Christmas feels shame in the details of his relation with Bobby, the waitress—the discovery that pie and coffee cost fifteen cents instead of the dime he had, his return to repay the extra nickel, his ignorance about "woman's sickness" and of "what one does" in the sex act, his first gift to Bobby of the stale and fly-specked box of candy. The newness and uniqueness of his gift was as important as the newness and uniqueness he felt in her body. After his discovery that she was a prostitute he had to regain his position *with himself* by repudiating his own shyness, decency, and tenderness.[58]

Because of the outwardly small occasion that has precipitated shame, the intense emotion seems inappropriate, incongruous, disproportionate to the incident that has aroused it. Hence a double shame is involved; we are ashamed because of the original episode and ashamed because we feel so deeply about something so slight that a sensible person would not pay any attention

[55] *The Eternal Husband* in *The Short Novels of Dostoevsky*, p. 354.
[56] Dostoyevsky, *The Devils* (*The Possessed*), Penguin, 1953, pp. 66, 191–2, 305.
[57] Dostoyevsky, *The Idiot*, Penguin, 1955.
[58] William Faulkner, *Light in August*, Modern Library, 1933, pp. 168–87.

to it. "We no more forgive an emotion for showing itself completely than we forgive a man for not having a cent," says Balzac.[59]

Various interpretations can be made of the fact that a seemingly trivial occurrence can give rise to feelings of intense shame. Some people would regard feeling acute shame over a slight gaucherie as neurotic.[60] Others think that trivial shame and neurotic shame should be placed in separate categories distinct from real shame and existentialist shame.[61] I believe that both of these interpretations miss the importance of the way in which a trifling incident can touch off a deep sense of shame. It is true that a consistent and excessive response of shame over using the wrong fork or mispronouncing a word may in some cases be a sign of neurotic or even psychotic tendencies. It is also true that a trivial incident will presumably produce less shame in a situation and with persons where one feels relatively secure and at home. But to assume that any feeling of deep shame over a seemingly trivial incident is neurotic is to miss the point that it is characteristic of shame, as experienced by normal, healthy persons, that a seemingly insignificant occurrence can set off a train of associations that have profound significance for the whole self.[62] Freud made this very clear in the *Psychopathology of Everyday Life*.[63] It is also the case that the very fact of feeling at home in a situation and then suddenly discovering that it is alien can be disconcertingly touched off by a slight occurrence.

One other point should be mentioned in connection with shame as sudden awareness of discrepancy. The same situation of suddenly exposed incongruity can give rise to shame or to laughter. Different explanations of this fact according to different theories of personality will be discussed later.

Threat to Trust

In an experience of shame trust is seriously jeopardized or destroyed. Emphasis may fall on one side or the other: on the ques-

---

[59] *Père Goriot*, p. 80. Cf. T. S. Eliot's discussion of Hamlet's emotion as "exceeding its object." ("Hamlet" in *Selected Essays*, Faber and Faber, 1932, pp. 145–6.) One may disagree with Eliot's interpretation of Hamlet and still recognize the importance of the kind of emotional discrepancy he describes.

[60] Robert K. Merton has suggested this view as a possibility.

[61] This classification has been suggested by Herbert C. Kelman.

[62] For precisely this effect of a trivial incident see the discussion of Virginia Woolf's "The New Dress," pp. 184–5. The normality of the character pictured there may be questioned, but not, I think, the normal nature of the experience.

[63] Freud, *The Psychopathology of Everyday Life*, in A. A. Brill, *The Basic Writings of Sigmund Freud*, Modern Library, 1938.

tioning of one's own adequacy or on the questioning of the values in the world of reality which so contradict what one has been led to expect. Or both may be doubted. In any case, suddenly exposed discrepancy threatens trust. Part of the difficulty in admitting shame to oneself arises from reluctance to recognize that one has built on false assumptions about what the world one lives in is and about the way others will respond to oneself. There is a failure to meet on common ground, as, for example, when adolescent children suddenly find their parents strangers, or when one meets a trusted friend after a separation and finds that the years have taken each person in a different direction.

Shame over a sudden uncovering of incongruity mounts when what is exposed is inappropriate positive expectation, happy and confident commitment to a world that proves to be alien or nonexistent.

> *They are confused because of their trust;*
> *They come to the spot and are put to shame.*[64]

Even more than the uncovering of weakness or ineptness, exposure of misplaced confidence can be shameful — happiness, love, anticipation of a response that is not there, something personally momentous received as inconsequential. The greater the expectation, the more acute the shame; the greater the discrepancy between one's image of oneself and the image others have of one, the more one has to "put on a brave face."

The gift-giving of a child to an older person whose orientation is different offers special occasions for such shame. A child spent a whole morning and infinite care constructing a necklace of paper discs and links as a surprise for an old lady who was to be an afternoon guest. With the construction went the blissful anticipation of the delight of the recipient, and debate as to the best way to present the gift. She finally decided that the surprise and pleasure would be greater if she slipped the necklace over the head of the guest. The years of a lifetime would not be enough to erase the shame aroused by the guest's impatient response. "Take this thing off my head, Jenny, it's tearing my hair net."

A small girl pictured the delight of her older brother when she presented him with a jigsaw puzzle of a mountain scene, found after much search, and paid for out of her allowance — but he had outgrown puzzles. "Do you still like detective stories?" she asked eagerly, producing a pocket Sherlock Holmes — but he was reading Malraux. Similar violation of expectation occurs if an adult

[64] Job 6:20. (Jastrow translation.)

treats casually or indifferently an event such as a school or Scout ceremony of momentous importance to a child.

Not only children experience the confusion resulting from such blocking of a vital act of special importance, or such careless dismissal of a value-loaded gift. A mother may offer to her daughter a set of china or fine damask, the treasure of a lifetime, as a supreme gesture of devotion—to be met with an open or disguised response that this is unwanted, old-fashioned junk.

Aldous Huxley's despair of human beings arises in part from his belief that any expectation of positive response from other persons inevitably ends in humiliation.

At the sound of that telephone voice Elinor quickly drew away from him. To press yourself against someone who turns out simply not to be there is not only disappointing; it is also rather humiliating. Which evenings, indeed![65]

In a very different mood Turgenev describes expectation unrealized. The aging composer Lemm thought he had for once captured his dreams in a song composed to express his love and admiration for Lisa.

... Lisa sat down ... to the piano and played ... the song. ... Alas! the music turned out to be complicated and painfully strained; it was clear that the composer had striven to express something passionate and deep, but nothing had come of it; the effort had remained an effort. Lavretsky and Lisa both felt this, and Lemm understood it. Without uttering a single word, he put his song back into his pocket, and in reply to Lisa's proposal to play it again, he only shook his head and said significantly: 'Now —enough!' and shrinking into himself he turned away.[66] (*Roman mine.*)

Basic trust in the personal and in the physical world that surrounds him is the air that the child must breathe if he is to have roots for his own sense of identity and for the related sense of his place in the world. As he gradually differentiates the world of in here from the world of out there he is constantly testing the coherence, continuity, and dependability of both.[67] Things that for an adult have defined outlines and constancies for a child remain fluid and must slowly coalesce. Schachtel beautifully

[65] Aldous Huxley, *Point Counter Point*, Doubleday, Doran, 1928, p. 72.
[66] Turgenev, *A House of Gentlefolk*, Macmillan, 1906, pp. 154–5.
[67] Cf. Erikson, *Childhood and Society*, p. 219 and throughout.

describes the way in which a child's insistence on the word-for-word repetition of a familiar story is a demand for assurance that it is *there*,[68] to be depended upon; alteration may be as disconcerting for him as it would be for an adult to see a familiar house or mountain suddenly standing on its apex. The developing sense of himself and the developing sense of the world about him increase concurrently. Expectation and having expectation met are crucial in developing a sense of coherence in the world and in oneself.

Sudden experience of a violation of expectation, of incongruity between expectation and outcome, results in a shattering of trust in oneself, even in one's own body and skill and identity, and in the trusted boundaries or framework of the society and the world one has known. As trust in oneself and in the outer world develop together, so doubt of oneself and of the world are also intermeshed.

The rejected gift, the joke or the phrase that does not come off, the misunderstood gesture, the falling short of our own ideals, the expectation of response violated—such experiences mean that we have trusted ourselves to a situation that is not there. We have relied on the assumption of one perspective or *Gestalt* and found a totally different one. What we have thought we could count on in ourselves, and what we have thought to be the boundaries and contours of the world, turn out suddenly not to be the "real" outlines of ourselves or of the world, or those that others accept. We have become strangers in a world where we thought we were at home. We experience anxiety in becoming aware that we cannot trust our answers to the questions Who am I? Where do I belong?

A child taken abroad at four had just begun to become accustomed to the strangeness of life on shipboard when there began to be talk of landing in a strange country, of going to a strange hotel. She protested, "I don't want to go there. Nobody will know me."

Few people have realized as deeply as George Eliot the irreplaceable character of trusted early surroundings. She describes

> ... *that familiar hearth, where the pattern of the rug, and the grate, and the fire irons were "first ideas" that it was no more possible to criticize than the solidity and extension of matter.*
>   ... *There is no sense of ease like the ease we felt in those scenes where we were born, where objects became dear to us*

[68] Ernest Schachtel, "The Development of Focal Attention and the Emergence of Reality," *Psychiatry*, Vol. 17, No. 4, Nov. 1954, pp. 313–6.

before we had known the labor of choice, and where the outer world seemed only an extension of our own personality: we accepted and loved it as we accepted our own sense of existence and our own limbs.[69]

Because personality is rooted in unconscious and unquestioned trust in one's immediate world, experiences that shake trusted anticipations and give rise to doubt may be of lasting importance. In Elizabethan English doubt and fear were synonymous. "Do not doubt that," says Desdemona[70] meaning "Trust; do not fear." Doubt replacing basic trust in the way of life of one's social group or in one's place in it can undermine the sense of one's own identity. Thus shame, an experience of violation of trust in oneself and in the world, may go deeper than guilt for a specific act. The emphasis on strict moral codes and hatred of sin which characterize certain cultures and certain periods of history may actually arise from a basic distrust of life.

Shattering of trust in the dependability of one's immediate world means loss of trust in other persons, who are the transmitters and interpreters of that world. We have relied on the picture of the world they have given us and it has proved mistaken; we have turned for response in what we thought was a relation of mutuality and have found our expectation misinterpreted or distorted; we have opened ourselves in anticipation of a response that was not forthcoming. With every recurrent violation of trust we become again children unsure of ourselves in an alien world.

An old volume, little known now, gives an exceptionally sensitive account of a child trustingly and earnestly trying to find her way in the bewildering adult world of arbitrary signs.

It was when a bell rang one must stand up. But what for, Emmy Lou never knew, until after the others began to do it.

. . . to be told crossly to sit down was bewildering, when in answer to c, a, t, one said "Pussy." And yet there was Pussy washing her face on the chart, and Miss Clara's pointer pointing to her[71] *. . . the music man drew . . . five lines on the blackboard, and made eight dots. . . . "This," said Mr. Cato, "is A," and he pointed to a dot. . . . "A," said Emmy Lou, obediently . . . she*

[69] George Eliot, *The Mill on the Floss*, Harper Library Edition, p. 136.

[70] *Othello*, III, iii, 19.

[71] George Madden Martin, *Emmy Lou, Her Book and Her Heart*. Copyright 1902 by McClure, Phillip and Company, reprinted by permission of Doubleday & Company, Inc., pp. 6–8.

*had met A in so many guises of print and script that she accepted
any statement concerning A. And now a dot was A.*

*". . . but we are not going to call them A, B, C, D, E, F, G, A
[said Mr. Cato] . . . we are going to call them do, re, mi, fa, sol,
la, si. . . . A is do here. Always remember the first letter in the
scale is do."*

*. . . [In spelling class] the rest might forget, but Emmy Lou
would not. It came her turn.*

*She stood up. Her word was Adam. And A was dough. Emmy
Lou went slowly to get it right. "Dough-d-dough-m, Adam," said
Emmy Lou.*

They laughed.[72]

Norbert Wiener describes the bewilderment of a child when
trusted interpretations of his world fail him:

*Christmas of 1901 was hard for me. I was just seven. It was then
that I first discovered that Santa Claus was a conventional invention of the grownups. At that time I was already reading scientific books of more than slight difficulty, and it seemed to my
parents that a child who was doing this should have no difficulty
in discarding what to them was obviously a sentimental fiction.
What they did not realize was the fragmentariness of the child's
world. The child does not wander far from home, and what may
be only a few blocks away is to him an unknown territory in which
every fancy is permissible.*

*What is true concerning the physical map is also true concern-
ing the chart of his ideas. He has not yet had the opportunity to
explore very far from the few central notions that are his by experience. In the intermediate regions, anything may be true; and
what for his elders is at least an emotional contradiction is for
him a blank which may be filled in any one of several ways.*[73]

The discovery that our parents are not all-wise and all-good
and that we must face the uncertainties of our own judgment
and our own interpretations of the world is a lonely experience.
It becomes still more lonely and poignant, and in a real sense
shameful, when it is followed by the realization that, instead of
our elders being our interpreters of the world, our protectors,
we must, instead, protect them from their own fallibilities and

[72] *Ibid.*, pp. 56–60.
[73] Norbert Wiener, *Ex-Prodigy: My Childhood and Youth*, Simon and Schuster,
1953, pp. 81–2.

shortcomings, and from the shameful knowledge that we are aware of them.

This painful transformation of roles appears in Rilke's account of the metamorphosis of birthdays.

> . . . on [one's birthday] one arose with a right to joy which was not to be doubted. . . .
>
> But suddenly come those remarkable birthdays when . . . you see others becoming uncertain. . . . You are hardly awake when someone shouts . . . that the cake hasn't arrived yet; . . . or somebody comes in and leaves the door open, and you see everything before you should have seen it. That is the moment when something like an operation is performed on you: a brief but atrociously painful incision. . . . You have scarce got over it when you no longer think about yourself; you must rescue the birthday, watch the others, anticipate their mistakes, and confirm them in the illusion that they are managing everything admirably. . . . They want to surprise you and . . . [they] open the lowest layer of a toy-box which contains nothing more, only cotton-wool; then you have to relieve their embarrassment.[74]

To some extent everyone experiences a loss of early trust,[75] which may leave a nostalgia for familiar images unmarred by change. But the extent to which some form of early trust continues for a person, and the way in which it is transmuted into more mature and understanding confidence, determine in important ways his future sense of identity.

Involvement of the Whole Self

Shame is an experience that affects and is affected by the whole self. This whole-self involvement is one of its distinguishing characteristics and one that makes it a clue to identity.

Separate, discrete acts or incidents, including those seemingly most trivial, have importance because in this moment of *self*-consciousness, the self stands revealed. Coming suddenly upon us, experiences of shame throw a flooding light on what and who we are and what the world we live in is.

---

[74] Rainer Maria Rilke, *The Journal of My Other Self,* trans. by M. O. Herter Norton and John Linton, Norton, 1930, pp. 138–9.

[75] This collapse of trust in other people and in their interpretations of the world is, Hilde Lewinsky believes, an essential element in shyness. It results in inhibition that is not volitional, but compulsory, a feeling of not being wanted, a fear of being misunderstood, of being an outsider, mistrusting one's power to understand what is told him. ("The Nature of Shyness," *British Journal of Psychology,* Vol. 32, Part 2, Oct. 1941, pp. 105–06.)

This gives at least a partial answer to the question as to whether shame is something that one voluntarily brings on oneself or something that comes upon one from without. It is both. One does not, as in guilt, choose to engage in a specific act, a sin. Guilt frequently involves a sort of haggling anxiety, a weighing of pros and cons prolonged over a period of time. The shameful situation frequently takes one by surprise. But one is overtaken by shame because one's whole life has been a preparation for putting one in this situation. One finds oneself in a situation in which hopes and purposes are invested and in which anxiety about one's own adequacy may also be felt. In shame the inadequacy becomes manifest; the anxiety is realized. It is because of this whole-life involvement that one can speak of an over-all ashamedness. Jean-Paul Sartre makes basic in shame the way one appears in the eyes of others (others as audience), rather than in one's own eyes. But he recognizes that what is exposed in shame is oneself. I am ashamed of what I am.[76]

Because of this over-all character, an experience of shame can be altered or transcended only in so far as there is some change in the whole self.[77] No single, specific thing we can do can rectify or mitigate such an experience. Unlike guilt it is—in specific terms—irreversible. "In shame there is no comfort, but to be beyond all bounds of shame." It is too small to refer to; but it pervades everything. There it is. An experience that arouses guilt, from a slight misdemeanor to a crime, can be followed by appropriate mitigating or nullifying sequences—confession, repentance, punishment, atonement, condemnation, restoration. "Even the misery of guilt doth attain to the bliss of pardon." At least in our culture, guilt is a culturally defined wrong act, a part of oneself that is separable, segmented, and redeemable.

But an experience of shame of the sort I am attempting to describe cannot be modified by addition, or wiped out by subtraction, or exorcised by expiation.[78] It is not an isolated act that can be detached from the self. It carries the weight of "I cannot have done this. But I have done it and I cannot undo it, because this is I." It is pervasive as anxiety is pervasive;[79] its focus is not a

[76]Jean-Paul Sartre, *Being and Nothingness: An Essay on Phenomenological Ontology,* trans. by Hazel E. Barnes, Philosophical Library, 1956, p. 221. See also pp. 235, 237, 249, 364, 368, 377. Sartre says, "the Other is the indispensable mediator between myself and me. I am ashamed of myself *as I appear* to the Other." (*Ibid.,* p. 222.) See also Erikson, "The Problem of Ego Identity," *Journal of the American Psychoanalytic Association,* Vol. IV, No. 1, Jan. 1956, p. 99. Alastair Reid has pointed out that having a sense of identity is having "good faith."

[77]Cf. Kurt Lewin, "Intention, Will and Need," in David Rapaport, *Organization and Pathology of Thought,* Columbia University Press, 1951, p. 138.

[78]Cf. Isenberg, "Natural Pride and Natural Shame," pp. 19–20.

[79]Cf. pp. 150–2 on anxiety.

separate act, but revelation of the whole self. The thing that has been exposed is what I am.

To describe these experiences as loss of face or acting in an unsuitable role is inadequate, because these formulations are relatively external. The German language, as noted earlier, reflects the direction of the quality of shame, inseparable from the depths of the self, in contrast to guilt, as it reflects the similar distinction between anxiety and fear: *Ich schäme mich,* but *Ich bin schuldig; Ich ängste mich,* but *Ich fürchte etwas.* Guilt can be expiated. Shame, short of a transformation of the self, is retained. This transformation means, in Plato's words, a turning of the whole soul toward the light.

Piers' distinction between shame and guilt, quoted above, is rooted in the shattering of one's sense of self in shame, in the failure to reach one's ideal:

> *Whereas guilt is generated whenever a boundary . . . is touched or transgressed, shame occurs when a goal . . . is not being reached. It thus indicates a real "short-coming." Guilt anxiety accompanies transgression; shame, failure.*
>
> *. . . the Ego-Ideal is in continuous dynamic interfunction with the unconscious and conscious awareness of the Ego's potentialities.*
>
> *Shame . . . occurs whenever goals and images presented by the Ego-Ideal are not reached.*[80]

With all the emphasis on codified guilt that is part of our Western heritage, there is abundant evidence in our literature of recognition of the distinction between specific acts that are, in a sense, detachable from the self because they may be punished or expiated and those acts and feelings that reveal the whole person. Alcibiades says of his feeling in the presence of Socrates:

> *When I hear him my heart leaps in me more than that of the Corybantes; my tears flow at his words. . . . And with this man alone I have an experience which no one would believe was possible for me—the sense of shame. . . . Often I would be glad if I should not see him again in this world, but if this should happen I know very well that I should be more miserable than ever. . . .*[81]

---

[80] Piers and Singer, *Shame and Guilt,* pp. 11, 14, 16. This is in contrast to Fromm, who uses "guilt" to denote a failure to reach one's own ideals.

[81] Plato, *The Symposium.*

Othello makes clear the difference between shame in the Freud-Benedict sense of reaction to the ridicule of others,

> . . . *to make me*
> *A fixed figure for the time of scorn*
> *To point his slow unmoving finger at!*[82]

and the far deeper, more unbearable wound which cuts to the center of the self,

> . . . *there where I have garner'd up my heart,*
> *Where either I must live or bear no life,*
> *The fountain from the which my current runs*
> *Or else dries up. . . .*[83]

This cry of Othello's also points again to the relation between being overtaken by a situation of shame and a voluntary act of choice. The circumstances of Desdemona's supposed betrayal came upon Othello; the situation was not the result of an immediate act of choice. But he was in this situation because he was the kind of person he was, a person who had chosen Desdemona and chosen Iago.

This feeling of a crumpling or failure of the whole self appears in Dmitri Furmanov's description of his hero Klychkov, who has experienced cowardice in his first hours under fire.

Oh! Shame, unspeakable, unutterable shame! It was bitter to realize that his heart had failed him in the first battle, that he had fallen short of his own expectations. Where had been the boldness, the heroism of which he had dreamed so much when he was still far from the front line?[84]

A similar sense of shame at failure to be what one thought one was, although no one else was aware of the incident, appears in a recent American volume of science fiction. The seventeen-year-old hero sees a Negro boy pursued by a man on horseback with the clear intent of riding him down. He did not hold on to the rein and delay the hunter:

I had been immobilized by the fear of asserting my sympathies, my presumptions, against events.

---

[82] *Othello*, IV, ii, 53–5.

[83] *Ibid.*, 57–60.

[84] Dmitri Furmanov, *Chapaev*, Moscow, 1934, p. 124, quoted in Rufus Mathewson, "The Hero in Soviet Literature" (manuscript), p. 323.

*. . . Walking slowly down the road I experienced deep shame.
I might, I could have saved someone from hurt; I had perhaps
had the power for a brief instant to change the course of a whole
life.*

*. . . I couldn't excuse my failure on the grounds that action
would have been considered outrageous. It would not have been
considered outrageous by me.*[85]

Samuel Stouffer describing the common experience of fear
in battle—often known only to oneself—makes it clear that this
failure to live up to one's expectations of oneself is related not
to one particular aspect of personality but to a whole cluster of
ideals.[86]

*Conceptions of masculinity vary among different American
groups, but there is a core which is common to most: courage,
endurance and toughness, lack of squeamishness . . . avoidance
of display of weakness in general, reticence about emotional or
idealistic matters, and sexual competency. . . .*

*A code as universal as "being a man" is very likely to have
been deeply internalized. So the fear of failure in the role, as by
showing cowardice in battle, could bring not only fear of social
censure on this point as such, but also more central and strongly
established fears related to sex-typing:*

*. . . behavior in combat was recognized as a test of being a
man . . . a man once in combat had to fight in order to keep his
own self-respect: "Hell, I'm a soldier."*[87]

In "The New Dress" Virginia Woolf shows how one incident
takes on an unbearably wounding character because this single
occasion partakes of and reveals what one's whole life has been
and is. It was not only that Mabel's new yellow dress, so carefully contrived with the little dressmaker, stood out at Mrs.
Dalloway's party as conspicuous, ridiculous, "not *right*." Since
it was not right, it made Mabel question her feeling for Miss

---

[85] Ward Moore, *Bring the Jubilee,* Farrar, Straus, and Young, 1952, pp. 15–16.

[86] Grinker and Spiegel say that men who leave combat because of overpowering
anxiety are haunted by depression over failure to live up to their own and the group's
standards of courageous performance. The effect of military service is, not only to
create resentment of discipline and of curtailment of personal interest, but even
more to lead to the incorporation of military demands into the personality of the
soldier. (Roy R. Grinker and John P. Spiegel, *Men Under Stress,* Blakiston, 1945,
pp. 40, 114, 279.)

[87] Samuel A. Stouffer and Associates, *The American Soldier: Combat and Its
Aftermath,* Princeton University Press, 1949, Vol. II, pp. 131–2. Cf. *ibid.,* pp. 196 ff.
on teaching soldiers to accept fear in combat as normal. One thing apparent from
this and similar studies is that shame can be somewhat eased if it is shared and if
one can be assured that what one feels is perfectly natural under the circumstances.

Milan, who had made it, and her own earlier happiness in the making of it; it made her question her "safe" marriage to Hubert, her "fretful, weak, unsatisfactory" motherhood, her "wobbly" feeling as a wife; her own appalling inadequacy; her cowardice; her "mean, water-sprinkled blood."[88]

Because of the pervasive and specifically unalterable character of experiences of shame, shame for one's parents can pierce deeper than shame for oneself, and sense of continuity with one's parents is correspondingly important. No matter how disgusted I am with myself, in some respects I can perhaps change. But the fact that these are my parents, that I am the fruit of their loins, is unchangeable. "Shame in a kindred cannot be avoided," says a seventeenth-century proverb.

Myth and literature recognize the special character of shame felt by children for their parents. Noah's sons felt this shame when

Noah . . . drank of the wine, and was drunken; and he was uncovered within his tent. . . . And Shem and Japheth took a garment, and laid it upon both their shoulders, and went backward, and covered the nakedness of their father; and their faces were backward, and they saw not their father's nakedness.[89]

Albany, upbraiding Goneril for her treatment of her father, says

> *That nature which contemns its origin*
> *Cannot be bordered certain in itself.*
> *She that herself will sliver and disbranch*
> *From her material sap, perforce must wither*
> *And come to deadly use.*[90]

Pierre's whole life and self were uprooted when he discovered that he had all his life been cherishing a false image of the integrity of his father.

He looked up, and found himself fronted by the no longer wholly enigmatical, but still ambiguously smiling picture of his father . . . endure the smiling portrait he could not; and obeying an irresistible nameless impulse, he rose, and without unhanging it, reversed the picture on the wall.[91]

---

[88] Virginia Woolf, "The New Dress," in *A Haunted House and Other Short Stories*, Harcourt, Brace, 1944, pp. 47, 50, 55.

[89] Genesis 9:21 and 23.

[90] *King Lear*, IV, ii, 32–6.

[91] Herman Melville, *Pierre, or the Ambiguities*, Dutton, 1929, p. 121.

The Brothers Karamazov is a delineation of the varieties of shame that bound each son to his father. Elsewhere Dostoevski explores the same theme.

Velchaninov . . . guessed that [Liza] was ashamed before him, that she was ashamed of her father's having so easily let her go with him, of his having, as it were, flung her into his keeping.[92]

Flora de Barral felt such shame for her father:

The girl was like a creature struggling under a net. "But how can I forget she called my father a cheat and a swindler? It can't be true. How can it be true?"
. . . Flora . . . who felt the shame but did not believe in the guilt of her father, retorted fiercely: "Nevertheless, I am as honourable as you are."[93] (Roman mine.)

The enormous perceptiveness of children in sensing unease or hypocrisy in their parents and their shame when they are aware that their parents are acting a part appears in *Anna Karenina:*

The little girl well knew that there was trouble between her father and her mother, and that her mother could not be cheerful, and that her father ought to know it, and that he was dissembling when he questioned her so lightly. And she blushed for her father.[94]

Elizabeth Bennet "blushed and blushed again with shame and vexation" at her mother's improprieties at the Netherfield ball, but, because of her greater closeness to her father, felt an even deeper pang at his complacency when it seemed to her that "her family [had] made an agreement to expose themselves."[95]
For Virginia Woolf it was a terrible experience, when her father made a scene, to have to excuse him for being "so majestic and so unreasonable." "It was also belittling to his real dignity that they knew he would be sorry later on and would reproach himself bitterly and need to be comforted because he was such an unkind father."[96] Of the description of her father as Mr. Ramsay in *To the Lighthouse* Virginia Woolf said, "I am more like him than [my mother] and therefore more critical."[97]

[92] *The Eternal Husband*, p. 384.
[93] *Chance*, pp. 147, 192.
[94] *Anna Karenina*, p. 12.
[95] Jane Austen, *Pride and Prejudice*, Nelson, pp. 89–91.
[96] Quoted in Aileen Pippett, *The Moth and the Star*, p. 26.
[97] *Ibid.*, p. 14.

For a child of immigrant parents there is often acute conflict between the desire to look up to his parents and the shame he feels for the exposure of their different ways and their uncertainty and unseemliness in a strange land.[98] Estranged from both cultures he may manifest his own insecurity about where he belongs by overzealousness in taking on the ways of the school and the neighborhood alien to his elders, and by impatience with their foreignness and slowness of adaptation.

Less extreme than the predicament of the child of immigrant parents is the widely felt, if not widely acknowledged, shame of children who become aware that their parents are not secure or at home in their social environment. That may occur with parents of modest financial means who are ill at ease with or accept favors from those who have more; or with parents who are gentle in a society that demands efficiency, or who place other values before achievement and success but show diffidence in doing so. Deference toward other persons on the part of parents, their not "knowing what to do" in a situation that calls for competence, their smiling acquiescence in place of strength, may arouse in their children pity or protectiveness when they want to give respect—a feeling hard to acknowledge and hard to bear.

Such feeling toward one's parents may be in varying degrees a more common human experience than we realize. The over-all quality of shame involves the whole life of a person, all that he is, including the parents who have created and nurtured that life.

Confronting of Tragedy

The import of shame for others may reach even deeper than shame for ourselves.[99] This is true not only of shame for our parents, but in very different ways of feeling shame with other persons less close to us, and, in still different ways, of feeling shame for and with our children.

Identifications with other persons in situations that make them feel ashamed lead beyond such experiences of shame as have been described to the confrontation of the human condition and the possibilities and the tragic limitations of man's lot. This con-

---

[98] This attitude of immigrant children toward their parents has been described many times. See, for example, Everett V. Stonequist, *The Marginal Man*, Scribner's, 1937; Oscar Handlin, *The Uprooted: The Epic Story of the Great Migrations that Made the American People*, Little, Brown, 1951.

[99] "The person who can witness another person's humiliation is said in our society to be 'heartless' just as he who can unfeelingly participate in his own defacement is thought to be 'shameless.'" (Erving Goffman, "On Face-Work," p. 215.)

frontation may be the beginning of the realization of shame as revelation—of oneself, of one's society, and of the world—and of the transcending of shame.

Loss of trust, exposure, failure, the feeling of homelessness—these experiences of shame—become still more unbearable if they lead to the feeling that there is no home for anyone, anywhere. Paradoxically, shame, an isolating, highly personal experience is also peculiarly related to one's conception of the universe, and of one's place in it. Apprehension that one's own life may be cut off from others, empty, void of significance, is a terrifying thing; but fear that this same isolation is true for others, and that the world itself may hold no meaning is infinitely worse. Experience of shame may call into question, not only one's own adequacy and the validity of the codes of one's immediate society, but the meaning of the universe itself.

It is one thing to recognize the inevitable limitations of man's lot—that even the longest life of man is no more than a hundred years and ends in death; that death separates us from those we love; that in a single life we can realize only a few of the possibilities within us for creative work and love; that in imagination we can go backward and forward in time and space but are actually alive in only limited parts of the world and in only one age. It is a wholly different thing to say that life is nothing but tragedy, that life holds, or can discover, no meaning except that it leads toward death. We may not be able to affirm with St. Augustine that

He who knows the Truth knows that [Unchangeable] Light; and he that knows it knoweth eternity. . . . I should more readily doubt that I live than that Truth [exists]. . . . For that truly is which remains immutably.[100]

But the demand to discover or to create significance in life asserts itself no less insistently. There are times when we feel that more than anything else in the world we should like to have—for just a few moments—the perspective of a God's-eye view of situations in which we are involved. Depending on initial premises, we can sort experiences this way or that with logic and validity. But what is the True, the Right, way to sort them? "I want to be there when every one suddenly understands what it has all been for," says Ivan Karamazov.

---

[100] St. Augustine, *Confessions*, trans. by J. G. Pilkington, in *A Select Library of the Nicene and Post-Nicene Fathers*, Christian Literature Company, 1886, Vol. I, Book VII, Chaps. 10, 11.

Feeling with others in situations of exposure, estrangement, forces us to face the questions of whether there is meaning and where truth and meaning lie. Lionel Trilling in his story "The Other Margaret" beautifully describes the way in which shame for another may lead to a questioning of meaning in life. Such questions come to the fore when we feel shame for and with others in circumstances from the most humble to the most august.

The child depicted in *Emmy Lou* painfully, if dimly, felt these questions through seeing the humiliation of Lisa Schmit, the daughter of a German grocer.

One day the air of the Fourth Reader room . . . was most unpleasant.

"Who in this room has lunch?" said Miss Lizzie. . . . "File by the platform in order, bringing your lunch." . . . Some were in newspaper. Emmy Lou's heart ached for those. . . . Miss Lizzie bent and deliberately smelled of each package in turn. . . . Most of the faces of the little girls were red.

Then came Lisa — Lisa Schmit. Her lunch was in paper — heavy brown paper. . . .

"Open it," said Miss Lizzie.

. . . The unpleasantness wafted heavily. There was sausage and dark gray bread and cheese. It was the cheese that was unpleasant.

"Go open the stove door," said Miss Lizzie. "Now, take it and put it in. . . ."

Lisa took her lunch and put it in. . . . When she got back to her seat, Lisa's head went down on her arm on the desk, and . . . even her yellow plaits shook with the convulsiveness of her sobs.

It wasn't the loss of the sausage or the bread or the cheese, Emmy Lou . . . knew.[101]

Acknowledgment of personal sin or confession of guilt may sometimes be a defense against the possibility that there may be no meaning in the world. After some experiences of shame and fear of emptiness we may welcome guilt as a friend. Sin, guilt, punishment — each is, in one sense, an affirmation of order and significance. Shame questions the reality of any significance. Guilt in oneself is easier to face than lack of meaning in life.

Philip, praying with utter faith that his clubfoot would be made whole, found it better to believe that he lacked faith than that God had failed him.

[101] *Emmy Lou*, pp. 144–8.

"D'you mean to say [said Philip] that if you really believed you could move mountains you could?"

"By the grace of God," said the Vicar.

. . . he . . . prayed to God with all his might that He would make his club-foot whole. It was a very small thing beside the moving of mountains. . . .

"Oh, God, . . . if it be Thy will, please make my foot all right on the night before I go back to school."

. . . No doubts assailed him. He was confident in the word of God . . . the morning for the miracle. . . . His first instinct was to put down his hand and feel the foot which was whole now, but to do this seemed to doubt the goodness of God. He knew that his foot was well. But at last he made up his mind, and with the toes of his right foot he just touched his left. Then he passed his hand over it. . . .

. . . perhaps he had not given God enough time. . . . But presently the feeling came to him that this time also his faith would not be great enough.

"I suppose no one ever has faith enough," he said.[102]

George Eliot's Dorothea in Rome showed a similar eagerness to exaggerate her own guilt rather than to admit inadequacy in the possibilities of love or loss of faith in the people and the world she had trusted. However just her indignation might be, "her ideal was not to claim justice, but to give tenderness."[103] So, too, Anna Karenina would go to any length in order not to recognize that the love between her and Vronsky was less than she had believed.

Having read the letter, [Vronsky] raised his eyes to her, and there was no determination in them. . . . She knew that whatever he might say to her, he would not say all he thought. And she knew that her last hope had failed. . . .

"You say degrading . . . don't say that . . ." she said in a shaking voice. She did not want him now to say what was untrue. Her love for him was trembling in the balance. . . . "If [your love] is like mine, I feel so exalted, so strong, that nothing can be humiliating to me. I am proud of my position, because . . ." She could not say what she was proud of. Tears of shame and despair choked her utterance.[104]

[102] *Of Human Bondage*, pp. 58–61.
[103] *Middlemarch*, Chatto and Windus, Zodiac Press, 1950, pp. 196, 204–05.
[104] *Anna Karenina*, pp. 374–5.

Shame for one's children raises other searching questions. Just as shame for and with one's parents in some ways tests the limits of one's acceptance of oneself, so shame for and with one's children — their feelings of inferiority and failure, their disappointment in positive expectations of other people and of the world — comes near to testing the limits of one's faith in the possibilities of life. The sensitivity of this area of awareness is suggested by the fact that many people would hesitate to speak of shame for their children. If the feeling of shame for one's children receives psychological recognition it is quickly codified as a parental defect.

At least two things obscure recognition of some of the implications of identifications with our children which partake of the nature of shame.

The first takes the more obvious forms of desiring the success of our children in terms of the standards of the culture or of our particular group in the culture ("intellectuals" may repudiate the cruder and more common success norms and set up their own even more exigent ones) and of feeling some sort of shame for our children if these are not attained. This is a phenomenon widely recognized and discussed as a characteristic of American life.[105] Many of us do, more than we like to admit, want, among other values, such success for our children. It is undeniably true that many parents do want to realize themselves through pride in their children's achievements, to have their children succeed where they themselves have fallen short. But if we stop here we have barely touched the edge of what identifications with one's children imply.

A second factor that confuses entering into the deeper implications of these identifications is that the complex of feelings about our children's lives and hopes is one in which shame and guilt are peculiarly intermeshed. Consciousness of guilt and of where we have failed our children almost inevitably submerges awareness of the implications of shame. Few parents, as they watch the disappointments and frustrations, or the compromises and adjustments, of their children as they make their own choices in becoming related to social "reality" can escape some feeling that had they done certain things differently the path for their children might have been clearer.

Some of the social changes of the last quarter or half century

---

[105] Harold D. Lasswell, among others, has described the particularly confusing, and at the same time particularly coercive, standards that middle-class parents, implicitly or explicitly, set for their children. (*Power and Personality*, Norton, 1948, pp. 47–9 and throughout.)

have made growing up more difficult; and certain kinds of awareness of the way in which seemingly incidental aspects of behavior
of parents may affect their children's lives[106] have heightened
the parents' sense of responsibility and of wrongdoing.

Neither the obvious forms of what may be called shame if our
children fall short of our wishes for their achievement nor the
much more important guilt we feel over our own inadequacies
toward them, however, come near to the core of the implications
of our identifications with them. Something far deeper is involved
in our desires for our children and the putting to trial through
them of our faith in the possibilities of life. For ourselves we can
accept disappointment, rebuff, and failure. Recognizing and
accepting it for them becomes an almost wholly different experience.

> *O my son Absalom, my son, my son Absalom!*
> *Would God I had died for thee,*
> *O Absalom, my son, my son!*

The cry stands alone. The love and expectations of a father for
his son, the guilt of a father for the way his son's life grew and
ended, the treachery of a son toward his father[107] — it is beyond
them all.

Is there anything in the world of adult reality that is commensurate with the uncertain excitement of a child in taking his first
steps; the trust with which he holds out his arms to be taken up;
his eager intensity as he digs in the sand, his laughter as a wave
breaks over him; the expectancy overcoming self-doubt with
which an adolescent goes out to meet new people, new places,
new ideas; the hope of an expanding world with which a fresh-

---

[106] For the last twenty-five years or more, child psychologists have been warning
parents, especially mothers, of all the things they must not do or be lest them perma-
nently damage their children. Parents have been censured for being overstrict and
overpermissive, overdetached and overprotective, and for a thousand other mistakes of commission and omission. In recent years, not altogether pleased at the
results of these efforts, child psychologists have flown still another danger signal —
parents must, at all costs, not be "overanxious parents"! The Mental Health Materials
Center issues a pamphlet entitled "What Did I Do?" presenting "the case of a
mother" who through trying too hard missed some important clues from her child.
(Dorothy Barclay, "The Case of the Overanxious Parent," New York *Times Magazine*,
May 5, 1957.)

Much recent work of child psychologists tries specifically to correct the effect
of such guilt-producing injunctions.

[107] II Samuel 18:33. Cf. the statement of Admetos

> Men who never marry, men who have no children,
> Each of them has one life to live: his own;
> And a man can endure the pain of a single life.

(Euripides, *Alcestis*, an English version by Dudley Fitts and Robert Fitzgerald,
Harcourt, Brace, 1936, Scene IV, Kommos.)

man enters college; the wonder and dawning confidence of a first—and renewed—love?

Or, must we say that maturity involves the acceptance of frustrations of which earlier bewildered disappointments are prototypes: being excluded— "They're playing a game and I guess I'm not in it any more"; offering one's most cherished book, a much-read copy of *Treasure Island,* as a birthday present and having it disregarded among the new and costly gifts; the expectancy called forth by the words over a college entrance "The Pursuit of Truth" being met by rebuff and "scaling down to size"; open friendship met by formality; love by shrinking or betrayal?

And is the raising of such questions as these a mark of sentimentality and immaturity?

As shame of immigrant children for their parents highlights certain similar but less acute experiences of other children, so the feeling of these same parents for their children by its intensity illumines questions that present themselves in some form to many parents.

About the children [*the immigrant parents*] *can feel no certainty whatever.*

. . . It was difficult enough to show them the right ways around the corners of the city blocks; it was infinitely more difficult to show them the right ways around the twisting curves of the new way of life.

. . . It occurs to [*the parents*] *that they cannot possibly meet their obligations to the children . . . by the act of migration, they . . . have destroyed the birthright of their sons and daughters. . . . To each other, the parents acknowledge the guilt:* Yes, dear, and therefore let us sacrifice ourselves and live only for them. If there is any hope in this world, it is not for us but for them.

It was easier to bend the neck in readiness than to be certain that the yoke would fit. With bewilderment the immigrants learned that to be willing to sacrifice was not enough, that their children must be also willing to accept the sacrifice; and of that there could be no confidence.[108]

For these parents, too, their children's future could become one test of their faith in life. "From the depths of a dark pessimism they looked up at a frustrating universe ruled by haphazard, capricious forces."[109] For them, too, the feeling of per-

---

[108] Handlin, *The Uprooted,* pp. 240, 243–4.
[109] *Ibid.,* p. 108.

sonal guilt was easier to bear than facing lack of meaning in the world.

Hardy describes Clym's bitter self-reproach as a refuge from facing lack of trust in other persons and ultimate emptiness.

He did sometimes think he had been ill-used by fortune, so far as to say that to be born is a palpable dilemma, and that instead of men aiming to advance in life with glory they should calculate how to retreat out of it without shame. But that he and his had been sarcastically and pitilessly handled in having such irons thrust into their souls he did not maintain long. It is usually so except with the sternest of men. Human beings, in their generous endeavour to construct a hypothesis that shall not degrade a First Cause, have always hesitated to conceive a dominant power of lower moral quality than their own; and, even while they sit down and weep by the waters of Babylon, invent excuses for the oppression which prompts their tears.[110]

Shame for God or for the world is harder to bear than shame for ourselves. We may think that Gloucester lacked courage or was without sense of historic change, but there are no more fearful words than his

> *As flies to wanton boys are we to th' gods.*
> *They kill us for their sport.*[111]

Failure to reach our own aspirations, our own possibilities, is intimately related to the way we see our place in the universe, and hence to the way we conceive the universe itself. This leads to the question of how far disappointment and the failure of human effort lie in the unalterable nature of things and how far in the particular version of the nature of things presented by our society and this period of history. This question, which presents itself repeatedly, will be discussed further.

Difficulty in Communicating Shame

The characteristics that have been suggested as central in experiences of shame—the sudden exposure of unanticipated incongruity, the seemingly trivial incident that arouses overwhelming and almost unbearably painful emotion, the threat to the core of identity, the loss of trust in expectations of oneself, of other persons, of one's society, and a reluctantly recog-

[110] Thomas Hardy, *The Return of the Native*, Macmillan, 1922, p. 475.
[111] *King Lear*, IV, i, 36–7.

nized questioning of meaning in the world — all these things combine to make experiences of shame almost impossible to communicate.

We may say, "I had an experience of such and such a sort," recounting its aspects which belong to some named class of experiences. But the minute, concrete detail — of inappropriate facial expression, bodily awkwardness, inept shading of voice, choice of word revealing Philistine taste, the particular manner of shortcoming, or of reaching out and meeting no response — the actual thorn in the wound, this, although seemingly the smallest part of the whole experience, is almost unbearable to admit to recollection or to express in words to another. The possibility of having to communicate to another person a past experience of shame may bring into throbbing awareness of detail what one has attempted to shroud in general phrases.[112]

A particular situation may give rise to guilt or to shame or to both. But guilt is more concerned with the codified act involved, shame with the uncodified detail and with the diffused feeling. Stealing a dime, killing a man, committing adultery, however vague or various the codes that cover them, are nevertheless specific acts of guilt which can be fitted into a more or less coherent scheme and which carry recognized consequences that can, to some extent at least, be anticipated. Nothing comparable covers lack of beauty or grace, errors of taste and congruence, weakness and certain kinds of failure, feelings of meanness or envy, rejection of the gift of oneself — situations that are experienced as exposure of deeply personal inadequacy.

Codes or conventions, says Conrad, provide ways of assorting, assimilating, and bearing experience.[113] Recognition of this use of ritual or convention is widespread. "Yet he took [his bitter personal defeat] with dignity; he even laid on it a certain ritual in order to keep it from being a low and shameful experience."[114]

For many people no experience can produce more disturbance than that that fits into no discernible pattern. The association of shame with confounding and confusion and the use of familiar detail to surmount experiences of shame emphasize this common human phenomenon. The contemporary existence of *anomie*, literally being without a norm, has engaged the attention of such sociologists as Emile Durkheim and Robert K. Merton because, according to Merton's hypothesis, contemporary society with its "disassociation between culturally prescribed aspirations and socially structured avenues for realizing these aspirations" brings

[112] See George Eliot's account of Bulstrode, *Middlemarch*, pp. 586–7.
[113] *Chance*, p. 221.
[114] Nancy Wilson Ross, *The Left Hand Is the Dreamer*, William Sloane, 1947, p. 196.

about deviant, uncodified behavior. Imperfect co-ordination of goals and means in society leads to *anomie*.[115] Naming, structure, social norms, ritualized detail, and closure or correspondence between stated cultural goals and ways of realizing them give security and protection. Except for the person sufficiently deep-rooted in his own identity to be freely exploring, whatever cannot be codified, classified, labeled is potentially threatening, and càn lead to a sense of being lost, unconnected. The wood in *Through the Looking-Glass* where no creature bears a name is a place of terror.

It has been frequently pointed out that it is harder to recount daydreams than those that occur in sleep. In daydreams we retain or can recapture consciousness and therefore feel more personally responsible for these fantasies than for dreams that occur in sleep. There is no widely recognized pattern or explanation of waking fantasies that lifts the weight of personal responsibility.[116] The difference of feeling about waking and sleeping dreams has perhaps been accentuated since Freud has provided names and a code into which dreams in sleep can be fitted.

Shame sets one apart. There is no clear code of shame. Voluntarily or involuntarily, one has opened oneself and the openness has been misunderstood or rejected; there has been weakness and failure in one's own eyes. Guilt, at least in our culture, can be a form of communication. There is communication of a sort not only between penitent and confessor, but between criminal and judge. Condemnation or punishment is itself a form of communication, relation to one's fellows. It fits in; it gives a code to cling to even if one has violated it. Hawthorne says of Hester Prynne, "The very law that condemned her . . . had held her up through the terrible ordeal of her ignominy."[117] Punishment merited by a guilty act or even undeserved punishment for an act one has not committed may be a refuge from shame.[118] In the midst of a situation in which one is overwhelmed by shame one may confess to a crime of which one is innocent, inviting punishment in order to re-establish, even through condemnation, communication with others.[119]

---

[115] Robert K. Merton, "Social Structure and Anomie," in *Social Theory and Social Structure,* Free Press, 1949, pp. 125–49, especially pp. 128, 146, 149.

[116] It is notable that the only full-length study of daydreams is Varendonck's published in 1921 (J. Varendonck, *The Psychology of Daydreams,* Allen and Unwin, 1921). Cf. Ernst Kris, *Psychoanalytic Explorations in Art,* International Universities Press, 1952, pp. 310–11 and 314–15.

[117] *The Scarlet Letter,* p. 101.

[118] Cf. Piers and Singer, *Shame and Guilt,* pp. 20–1.

[119] See, for example, such confession of crimes one has not committed, after the mental torture of concentration camps, cited in William Sargant, *Battle for the Mind,* Chap. IX.

The very fact that shame is an isolating experience also means that if one can find ways of sharing and communicating it this communication can bring about particular closeness with other persons and with other groups. This can become the situation with minority groups or with minority positions in a particular historical situation. What is directed against a group as a label of shame can be converted into a mark of honor, and the group itself gains in strength.

There is no readily expressive language of shame, of identity, of mutuality, no accepted form by which these experiences can be communicated. Rebecca West believes that communication of such "living" experiences is impossible.

There is no such thing as conversation. . . . There are inter-secting monologues, that is all. We speak; we spread round us with sounds, with words, an emanation from ourselves. Some-times they overlap the circles that others are spreading around themselves. . . . I am talking now of times when life is being lived . . . not when the intellect is holding the field. Then, of course, ideas can be formulated . . . like handing round a pearl on which you wish an opinion to a circle of experts. You cup the palm to hold it, you keep the hand very steady. No such caution is pos-sible when one is really living. Then there is no conversation.[120]

Lack of a language may contribute to a sense of estrangement. Carson McCullers describes the effort to reach other people with words.

F. Jasmine could not speak the unknown words, so after a minute she knocked her head a last time on the door and then began to walk around the kitchen table. . . . She began to talk in a high fast voice, but they were the wrong words, and not what she had meant to say.[121]

Contrasting the emotional concomitants of shame and guilt, Piers says that the unconscious, irrational threat implied in shame anxiety is abandonment, in contrast to the fear in guilt of mutilation.

Behind the feeling of shame stands not the fear of hatred, but the fear of contempt which . . . spells fear of abandonment . . . the

---

[120] Rebecca West, "There Is No Conversation," in *The Harsh Voice*, Doubleday, Doran, 1935, p. 67.

[121] Carson McCullers, *The Member of the Wedding*, Houghton Mifflin, 1946, p. 141.

98** Guilt and Shame

*deeper rooted shame anxiety is based on the fear of the parent
who walks away "in disgust," and . . . this anxiety in turn draws
its terror from the earlier established and probably ubiquital
separation anxiety.*[122]

Important as is Piers' emphasis on the different kinds of anxi-
eties that are the outcome of shame and guilt, it seems to me
probable that the anguish of the experience of shame is not so
much the fear that isolation or alienation will be the *penalty*
for the shameful act as that the experience of shame is itself
isolating, alienating, incommunicable.

A small child allowed to play with the loom of an older girl
cut all the strings of the loom to remove her weaving and, when
questioned, lied about having done this. There was certainly
guilt over having destroyed the loom by cutting the strings and
over having lied about it; but deeper than this, I believe, there
was shame over the fact that she had cut the strings trustingly,
in good faith, thinking that that was the way to remove the
pattern, not knowing that it would damage the loom. The discovery left her alone and bewildered. The lie covered her inability to communicate the trust that had been shattered and
the confused doubt that replaced it.

Being isolated, cut off, unable to find any way of being recognized by oneself and others as part of humanity is a peculiarly
frightening experience. Donne's perception of this may be one
reason that lines from Donne appear as titles or themes of so
many novels in this present time of awareness of isolation.

*As Sicknes is the greatest misery, so the greatest misery of sicknes
is* solitude. . . . Solitude *is a torment which is not threatened in*
hell *it selfe. Meere* vacuitie *the first* Agent, God . . . *will not admit; Nothing can be utterly* emptie; *but so neere a degree towards*
Vacuitie *as* Solitude, *to bee but one, they* [God and Nature] *love
not.*[123]

For persons with certain forms of brain injury the desire for
human identity is so great and the need to avoid isolation so
strong that a person will go to almost any lengths to maintain
the first and avoid the second.[124] Using Piers' contrast between

---

22 Piers and Singer, *Shame and Guilt,* pp. 11, 16.

23 John Donne, *Complete Poetry and Selected Prose,* ed. by John Hayward,
Random House, 1930, p. 513.

24 See Kurt Goldstein, "The Effect Of Brain Damage On The Personality," pp.
256–7; see also his *The Organism: A Holistic Approach to Biology Derived from
Pathological Data in Man,* American Book Co., 1939, pp. 195–7, 292–5, and *Human
Nature in the Light of Psychopathology,* Harvard University Press, 1940, pp. 109,
140–2. Cf. Freud's association of certain psychotic states with fears of annihilation.
(Ruth Munroe, *Schools of Psychoanalytic Thought,* Dryden Press, 1955, pp. 288–9.)

consequences of guilt and shame, we recognize that one can exist and retain one's identity even if mutilated. If sufficiently isolated, estranged, one may question one's own existence.

When the threat of isolation is acute the need of establishing some sort of relationship is so great that there is an attempt to break through the barriers by any means however false or inadequate. In the extreme isolation of approaching schizophrenia a person desperately grasps any signals that it is thought "They" may understand:

One day we were jumping rope . . . when it came my turn and I saw my partner jump toward me. . . . I was seized with panic; I did not recognize her. . . . Standing at the other end of the rope, she had seemed smaller, but the nearer we approached each other . . . the more she swelled in size.

I cried out, "Stop, Alice, you look like a lion; you frighten me!" . . . I tried to dissemble [my fear] under the guise of fooling . . . actually, I didn't see a lion at all: it was only an attempt to describe the enlarging image of my friend and the fact that I didn't recognize her.[125]

Even in more usual predicaments a person sometimes adopts a means of communication that he thinks "They" may understand when he can find no way of expressing what is to him the reality. Collingwood describes the means he adopted in boyhood to pacify the adults when he was wrestling with "a formless and aimless intellectual disturbance" that he could not name.

I know now that this is what always happens when I am in the early stages of work on a problem. Until the problem has gone a long way towards being solved, I do not know what it is . . . anyone who observed me must have thought, as my elders did think, that I had fallen into a habit of loafing. . . . My only defence against this opinion . . . was to cover these fits of abstraction with some bodily activity, trifling enough not to distract my attention from my inward wrestling. . . . So when the fit was upon me I would set myself to make something quite uninteresting, like a regiment of paper men. . . . It was painful to be laughed at for playing with paper men; but the alternative, to explain why I did it, was impossible.[126]

Awareness of loneliness, of isolation, is one of the most characteristic experiences of the contemporary world. Marx's chief

[125] *Autobiography of a Schizophrenic Girl*, with Analytic Interpretation by Marguerite Sechehaye, Grune and Stratton, 1951, pp. 4, 5.
[126] R. G. Collingwood, *An Autobiography*, Oxford University Press, 1939, pp. 4–5.

condemnation of capitalism is that it alienates the individual.[127] The phenomenon of individual isolation is a cornerstone of existentialist philosophy, and the fact of alienation in the contemporary world is one thing that gives existentialism its contemporary appeal.[128] Freud regards separation and fear of separation as one of the main factors in anxiety.[129] The situation of isolation is a central theme in Fromm's *Escape from Freedom*,[130] in Sullivan's psychology of interpersonal relations, and in Durkheim's and Merton's analysis of *anomie*.

The search for ways to transcend loneliness pervades much contemporary writing, and the study of different kinds and degrees of isolation engages much attention in recent social science. It is possible that this indicates more belief in the possibilities of communication and personal relations, less acceptance of the finality of individual estrangement, than was characteristic of the generation of Chekhov or even of Proust.

Estrangement and betrayal and ways of meeting them constantly recur as themes in Graham Greene's novels. Portrayal of loneliness and of ways of overcoming it is central in the work of Carson McCullers and helps to explain her wide appeal. Of F. Jasmine she says, "She was not afraid of Germans or bombs or Japanese. She was afraid because in the war they would not include her, and because the world seemed somehow separate from herself."[131]

Elizabeth Bowen describes the search for a language in which the deepest, most individual experiences can be expressed:

Innocence so constantly finds itself in a false position that inwardly innocent people learn to be disingenuous. Finding no language in which to speak in their own terms, they resign themselves to being translated imperfectly. They exist alone; when they try to enter into relations they compromise falsifyingly—

---

[127] Karl Marx and Friedrich Engels, *The German Ideology*, Parts I and II, International Publishers Company, 1939, pp. 74–5; Marx, "Alienated Labor," *Three Essays Selected from the Economic Philosophical Manuscripts*, mimeographed, trans. by Rita Stone.

[128] See Edith Weigert, "Existentialism and Its Relations to Psychotherapy," *Psychiatry*, Vol. 12, No. 4, Nov. 1949, pp. 399–412.

[129] Freud, *The Problem of Anxiety*, Psychoanalytic Quarterly Press and Norton, 1936, pp. 67–8 and throughout.

[130] Ruth Munroe believes that Fromm overstresses the fear of being alone and insignificant until it becomes a kind of primary drive like Horney's need for security and Adler's need for superiority. (*Schools of Psychoanalytic Thought*, p. 397.) An outcome of this is what she regards as his overemphasis on the emptiness of the marketing orientation which, in her view, describes the era of Kafka and Ibsen rather than the present. (*Ibid.*, p. 476.)

[131] *The Member of the Wedding*, p. 28. See also Carson McCullers, *The Heart Is a Lonely Hunter*, Houghton Mifflin, 1940, p. 257.

through anxiety, through desire to impart and to feel warmth. . . .
They are bound to blunder, then to be told they cheat. . . .[132]

Virginia Woolf herself felt, and also expressed through the characters with whom she identified, the conflict between wanting to come out of isolation and hesitancy to trust herself to communication. "Her strength and her limitations were that she didn't know really how it felt to be someone else. What she did know was how it felt to be alone, unique, isolated. . . ."[133]

After all [Katharine] considered, why should she speak? Because it is right, her instinct told her; right to expose oneself without restraint to other human beings. She flinched from the thought. . . . Something she must keep of her own. But if she did keep something of her own? Immediately she figured an immured life . . . the same feeling living for ever, neither dwindling nor changing within the ring of a thick stone wall. The imagination of this loneliness frightened her.[134]

Protection against isolation and the difficulty of communicating such experiences as shame may take the form of impersonalization and dehumanization. If I cannot communicate with others, then I will at least not risk openness; I will deny the possibility of openness; I will protect myself against it.

K. had a large room in the Bank with a waiting-room attached to it and could watch the busy life of the city through his enormous plate-glass window.[135]

Discussing Maupassant's protective plate glass of impersonality V. S. Pritchett says:

It is impossible to know what hardens the heart, what checks the impulse to "look inside." . . . We can surmise that the broken home of the Maupassants had fixed the detachment, the watchfulness, the habit of surveillance *in the child. . . . It is the outside that must be watched and . . . the very title of* Le Horla — *what is outside — shows that the horrors come from* an outside world that cannot be trusted . . . *this was Maupassant's terror: that the world would crash inwards upon a nature that . . . could not*

[132] Elizabeth Bowen, *The Death of the Heart,* Knopf, 1939, p. 133.
[133] Stephen Spender, *World Within World,* Harcourt, Brace, 1951, p. 141.
[134] Virginia Woolf, *Night and Day,* Harcourt, Brace, 1920, pp. 274–5.
[135] Kafka, *The Trial,* p. 75.

*make itself hard, efficient, drastic, sealed off, and settled enough
. . . he was at home only in the disconnected episode.*[136] *(Roman
mine.)*

*As one of his letters says: "Men, women or events — they mean
nothing to me. I don't even care about myself." Life, he decided,
was meaningless; it is a philosophy that leaves the door wide
open for loneliness, melancholy — and personal push.*[137]

The difficulty of communicating experiences of shame and the
markedly different ways of responding to such experiences
suggest that they can lead in two different directions: 1. They can
lead to protection of the exposed self and of the exposed society
at all costs — refusing to recognize the wound, covering the
isolating effect of shame through depersonalization and adaptation to any approved codes. 2. If experiences of shame can be
fully faced, if we allow ourselves to realize their import, they can
inform the self, and become a revelation of oneself, of one's
society, and of the human situation.

In attempts to understand diffused experiences of which
shame is one example the development of a language that can
express such experiences becomes of great importance. Certain
current methods in the study of personality may hamper, not
help, the creation of such a language. Other emerging methods
may contribute more toward it.

[136] V. S. Pritchett, review of Guy de Maupassant, *A Woman's Life, New Statesman
and Nation,* December 3, 1949.

[137] V. S. Pritchett, "The Cat's Eye View," *New Statesman and Nation,* June 4, 1955.
Pritchett also says that this is not the whole of de Maupassant.

Bibliography

Adkins, A. W. H., *Merit and Responsibility*, 1960.   **203**

Alexander, F., *Fundamentals of Psychoanalysis*, 1963.

Alston, W., "Feelings," *Philosophical Review*, 77 (January 1969).

Arnold, M., *Emotion and Personality*, 1960.

Aronfreed, J. M., *Conduct and Conscience*, 1968.

Augustine, *The City of God; Confessions.*

Beardsley, E., "A Plea for Deserts," *American Philosophical Quarterly*, 6, 1 (January 1969).

Bedford, E., "Emotions," *Proceedings of the Aristotelian Society* (1956–1957).

Benedict, R., *The Chrysanthemum and the Sword*, 1946.

Bergler, E., *The Battle of Conscience*, 1948.

Bergson, H., *The Two Sources of Morality and Religion*, 1935.

Bonhoeffer, D., *Ethics*, 1955; *Creation and Fall* and *Temptation*, 1959.

Bradley, F. H., *Ethical Studies*, 1927.

Brett, P., *An Inquiry into Criminal Guilt*, 1963.

Broad, C. D., "Conscience and Conscientious Action," *Philosophy*, 15, 58 (April 1940).

Brown, N. O., *Life against Death*, 1959; *Love's Body*, 1966.

Brunner, F., *Justice and the Social Order*, 1945.

Buber, M., *Good and Evil*, 1952.

Buchler, A., *Studies in Sin and Atonement in the Rabbinic Literature of the First Century*, 1967.

Butler, J., *Sermons*, 1897.

Camus, A., *The Myth of Sisyphus*, 1955.

Daube, D., *Studies in Biblical Law*, 1969.

Durkheim, E., *The Division of Labor in Society*, 1947.

Eberhard, W., *Guilt and Sin in Traditional China*, 1967.

Emmet, D., *Rules, Roles and Relations*, 1966.

Erikson, E. H., *Insight and Responsibility*, 1964.

Feinberg, J., *Doing and Deserving*, 1970.

Fingarette, H., *The Self in Transformation*, 1963; *Self-Deception*, 1970.

Flugel, J. C., *Man, Morals and Society*, 1955.

Freud, S., *Totem and Taboo*, 1952.

Fromm, E., *Man for Himself*, 1947; *You Shall Be as Gods*, 1966.

Fuss, P., "Conscience," *Ethics*, 74 (1964).

Glover, J., *Responsibility*, 1970.

Hartmann, H., *Psychoanalysis and the Moral Values*, 1960.

Hegel, G. W. F., *Phenomenology of Mind*, 1966.

Heidegger, M., *Being and Time*, 1962.

Humanitas (Issue in *guilt and self-renewal*) (Fall 1969).

Hume, D., *Treatise of Human Nature*, 1888.

Hunter, J. F. M., "Conscience," *Mind*, 72, 287 (July 1963).

Isenberg, A., "Natural Pride and Natural Shame," *Philosophy and Phenomenological Research*, 10, 1 (September 1949).

Jankélévitch, V., *La Mauvaise Conscience*, 1951.

Jones, D. H., "Freud's Theory of Moral Conscience," *Philosophy*, 41, 155 (January 1966).

Jones, E., *Papers in Psychoanalysis*, 1950.

Kant, I., *Religion within the Limits of Reason Alone*, 1960; *The Metaphysic of Morals*, 1964.

Kierkegaard, S., *The Concept of Dread*, 1946; *The Sickness unto Death*, 1954.

Klein, M., *Envy and Gratitude*, 1957.

Klein, M., J. and Riviere, *Love, Hate and Reparation*, 1967.

Knight, J. A., *Conscience and Guilt*, 1969.

Laing, R. D., *The Divided Self*, 1959.

Lewis, H. D., *Morals and the New Theology*, 1947; *Morals and Revelation*, 1951.

Lindsay, A. D., *The Two Moralities*, 1940.

McKenzie, J. G., *Guilt*, 1962.

Marcuse, H., *Eros and Civilization*, 1955.

Margolis, J., *Psychotherapy and Morality*, 1966.

Maslow, A., *Toward a Psychology of Being*, 1962.

Mead, M., *Cooperation and Competition among Primitive Peoples*, 1938.

Moberly, W., *The Ethics of Punishment*, 1968.

Moore, G. F., *Judaism*, 1927.

Morris, H. (ed.), *Freedom and Responsibility*, 1961; "Persons and Punishment," *The Monist*, 52, 4 (October 1968).

Niebuhr, R., *The Nature and Destiny of Man*, 1942.

Nunberg, H., "The Feeling of Guilt," *The Psychoanalytic Quarterly*, 3 (1934).

Oraison, M., *et al.*, *Sin*, 1962.

O'Shaughnessy, R. J., "Forgiveness," *Philosophy*, 42, 162 (October 1967).

Peristiany, J. G. (ed.), *Honour and Shame*, 1966.

Perkins, M., "Emotion and Feeling," *Philosophical Review*, 75 (April 1966); "Emotion and the Concept of Behavior: A Disproof of Philosophical Behaviorism," *American Philosophical Quarterly*, 3, 4 (October 1966).

Pettazzoni, R., *Essays on the History of Religions*, 1954.

Piaget, J., *The Moral Judgment of the Child*, 1965.

Plutchik, R., *The Emotions*, 1962.

"The Problem of Guilt," *Aristotelian Society Proceedings*, Supplementary Volume 21 (1947).

Reider, N., "The Sense of Shame," *Samiska*, 3, 3 (1950).

Reik, T., *Myth and Guilt*, 1957.

Ricoeur, P., *The Symbolism of Evil*, 1967.

Rieff, P., *Freud: The Mind of the Moralist*, 1961.

Rotenstreich, N., "On Shame," *Review of Metaphysics*, 19, 1 (1965).

Sartre, J. P., *The Emotions: Outline of a Theory*, 1948; *Being and Nothingness*, 1956; *Saint Genet*, 1963.

Scheler, M., *The Nature of Sympathy*, 1954; *On the Eternal in Man*, 1960; *Ressentiment*, 1961.

Skinner, B. F., *Walden Two*, 1948.

Smith, A., *Theory of Moral Sentiments*, 1767.

Smith, T. V., *Beyond Conscience*, 1934.

Spinoza, *Ethics*, 1951.

Stephenson, G., *The Development of Conscience*, 1966.

Stuart, G., *Conscience and Reason*, 1951.

Tarde, G., *Penal Philosophy*, 1912.

Tennant, F. R., *The Sources of the Doctrine of the Fall and Original Sin*, 1903.

Thalberg, I., "Remorse," *Mind*, 72, 288 (October 1963).

Tillich, P., *Love, Power and Justice*, 1954; *Systematic Theology*, 1957; *Morality and Beyond*, 1963.

Tournier, P., *Guilt and Grace*, 1962.

Walsh, W. H., "Pride, Shame and Responsibility," *The Philosophical Quarterly*, 20, 78 (January 1970).

Westermarck, E., *The Origin and Development of Moral Ideas*, 1912.

Wieman, H. N., and R. W. Weiman, *Normative Philosophy of Religion*, 1935.

Basic Problems in Philosophy Series

A. I. Melden and Stanley Munsat
University of California, Irvine
General Editors

Morality and the Law
Richard A. Wasserstrom

Introduction   On Liberty, *John Stuart Mill*   Morals and the Criminal Law, *Lord Patrick Devlin*   Immorality and Treason, *H. L. A. Hart*   Lord Devlin and the Enforcement of Morals, *Ronald Dworkin*   Sins and Crimes, *A. R. Louch*   Morals Offenses and the Model Penal Code, *Louis B. Schwartz*   Paternalism, *Gerald Dworkin*   Four cases involving the enforcement of morality   Bibliography

War and Morality
Richard A. Wasserstrom

Introduction   The Moral Equivalent of War, *William James*   The Morality of Obliteration Bombing, *John C. Ford, S.J.*   War and Murder, *Elizabeth Anscombe*   Moral Judgment in Time of War, *Michael Walzer*   Pacifism: A Philosophical Analysis, *Jan Narveson*   On the Morality of War: A Preliminary Inquiry, *Richard Wasserstrom*   Judgment and Opinion, The International Tribunal, Nuremberg, Germany   Superior Orders, Nuclear Warfare, and the Dictates of Conscience, *Guenter Lewy*   Selected Bibliography